Office 2010

VISUAL™

Quick Tips

Visual

by Sherry Kinkoph Gunter

WILEY

Wiley Publishing, Inc.

Office 2010 Visual™ Quick Tips

Published by
Wiley Publishing, Inc.
10475 Crosspoint Boulevard
Indianapolis, IN 46256
www.wiley.com

Published simultaneously in Canada

Trademark Acknowledgments

Contact Us

For general information on our other products and services or to obtain technical support, please contact our Customer Care Department within the U.S. at (877) 762-2974, outside the U.S. at (317) 572-3993 or fax (317) 572-4002.

For technical support please visit www.wiley.com/techsupport.

Disclaimer

In order to get this information to you in a timely manner, this book was based on a pre-release version of Microsoft Office 2010. There may be some minor changes between the screenshots in this book and what you see on your desktop. As always, Microsoft has the final word on how programs look and function; if you have any questions or see any discrepancies, consult the online help for further information about the software. For purposes of illustrating the concepts and techniques described in this book, the author has created various names, company names, mailing, e-mail, and Internet addresses, phone and fax numbers, and similar information, all of which are fictitious. Any resemblance of the fictitious names, addresses, phone and fax numbers, and similar information to any actual person, company and/or organization is unintentional and purely coincidental.

WILEY

Wiley Publishing, Inc.

Sales

Contact Wiley
at (877) 762-2974 or
fax (317) 572-4002.

Credits

Executive Editor
Jody Lefevere

Sr. Project Editor
Sarah Hellert

Technical Editor
Joyce Nielsen

Copy Editor
Scott Tullis

Editorial Director
Robyn Siesky

Business Manager
Amy Knies

Sr. Marketing Manager
Sandy Smith

Vice President and Executive Group Publisher
Richard Swadley

Vice President and Executive Publisher
Barry Pruett

Sr. Project Coordinator
Kristie Rees

Proofreader
Susan Hobbs

Indexer
Estalita Slivoskey

Screen Artists
Ana Carrillo
Jill A. Proll

About the Author

Sherry Kinkoph Gunter has written and edited oodles of books over the past 18 years covering a wide variety of computer topics, including Microsoft Office programs, digital photography, and Web applications. Her recent titles include *Teach Yourself VISUALLY Office 2007*, *Microsoft Office 2008 for Mac Bible*, and *Master VISUALLY Dreamweaver CS3 and Flash CS3 Professional*. Sherry began writing computer books back in 1992, and her flexible writing style has allowed her to author for a varied assortment of imprints and formats. Sherry's ongoing quest is to aid users of all levels in the mastering of ever-changing computer technologies, helping users make sense of it all and get the most out of their machines and online experiences. Sherry currently resides in a swamp in the wilds of east central Indiana with a lovable ogre and a menagerie of interesting creatures.

Table of Contents

chapter 1 — General Office 2010 Maximizing Tips

chapter 2 — Timesaving Tips for Office Files

chapter 3 Boosting Your Productivity in Word

chapter 4 Utilizing Word's Document Building Tools

Table of Contents

chapter 5   Optimizing Excel

chapter 6   Polishing Your Spreadsheet Data

chapter 7 Increasing PowerPoint's Potential

Table of Contents

chapter 8 — Enhancing Your Presentations

chapter 9 — Harnessing Access

chapter 10   Customizing Your Database and Forms

chapter 11   Streamlining Outlook Tasks

Table of Contents

General Office 2010 Maximizing Tips

The various applications in Microsoft Office 2010 — in particular, Word, Excel, PowerPoint, Access, and Outlook — share a common look and feel. Indeed, you can find many of the same features in each program, such as the Ribbon feature, the Quick Access toolbar, various program window controls, and the File tab.

This common look and feel is helpful when you perform certain tasks within Office applications. For example, creating a new document in Word is similar to creating a new document in Excel. The same goes for

more complicated tasks, such as encrypting documents, tracking changes to a document, adding a digital signature, marking a document as final, and so on. This commonality makes mastering Office 2010 a snap.

This chapter focuses on tasks that transcend applications. That is, these tasks can be performed in more than one Office program. Although some of these tasks do apply to Access and Outlook, most relate only to Word, Excel, and PowerPoint.

Quick Tips

Customize the Quick Access Toolbar

Located in the top left corner of the program window sits the often underutilized Quick Access toolbar. The Quick Access toolbar provides easy access to often-used commands such as Save and Undo. In fact, it starts out with just a few default buttons. You can customize the Quick Access toolbar to change what commands are available and essentially make the toolbar into something that works for you.

Office enables you to add commands to the Quick Access toolbar three different ways. One is to select the desired command from the Customize Quick Access Toolbar menu. The menu only lists a few of the popular commands

and displays check marks next to each button that is actively in the toolbar. You can choose which of the common commands you want to display or hide.

Another way to add commands is to use the program's Options dialog box. You can simply right-click the command you want to add in the Ribbon and click Add to Quick Access Toolbar.

In addition to adding commands to the Quick Access toolbar, you can also move it from its default spot above the Ribbon to a spot below the Ribbon. To do so, click the arrow in the Quick Access toolbar and click Show Below the Ribbon from the menu that appears.

---

① Click the arrow to the right of the Quick Access toolbar.

Office displays the Customize Quick Access Toolbar menu.

② Click the command you want to add to the toolbar.

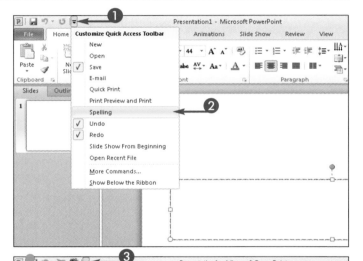

● A button for the selected command appears on the toolbar.

In this example, the Spelling button was added.

③ If you do not find the command you want to add, display the Customize Quick Access Toolbar menu again.

④ Click More Commands.

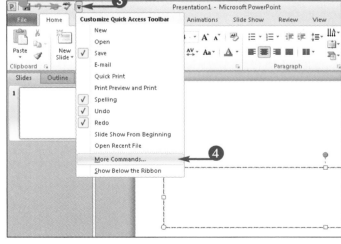

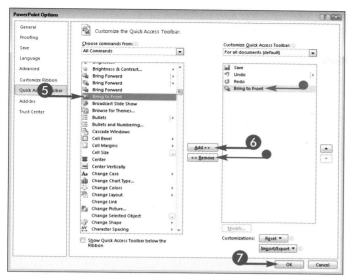

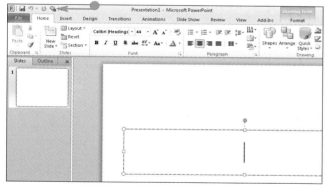

The program's Options dialog box opens with Quick Access toolbar options displayed.

⑤ In the left pane, click the command you want to add.

Note: *If the command you want to add is not shown, click the Choose Commands From drop-down arrow and select All Commands.*

⑥ Click Add.

● The command is added to the window's right list pane.

● To remove a command you do not want on the toolbar, click the command and click Remove.

⑦ Click OK to exit the dialog box.

● The Office program adds the new button to the toolbar.

TIPS

Did You Know?	Customize It!
You can add groups of commands in the Ribbon to the Quick Access toolbar. To do so, right-click the group name in the Ribbon and click Add to Quick Access Toolbar. The group is stored under a single button; click the button to reveal the available commands in the group.	You may want the customized toolbar for use with the current document only. In the program's Options dialog box with the Quick Access Toolbar settings showing, you can specify whether you want the customized toolbar available for all documents or just the current one you are working on. Click the Customize Quick Access Toolbar drop-down arrow located over the right pane listing all the buttons you have added and choose an option. In PowerPoint, for example, you can customize the toolbar for the current presentation, or in Word, you can apply the toolbar to the current document. The exact wording of the option varies based on what Office program you are using.

Customize the Ribbon

In Office 2010, the Ribbon is back and better than ever. The Office 2010 suite now offers a Ribbon of tools in every program. Designed to enable you to find the command necessary to complete a task more quickly and more intuitively than the menus and toolbars of old, the Ribbon is the go-to spot for accessing commands.

The Ribbon groups related commands together, placing them under clickable tabs. Each tab pertains to a certain type of task, such as formatting text, inserting items into a

document, laying out a page, reviewing a document, and so on. The tabs shown depend on what Office program is open, and what type of task is being performed.

You will be happy to know you can retool the Ribbon to suit the way you work in an Office program. You can add your own tab and populate it with buttons for not-so-common commands, add new groups to existing tabs, and reorder the tabs in the Ribbon. All buttons you add to a tab are organized into groups.

---

① **Right-click an empty area of the Ribbon.**

Office displays a context menu.

② **Click Customize the Ribbon.**

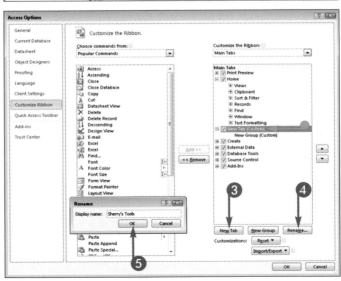

The program's Options dialog box opens with Ribbon options displayed.

③ **Click New Tab.**

● A new unnamed tab and group are added to the list.

④ **With the new tab selected, click the Rename button to give the new tab a distinctive name.**

Note: *You can also rename any groups you add to the new tab; click the group name and click the Rename button.*

The Rename dialog box opens.

⑤ **Type a new name and click OK.**

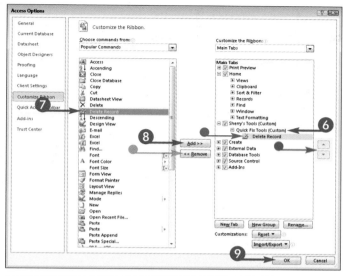

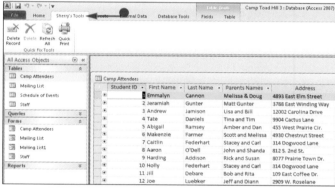

⑥ Click the new group name to select the group.

⑦ In the window's left pane, click a command you want to add to the new tab and group.

Note: *If the command you want to add is not shown, click the Choose Commands From drop-down arrow and select All Commands.*

⑧ Click Add.

● The command is added to window's right pane.

● You can use the Move Up and Move Down buttons to reposition a tab in the Ribbon, or reposition button order within a group or reposition groups within a tab.

● To remove a command, select it in the right pane and click Remove.

⑨ Click OK to exit the dialog box.

● The Office program adds the new tab and buttons to the Ribbon.

Reverse It!

If you ever want to revert back to the original default Ribbon, open the program's Options dialog box and click the Reset button and choose whether you want to restore a single customized tab or all the customizations. If you choose the latter option, a prompt box opens and asks if you really want to delete all Ribbon and Quick Access Toolbar customizations. Click Yes to complete the process.

Did You Know?

Another way to open the program's Options dialog box is through the File tab. Click the File tab on the Ribbon, and then click Options. The nice thing about using the right-click method to open the dialog box is that it displays the Customize Ribbon settings automatically for you. If you use the File tab to open the dialog box, it displays the last set of options you edited.

Control the Ribbon Display

The Ribbon feature in Office 2010 is docked at the top of the program window where you can easily access all the many commands and features it offers. This location seems practical and efficient, but there may be times when the Ribbon is simply in the way. For example, you may want to view more of the document window you are working on. Although you cannot permanently remove the Ribbon, move it, or turn it off like you used to do with toolbars in Office 2003 and earlier, you can minimize it to get it out of the way. Anytime

you need to utilize the commands again, you can summon the Ribbon back for display.

You can use two techniques to quickly minimize and summon the Ribbon. You can use the button located on the Ribbon itself, or you can right-click to display a context menu. Regardless of which method you employ, the Ribbon is significantly reduced in size, displaying only the tab names. This makes it extremely easy to bring the full Ribbon back again; just click a tab name.

Control the Ribbon with the Arrow Button

① Click the arrow button located next to the Help icon at the far right end of the Ribbon.

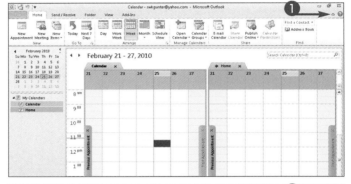

The Ribbon is minimized.

● Notice that the Ribbon's tabs are still present; to reveal options in a tab, click it; to hide them again, click the tab a second time.

② Click the arrow button again to redisplay the Ribbon.

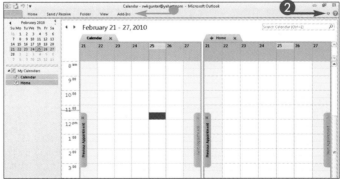

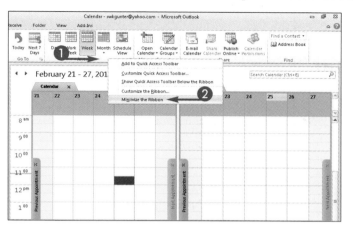

Control the Ribbon with the Context Menu

1 Right-click an empty area of the Ribbon.

A context menu appears.

2 Click Minimize the Ribbon.

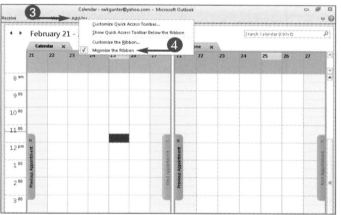

The Ribbon is minimized.

3 Right-click a tab name.

4 Click Minimize the Ribbon to remove the check mark from the command and restore the Ribbon display.

TIPS

Did You Know?

Once you minimize the Ribbon, it stays that way even after you activate it to use a command. As soon as you finish the task at hand and move the mouse pointer off the Ribbon, it is minimized again automatically. To turn this minimizing effect off, click the arrow button ([⌂]) at the end of the Ribbon.

Customize It!

If Microsoft's order of tabs on the Ribbon does not fit into your left-handed style, you can move the tabs around on the Ribbon to better work for your personal usage. In the Options dialog box for customizing a Ribbon, you can use the Move Up and Move Down buttons ([▲] and [▼]) to change the order of tabs or of groups and commands. See the previous task, "Customize the Ribbon," to learn more.

Share a Customized Ribbon

Perhaps you tackled the previous task and spent a great deal of time customizing a Ribbon with a new tab and groups of buttons. After all that work, you may want to share your efforts. Perhaps you want to share your personalized Ribbon with your laptop computer, or share it with other people who use Office. For example, if you build a custom tab with unique tools tailored for a group work project, you can share the customized Ribbon with others on the project team. How handy is that?

When you save a customized Ribbon, you are actually creating an Office user interface file which someone else can import into his or her Office program to use. The exported Ribbon file is saved as an XML file. Recipients of your personalized Ribbon can use the same Options dialog box you used to create the personalized Ribbon to import the customized file into their Office suite.

1. **Right-click an empty area of the Ribbon.**

   Office displays a context menu.

2. **Click Customize the Ribbon.**

   The program's Options dialog box opens with Ribbon options displayed.

3. **Click Import/Export.**

4. **Click Export All Customizations.**

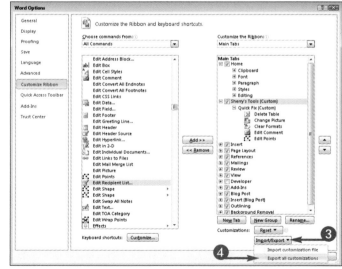

The File Save dialog box opens.

⑤ Type a unique file name.

⑥ Leave the file type set as Exported Office UI file.

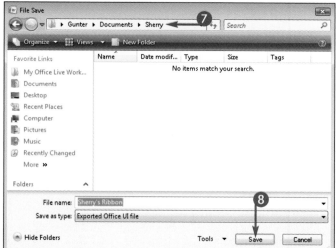

⑦ Navigate to the folder or drive where you want to save the file.

⑧ Click Save.

The file is saved and ready to share.

⑨ Click OK to exit the Options dialog box.

Apply It!

If you are the recipient of a customized Ribbon, simply open the Options dialog box to retrieve the file. Click the Import/Export button, click Import Customization File, and navigate to the XML file you want to open and use.

Remove It!

To remove a customized Ribbon, open the Options dialog box and click the Reset button, and then click Reset All Customizations.

Preview Paste Options

Pasting text, data, and other elements is one of the most-used Office commands. Cutting, copying, and pasting are basics in just about every computer application today. In past renditions of Office, however, it was not always easy to paste an item just the way you wanted. Sometimes formatting was included in the paste action, other times it was not. To help alleviate some of the frustration, Office 2010 has improved the Paste command to include a Paste Options gallery.

You can now choose exactly how you want the pasted data to appear. For example, you can choose to paste only the text without any

formatting ([A]), paste text along with its original formatting ([🖼]), or merge the formatting of both the original text and the new location where the pasted text appears ([🖼]). With the help of Live Preview, you can see what each potential application of the pasted element looks like before applying the command.

You can view the Paste Options gallery in three locations: through the Paste button on the Ribbon, through the pop-up that appears as soon as you paste an item, or through the right-click context menu. The options that appear in the Paste Options gallery are based on the type of data you are pasting.

---

① Cut or copy a piece of data in an Office program.

You can find the Cut, Copy, and Paste commands on the Home tab of the Ribbon or on the right-click context menu.

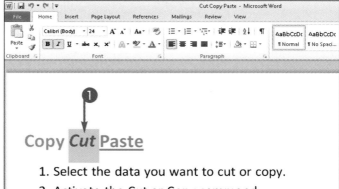

② Click where you want to paste the data in the document.

③ Click the Paste button's drop-down arrow.

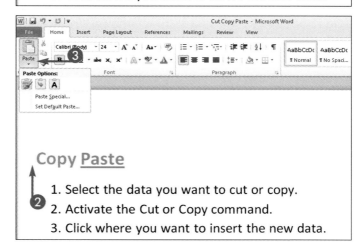

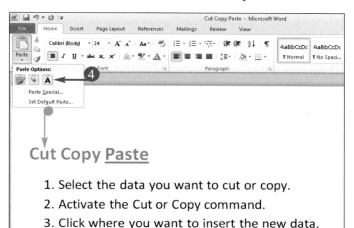

④ Position the mouse pointer over a paste option to preview it in the document.

● Its preview appears in the document. In this example, the Keep Text Only preview is shown.

Cut Copy Paste

1. Select the data you want to cut or copy.
2. Activate the Cut or Copy command.
3. Click where you want to insert the new data.

⑤ Click an option to apply it and paste the data.

● In this example, the Keep Source Formatting option is applied.

● Whenever you paste data, a Smart Tag appears briefly which you can also click to view the Paste Options gallery and choose a paste option. These options are the same as those listed in the Paste button's menu.

Cut Copy Paste

1. Select the data you want to cut or copy.
2. Activate the Cut or Copy command.
3. Click where you want to insert the new data.

TIPS

Customize It!

You can also control Paste options — such as whether to keep source formatting when pasting data between documents or between programs — through the Options dialog box, even setting up default paste preferences. To display the dialog box, click the Paste button's drop-down menu and click Set Default Paste. This opens the program's Options dialog box directly to the cut, copy, and paste options.

More Options!

If you prefer using keyboard shortcuts to cut, copy, and paste, you will be happy to know the Paste gallery is available through a keyboard shortcut. After pasting data using the Ctrl+V shortcut, press Ctrl again to view the Paste Options gallery.

Automate Office Tasks with Macros

If you frequently use an Office program to complete the same task — for example, to format the cells in a spreadsheet a certain way, or to insert a table in a Word document that contains a certain number of rows and columns — you can expedite the process by recording a macro. When you record a macro, you essentially record a series of actions; then you can run the macro you recorded to automatically perform the recorded actions.

One way to access the controls for recording a macro is from the Developer tab on the

Ribbon. This tab is not shown by default, however. To display the Developer tab, right-click an empty area of the Ribbon and click Customize the Ribbon to open the Options dialog box. Click the Developer tab check box in the right pane to turn the tab on. Click OK and you are ready to record your own macros.

Note that recording a macro in Access differs somewhat from recording macros in other Office programs, such as Word, Excel, and PowerPoint. For information on creating macros in Access, see Chapter 9.

---

1. Click the Developer tab in the Ribbon.

2. In the Code group, click Record Macro.

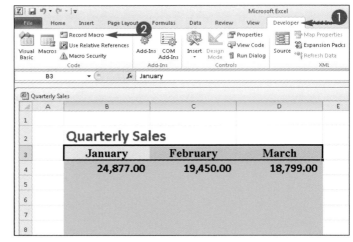

The Record Macro dialog box opens.

3. Type a name for the macro.

Note: No spaces are allowed in macro names.

4. Click here and select the template(s) in which you want the macro to be available.

5. Type a description of the macro.

6. Click OK.

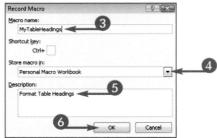

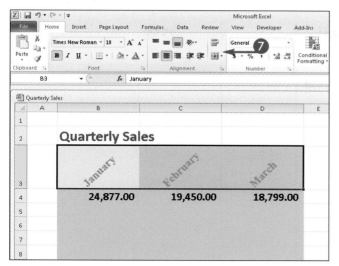

⑦ Perform the actions you want to record.

This example formats a series of headings.

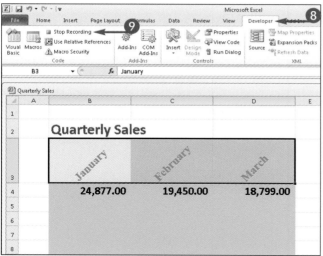

⑧ Click the Developer tab.

⑨ Click Stop Recording.

The application saves the macro.

TIPS

Apply It!

To run a macro you have recorded, click the Developer tab and click Macros in the Code group. In the Macros dialog box that appears, click the macro you want to run, and then click Run.

Caution!

Because macros can be created for malicious purposes, they are often disabled by default. To enable the use of macros in a particular document, click the File tab, click the Options button, click Trust Center, click Trust Center Settings, and then click Macro Settings. Finally, click Disable All Macros with Notification (⦿ changes to ◎). That way, when Office encounters a document that contains macros, it displays a security dialog box that enables you to specify whether the macros should be allowed.

You can control the font and size that Office automatically applies to every Word document or Excel workbook you open. By default, both programs apply a pre-set font and size to every new document or workbook you create. These settings are in place and ready to go so you can start entering data right away. You can certainly apply formatting to change the font and size as you add data, but if you use the same font and size for every file you create, why not instruct the program to assign those settings at startup?

In Word, you use the Font dialog box to assign new default settings. In Excel, you use the Excel Options dialog box to assign a new default font and size. Access, PowerPoint, Outlook, and Publisher do not utilize default sizes; however, you can set a default font and size for some of Outlook's features, such as the Calendar, Notes, and Journal. Use Outlook's Options dialog box to adjust settings.

Once you specify new default settings, those settings are in place for any new files you create.

Change Word's Default Font

① Click the dialog box launcher in the Font group on the Home tab.

Note: *Many of the tool groups in the Office Ribbons have icons in the corners you can click to open associated dialog boxes. In this example, the icon in the Font group, also called the Font dialog box launcher, opens the Font dialog box.*

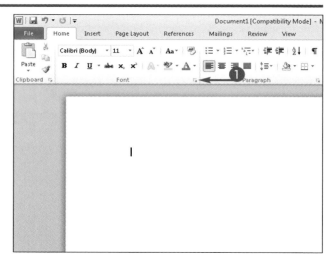

The Font dialog box opens.

② Select a new font and size from the available settings.

③ Click Set As Default.

A prompt box appears asking you whether you want the settings to apply to the current document or all documents.

④ Make your selection and click OK to apply the new settings.

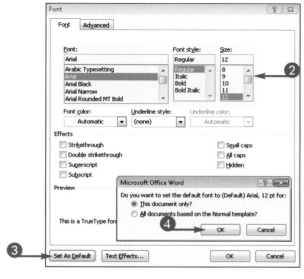

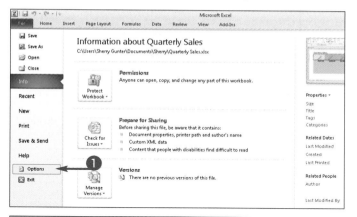

Change Excel's Default Font

① Click the File tab and click Options.

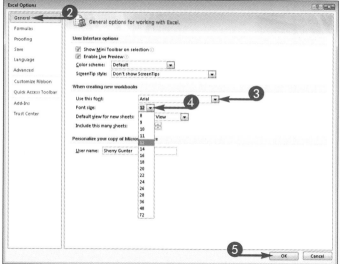

The Excel Options dialog box opens.

② Click General if it is not already shown.

③ Click the Use This Font drop-down arrow and choose another font.

④ Click the Font Size drop-down arrow and choose another size.

⑤ Click OK.

The new settings are assigned.

More Options!

Speaking of fonts, Word 2010 now supports OpenType ligatures. *Ligatures* refer to typography characters whose shape depends on surrounding characters, such as the letter f combined with the letter l or i. OpenType is a format for scalable fonts. OpenType ligatures are not enabled by default. To turn them on, open the Font dialog box by clicking the dialog box launcher in the Font group on the Home tab of the Ribbon. Click the Advanced tab and select a ligature from the OpenType features. Click OK to exit the dialog box and apply the new setting.

Organize Notes with OneNote

Often overlooked among the many programs in the Office suite, OneNote is a handy little organizer that may be just the thing you need to keep track of various pieces of information. Microsoft's OneNote application is a digital version of a 3-ring binder notebook. OneNote allows you to collect, store, and share notes, thoughts, scraps of information, text, and video and audio files, and organize all these various items so they are easy to find again. You can use OneNote to gather all kinds of elements into one place, then use word processing and annotation tools, search and indexing features, and drawing tools to work with the various elements.

Workbooks are organized into sections and tabs. Pages are stored in tabs and saved automatically. You can move pages in and out of a notebook, and share them with other users, making it ideal for collaborating with workgroups.

OneNote may look a little intimidating at first, but it is actually quite easy to use. The Getting Started information appears first thing, and you can view the various pages, learn how to use the features, and then start creating your own notebooks. Read through the pages to learn how to drag items from other windows into your notebook, insert screen clippings, paste pictures, and much more.

---

① Open the OneNote program.

② Click the One Note Guide tab to learn more about the application.

③ Click the various pages to read detailed information and instructions for using the program.

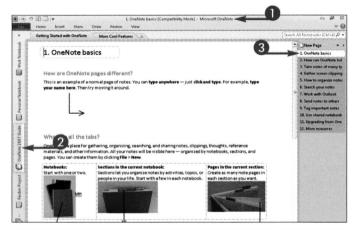

④ To start a new notebook, click the File tab and click New.

⑤ Click where you want to store the notebook.

⑥ Type a name for the notebook.

● You can choose a different destination in which to store the file by clicking the Browse button and navigating to another drive or folder.

⑦ Click Create Notebook.

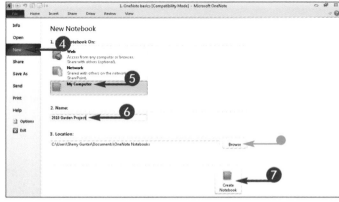

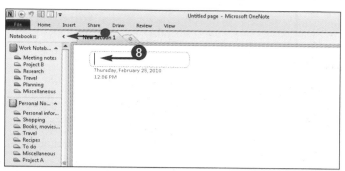

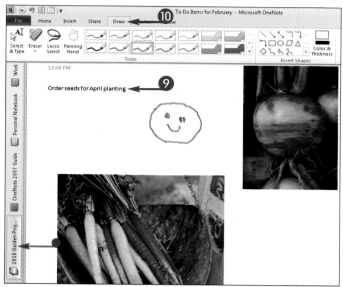

A new notebook opens with a blank page.

● You can use the navigation bar to view other notebooks, or minimize the bar to move it out of the way. Click here to minimize or display the bar.

⑧ Type a title for the page here.

● The page title appears on the Page Tabs bar for easy recall.

⑨ Click where you want to add a note and start typing.

Items you organize in your notebook do not have to be saved — OneNote does this automatically.

⑩ Use the OneNote tabs to find tools for drawing, inserting pictures, sharing pages, and more.

TIPS

Apply It!
To make it easier to add items to your notebook from other sources, you can dock OneNote to the side of your desktop, keeping it handy but slightly out of the way. You can then drag items over to it as needed. To dock OneNote, click the Dock to Desktop button (▢) on the Quick Access toolbar. To return it to full size again, click the Full Page View button (▢), also located in the Quick Access toolbar.

Try This!
You can use the View tab on the Ribbon to change the ways in which you view your Notebook. Normal view, the default view when you first open OneNote, includes the navigation bar on the left and the page tabs bar on the right. You can also find the docking command and Full Page View command on the View tab, too.

Timesaving Tips for Office Files

Office files come in several different "flavors" depending on the program. In Word, files you create are referred to as *documents*, but in Excel, they are called *workbooks*. In PowerPoint, files are *presentations*, whereas in Access, they are known as *databases*. In Publisher, the files you create are *publications*. In Outlook, you do not really create files, per se, although you can export various components, such as address books and calendars. Regardless of the official name, an Office file is simply the stored data you save in a program.

Because files are such a basic part of using an application, they share a lot of the same elements and tasks. For example, Word, Excel, PowerPoint, and Publisher share a similar Save As dialog box from which you control the file name, format type, and storage location. With the exception of Outlook, the Office programs also share a similar-looking Open dialog box from which you choose what file you want to open.

There are lots of other things you can do with your files besides just save them and open them again. For example, in Word, Excel, and PowerPoint you can control the default Save location for your files. If you always save your files to a particular work folder, for example, you can add the folder's path to the program so it saves files to that location by default, unless you direct otherwise.

You can also control the hidden data saved along with your files, called *properties*. You can activate security features, save files as PDF documents, and more.

This chapter shows you several different tasks that apply to Office files. Office 2010 has retooled the old Office button (introduced in Office 2007) into a File tab on the Ribbon that, when clicked, displays a whole screen full of options for working with your files, so make it your first stop in seeing what sort of tasks you can perform on or with your Office files.

Quick Tips

Change the Default File Save Location

You can tell Microsoft Office programs where you want to store files you create. Ordinarily, when you open the Save As dialog box to save your files in Word, Excel, PowerPoint, and Access, these programs select the Documents folder as the default working folder for storage. You may prefer to use a different destination folder. For example, you may have a work folder set up to hold all the Excel workbooks you create. Instead of manually selecting a different folder from the dialog box each time you save, you can tell the Office program to list a default folder instead. This can save you some time and effort when saving your files.

You can control the default file location through the Office program's Options dialog box. For Word, Excel, and PowerPoint, the default file location is listed under the Save options. In Access, you can find it in the General options, and the setting is called the Default database folder.

When specifying a new default folder, you can type the full path to the folder. In Word and Access, you can also use the Browse button to navigate to the destination folder. A folder path includes the drive label and any hierarchical folders the destination folder is listed under, such as C:\Users\Bob\Work Stuff.

---

① Click File.

② Click Options.

The program's Options dialog box opens.

③ Click the Save tab.

In Access, click the General tab, if it is not selected already.

④ In Word, click the Browse button next to the Default file location box.

In Excel and PowerPoint, you must type in the full folder path. You can triple-click inside the Default File Location box to select the existing text and type the new path.

In Access, click the Browse button next to the Default Database Folder box.

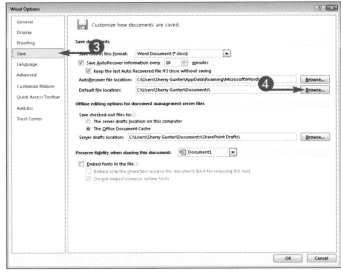

⑤ Navigate to the folder you want to use.

⑥ Click OK.

⑦ Click OK to exit the Options dialog box and apply the new setting.

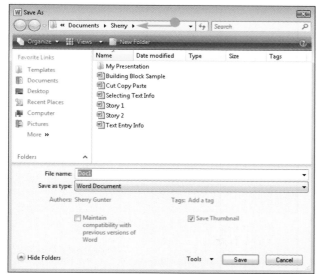

● The next time you use the Save As dialog box, the specified folder appears listed by default.

Customize It!

You can also specify a default file format to save to each time you save an Office file. Each Office program saves to a particular file type. For example, Word automatically saves documents as a Word Document file type (.docx) unless you choose otherwise. You may want to save all your documents as plain text files (.txt) or Microsoft Works files (.wps). You can set a different file type as the default type to save yourself a step. For Word, Excel, or PowerPoint, open the program's Options dialog box and click the Save tab. Display the Save Files in This Format drop-down menu and choose a different file format. For Access, open the Options dialog box and click the Default File Format for Blank Database drop-down arrow in the General tab to change the file format.

Check Document Compatibility

One of the first things users worry about with every new software release is compatibility. Will my old files work with the new program? Or more importantly, will my new Office files work for others who have older versions of Office? The answer is yes, but Office 2010 includes a feature you can use to check for compatibility issues in Word, Excel, and PowerPoint.

When you first open Word, for example, it opens a blank, new file in Compatibility mode; note the label [Compatibility Mode] next to the file name in the title bar. You can certainly work on the file as you normally would, but some of the newer Office 2010 features may not work with the file. If you convert the file to a 2010 format, the compatibility mode is removed and you can

utilize all the program's features. The good news is that any Office 2010 files you save are compatible with older versions of the program, so users with Office 2003 can still view your files.

If you frequently share files with others who use earlier versions of the software suite, you can check the file for compatibility issues. The Office Compatibility Checker scans your file for any features not supported by earlier versions of the program. Alas, the Compatibility Checker cannot fix any issues it finds; you must make sure any issues are resolved, but it does do a good job of telling you what impact the issues may have. This feature is available for Word, Excel, and PowerPoint.

Convert a Word File to 2010 Format

1. Click File.
2. Click Info.
3. Click Convert.

Note: *The Convert option only appears when you open a document saved in an earlier version of Word.*

A warning box opens letting you know the document's layout may change.

4. Click OK.

- The file is converted and [Compatibility Mode] is removed from the title bar.

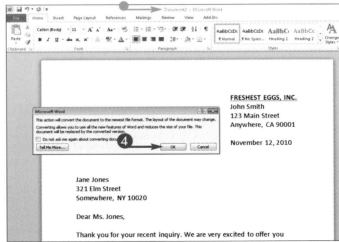

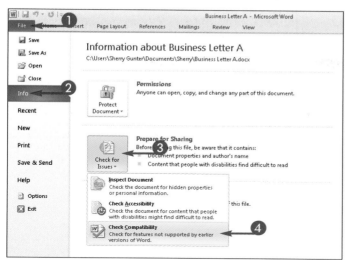

Check for Compatibility

1. Click File.
2. Click Info.
3. Click Check for Issues.
4. Click Check Compatibility.

The Compatibility Checker opens and checks the document.

● Any issues are listed here.

5. Click OK.

TIPS

Did You Know?

Documents you create with Office 2010 are saved with an x at the end of the file extension — for example, .docx for Word files, .xlsx for Excel files, and so on. The x extension was introduced with Office 2007 as part of the new XML formats. Earlier versions of Office files use a slightly different file extension. Office 2007 files were not backward-compatible unless you saved them in another format, but Office 2010 files are backward-compatible. Not all the new functions or layouts may work, but users can still read your 2010 files.

Try This!

You can save your Office files to other file formats that users of earlier versions of Office can read using the Save As dialog box. Click File, Save As, and change the Save as Type drop-down menu to the format you want to apply. For example, if you want to save a Word document as a file for Microsoft Works, change the format to Works 6-9 Document or Works 6.0 to 9.0.

Saving files as PDF documents is one way to keep a file's content intact without requiring the recipient to have a copy of Office 2010 installed on his or her computer. PDF (Portable Document Format) is a popular file format from Adobe for sharing documents just as they were intended to be viewed, including all the content, formatting, and page layout elements. In essence, the PDF format captures all the elements of a document much like an electronic image that you can view, navigate, and print.

Anyone can open a PDF file using the free Adobe Acrobat Reader software. PDF files are ideal for sharing on the Internet, easy to print using professional printer services, and the PDF open standard lets users share files regardless of

what program or platform was used to create the file. In previous versions of Office, you needed an add-in to convert documents. Office 2010 includes a built-in PDF writer to help you save your files to the PDF format.

When creating a PDF document, you have the option of creating an XPS document. Microsoft's own version of PDF-like documents are XML documents, commonly called XPS, short for XML Paper Specification. Like the PDF format, XPS documents include information defining the document's layout, appearance, and printing information. Unlike PDFs, however, XPS documents can be opened only by Windows XP, Vista, or Windows 7 users.

---

① Click File.

② Click Save & Send.

③ Click Create PDF/XPS Document.

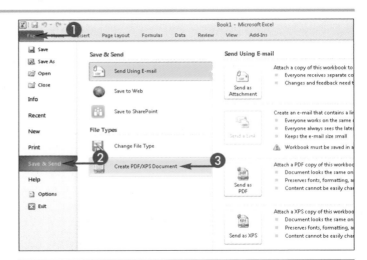

④ Click Create a PDF/XPS.

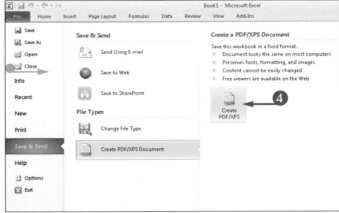

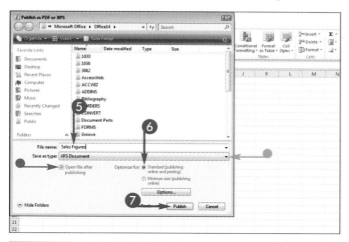

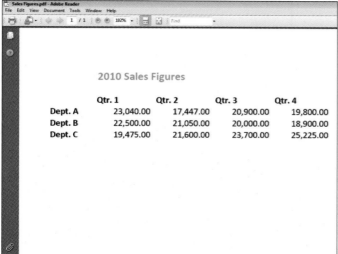

The program's Publish as PDF or XPS dialog box opens with the PDF file format selected by default.

⑤ Type a name for the file.

● To change the file type to PDF or XPS, click here and choose the correct file type.

⑥ Click an optimizing option (◯ changes to ◉). Choose Standard for printing, or Minimum size for online publishing.

● If you want to open the document in a PDF or XPS viewer after saving, leave this check box selected.

⑦ Click Publish.

The PDF document opens in the Adobe Reader window. If it is an XPS document, it opens in an XPS viewer.

More Options!

For more publishing options for PDF files, click the Options button in the Publish as PDF or XPS dialog box. This opens the Options dialog box where you find controls for setting the page range, choosing what items are published, and what nonprinting information is included. Click OK to apply any changes.

Did You Know?

You can also save your Office files as Web pages. In the Save As dialog box, click the Save as Type drop-down arrow and select either Single File Web Page or Web Page. The Single File Web Page option creates a single document without any supporting files for graphics and other elements. The Web Page option creates a folder for supporting elements along with the HTML file.

Assign Document Properties

Office automatically embeds certain document properties, or *metadata*, such as the size of the document, the date it was created, and so on, in the document file. In addition to these default properties, you can supply other document properties, which you can then use to organize and identify your documents, as well as search for documents at a later date. For example, you can enter an author name, a title, a subject, keywords, a category, status information, and comments. You can also add custom properties, such as the client name, department, date completed, and even typist.

You can view document properties through the Info tab, part of the new Backstage view that

appears when you click the File tab on the Ribbon. You can also open the Document Panel (Word, Excel, and PowerPoint) and add properties, or you can open the Properties dialog box (available in all the Office programs except for Outlook) to do the same and view additional properties.

In earlier versions of Office, you could control document properties only through the Properties dialog box. You can still access the dialog box, if you prefer, or you can use the Document Panel to enter properties such as keywords, comments, subject, and title. The panel opens directly on-screen, just below the Ribbon.

Open the Document Panel

① Click File.

② Click Info.

● The document's properties are listed on the right.

③ Click the Properties drop-down arrow.

Note: *Document properties are not available in Outlook.*

④ Click Show Document Panel.

Note: *The Document Panel is not available in Access or Publisher.*

● A Document Panel opens below the Ribbon.

⑤ Use the panel's fields to enter document properties.

⑥ Click the panel's Close button to exit the panel.

Gunter's Gourmet Garden

Offering fresh produce for the discerning palate

Open the Properties Dialog Box

① Click File.

② Click Info.

③ Click the Properties drop-down arrow.

In Access, click the View and Edit Database Properties link to open the Properties dialog box.

Note: *Document properties are not available in Outlook.*

④ Click Advanced Properties.

The Properties dialog box opens.

⑤ Click the Summary tab.

⑥ Fill in the properties you want to add.

⑦ Click OK to apply the new settings.

TIPS

Customize It!

You can use the Custom tab in the Properties dialog box to add custom fields to the properties. You can choose from existing fields or create a new one. To add a new field, click in the Name box and type the field name. Type a value for the property in the Value box, such as a name or number. Click the Add button to add it to the list, and then click OK to exit the dialog box and apply the new property to the document.

Did You Know?

In addition to enabling you to set custom properties, the Properties dialog box also enables you to see a general summary of the properties set, as well as statistics about the document, such as the page count, word count, and even whether the document has been printed. Some of this information already appears on the Info section of the File tab.

Remove Sensitive Document Information

If you plan to share an Office document with others, whether via e-mail or by some other method, you might want to first ensure that the document is void of personal, company, or other private information that may be stored in the document's metadata or in the document itself.

This information might include comments, tracked changes, or annotations; information about the document's author, status, category, keywords, and so on; hidden information (such as text, rows, columns, worksheets, or what have you) or content marked "invisible"; server properties; custom XML data; and more. This type of information is often called *metadata*.

(Note that if you remove hidden data from a document, you might not be able to restore it.) To locate and remove this data, you can use the Office Document Inspector. The Document Inspector is available only in Word, Excel, and PowerPoint.

When the Document Inspector dialog box opens, you can control what type of content is inspected. Once the information is inspected, the dialog box displays any potential issues and allows you to remove the items. Be aware that the particulars of using Document Inspector vary slightly depending on whether you are using it in Word, Excel, or PowerPoint.

---

① Click File.

② Click Info.

③ Click Check for Issues.

④ Click Inspect Document.

Note: *The Document Inspector is not available in Access or Publisher.*

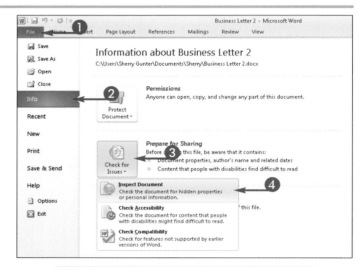

The Document Inspector dialog box opens.

⑤ Click what types of information you want inspected (☐ changes to ☑).

⑥ Click Inspect.

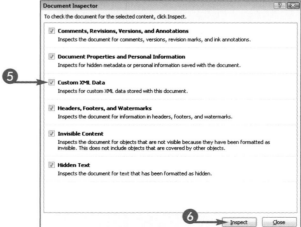

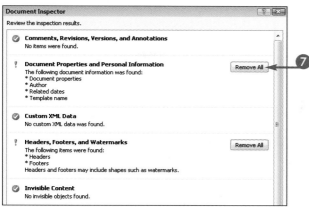

The document is inspected and any issues are listed.

⑦ Click Remove All to fix an issue.

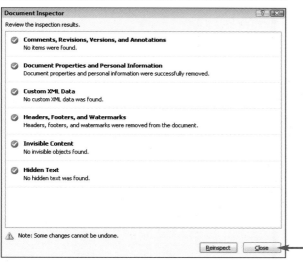

The Document Inspector removes the sensitive information.

⑧ Click Close.

Caution!
If you are not sure whether you want to remove the information flagged by Document Inspector, cancel the inspection and use the appropriate Office tools to view the information. For example, if document properties are flagged, view the document properties to see whether you want to eliminate them from the document. You cannot undo the effects of removing information with Document Inspector. You can, however, restore the removed information by closing the document without saving the changes that the inspection process made.

Important!
The Document Inspector does not remove metadata found in protected or restricted files, such as a document with a digital signature or restricted permissions. To get around this, be sure to run the Document Inspector before restricting or protecting the file.

If you are working on a document that contains sensitive information, you might want to encrypt it. That way, for someone to open the document and view its contents, he or she needs to enter a password, which you set. When you encrypt an Office document, you set a password for it; to open the document, the password is required.

Be aware that if you forget the password, you cannot open the document, even if you are the person who encrypted it. For this reason, it is imperative that you choose a password that

you will not forget, or that you write the password down and keep it in a safe place. That said, the password should not be easy for others to guess. The strongest passwords contain at least eight characters and are composed of a mixture of uppercase and lowercase letters, numbers, and symbols. Avoid using common passwords such as pet names, birth dates, and so on.

The encryption feature is not available in Publisher or Outlook.

① Click File.

② Click Info.

③ Click Protect Document, Protect Workbook, or Protect Presentation, depending on the program.

④ Click Encrypt with Password.

In Access, skip step 3 and click the Encrypt with Password button.

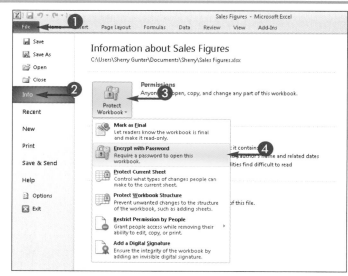

The Encrypt Document dialog box opens.

⑤ Type the password you want to use.

⑥ Click OK.

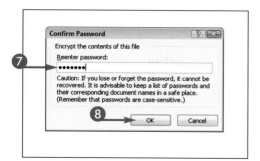

The Confirm Password dialog box opens.

⑦ Type the password again.

⑧ Click OK.

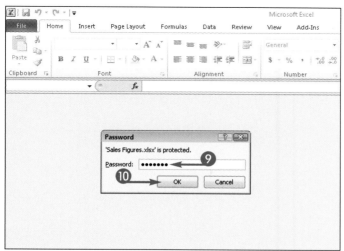

The next time you open the file, a prompt box appears for you to enter the new password.

⑨ Type the password.

⑩ Click OK.

Remove It!

To unencrypt a document, open it and revisit the Encrypt with Password feature. Click the File tab, click Info, and click a protection option (Protect Document, Protect Workbook, or Protect Presentation, depending on the program). Next, click Encrypt with Password. In the dialog box that opens, delete the password and click OK. This removes the password from the file.

Try This!

You can also assign a password to a file using the Save As dialog box. Click File, Save As to open the dialog box. After assigning a file name and storage location, click the Tools button and click General Options. Type a password in the Password to Open box and click OK. Retype the password again and click OK to assign it to the file. You can also use the General Options dialog box to restrict file sharing options for the document with a password to modify. Users cannot edit the document without knowing the password.

To authenticate an Office document, you can add a digital signature to it. First, however, you must create a digital ID and have a current digital certificate, which is a means of proving identity. A digital certificate is issued by a certificate authority, which is a trusted third-party entity. For a fee, you can get a digital signature from the Office Marketplace. (If you do not have a digital ID, you are prompted to create one as you complete this task.)

A digital signature contains a *message digest*, which contains a reduced version of the document's contents, and a *private key*, which is used to encrypt the message digest on the signer's computer. When you sign a document, the encrypted version of the message digest is appended to the document; the digest is then decrypted by the recipient using the *public key*, included in the digital certificate associated with the signature. In this way, the recipient can confirm the origin of the document and that the contents of the document did not change during transit.

① Click File.

② Click Info.

③ Click Protect Document, Protect Workbook, or Protect Presentation, depending on the program.

④ Click Add a Digital Signature.

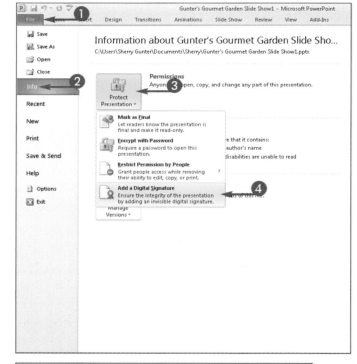

If you do not have a digital signature, this prompt box appears.

⑤ Click OK.

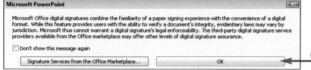

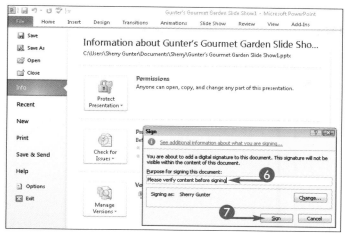

The Sign dialog box appears.

⑥ Type a note about the signature.

⑦ Click Sign.

A Signature Confirmation prompt box appears.

⑧ Click OK and the digital signature is added to the file and the file is marked as final.

● You can click View Signatures to review signatures assigned to the document.

Important!

You are not required to obtain a digital certificate from a certificate authority in order to create a digital ID and sign your Office documents; instead, you can create your own. To do so, click the Create Your Own Digital ID option instead of Get a Digital ID from a Microsoft Partner in the Get a Digital ID dialog box, which is shown automatically if no digital ID is present on your computer. Then, in the Create a Digital ID dialog box that appears, enter the requested information — name, e-mail address, organization, and location — and click Create. Note however, that when you share a file signed with a digital ID you created, it cannot be authenticated by users on other machines.

Control Author Permissions

When you create a file, anyone can access the file and make changes to the content. Office 2010 offers you several features you can use to control who else can work with your file. You already learned how to protect a file with a password in the task "Encrypt a Document" earlier in this chapter. Among the other options you can apply are restriction settings that limit who can access or what can be done to a file.

In Word, Excel, and PowerPoint, you can utilize the Restrict Permission by People feature to set up a Windows Live ID to restrict permissions. You need to create your own Windows Live ID in order to use this feature. You can restrict Read permissions to allow users to read the document, but not allow them to change, print, or copy the content. You can restrict Change permissions to allow certain users to read, edit, and change the content, but not print the document.

You can also set up additional options for setting an expiration date for the document, add printing and copying capability, and allow others to request permission to use the document.

---

① Click File.

② Click Info.

③ Click Protect Document, Protect Workbook, or Protect Presentation, depending on the program.

④ Click Restrict Permission by People.

⑤ Click Restricted Access.

If you do not have a Windows Live ID, you are prompted to create one before pursuing this feature any further.

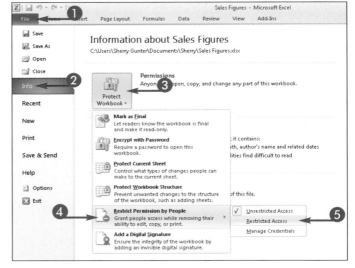

The Select User dialog box opens.

⑥ Select your account to open content with restricted permission.

⑦ Click OK.

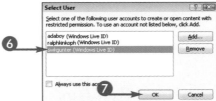

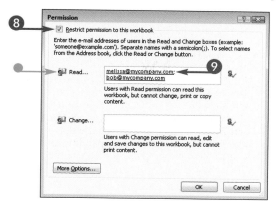

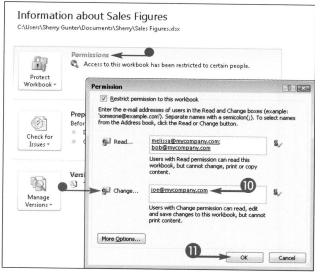

The Permission dialog box opens.

8 Click the Restrict Permission to This Document, Workbook, or Presentation check box (☐ changes to ☑).

9 Type the e-mail addresses of the users you want to allow file-reading access.

● To add users from your Address Book, click the Read button and choose people from your contacts list.

10 Type the e-mail addresses of the users you want to allow file-editing permission.

● To add users from your Address Book, click the Change button and choose people from your contacts list.

11 Click OK.

Permissions are now assigned to the file.

● The Permissions setting is highlighted in another color when permissions or passwords are assigned to the file.

More Options!
Because so many people author documents, Word offers an extra feature to control what types of changes other users can make to a file, called the Restrict Editing option (also listed under the Permissions options). When activated, this command opens the Restrict Formatting and Editing pane, and you can choose what formatting restrictions you want to apply to a document. You can restrict editing to certain styles, tracked changes, comments, and even specify what users can freely edit the document.

Remove It!
To remove restricted access, display the Info options in Backstage view again, click the Protect button, and then click Restrict Permission by People and Unrestricted Access. This returns the file to its unrestricted status again, which means anyone can view and edit the file.

After you finish working on a Word document, Excel workbook, or PowerPoint presentation — that is, you have proofread it and accepted any revisions made with the Track Changes feature — you can mark it as final. If you are working on a file in a group project situation, this technique is handy to let everyone know that work on the file is complete. You can find the Mark as Final option as part of the file's Permissions options.

Marking a document as final makes the file read-only, thereby preventing changes from being made to the file. The file can, however, be opened and read by others.

Keep in mind that marking a file as final is not a security feature. That is, it does not permanently and irrevocably lock the document to prevent further edits. Anyone with access to the document can revoke the Mark as Final status. Steps for revoking Mark as Final status appear among the tips at the end of this task.

① Click File.

② Click Info.

③ Click Protect Document, Protect Workbook, or Protect Presentation, depending on the program.

④ Click Mark as Final.

A prompt box appears telling you the file will be marked as final and saved.

⑤ Click OK.

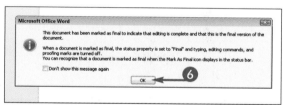

Another prompt box appears when the process is complete.

6 Click OK.

● If a document has been marked as final, it displays a special Marked as Final banner along the top of the document.

Notice the Ribbon is hidden from view because all the editing functions are disabled.

● To edit the document, click the Edit Anyway button.

TIPS

Remove It!

You revoke the Mark as Final status the same way you apply it: by clicking the File tab, clicking Info, clicking the Protect Document button, and clicking Mark as Final. Revoking Mark as Final status means the document can again be edited just like any other document.

Did You Know?

If you really want to lock down a document and prevent changes, you may want to restrict permissions or assign a password instead. When you restrict permissions, you can utilize the Windows Rights Management feature to assign read-only status to a document. To learn more about restricting permissions, see the previous task, "Control Author Permissions."

Office 2010 introduces a new feature to help you recover documents you did not save in Word, Excel, and PowerPoint. For example, perhaps you spent a great deal of time editing a Word document only to accidentally click Don't Save instead of Save when asked to save your changes. You can now recover your unsaved work with a few clicks.

By default, Word, Excel and PowerPoint are set up to automatically save versions of your file as you work on it, and keep a list of those autosaved files from your current session ready for recall. Autosaved drafts are stored in the DraftFiles folder. The autosaved versions are available only for a short time, however. Versions are kept for four days or until you reopen the file again.

If you close an editing session without saving, the Office program keeps the last auto saved version of the file and lists it in Backstage view among the Info settings. You can also find draft files listed in the Recent Documents list. A third way to locate drafts is through the Recover Unsaved Documents feature, which opens a dialog box where you can browse for files among the UnSavedFiles and DraftFiles folders.

① Click File.

② Click Info.

③ Click a recent draft listed here.

The recovered file opens.

④ Click Restore to restore the version.

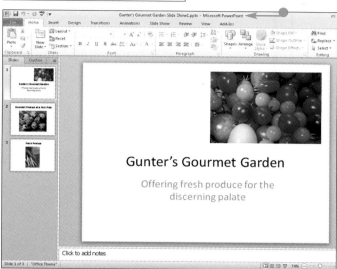

A prompt box appears warning you that you are about to overwrite the previously saved version of the file.

⑤ Click OK.

● The draft is now the current version of the file.

Customize It!

By default, Word, Excel, and PowerPoint are set up to automatically save a file every 10 minutes. You can change this setting, if needed. To do so, click the File tab and click Options to open the program's Options dialog box. Click the Save tab to view the AutoRecover settings. You can change the amount of time for auto-saving, or you can turn off the feature entirely.

Remove It!

If you have been working on the same file for quite a while, you may have accumulated many drafts. You can delete them all if you no longer need them. Open the Backstage view and click the Info tab. Click the Manage Versions button and click Delete All Draft Versions. A prompt box appears asking if you are sure; click Yes or No.

Boosting Your Productivity in Word

If you have a project that involves text of any kind — be it correspondence, a report, or what have you — you can harness the power of Word 2010 to quickly and easily generate a professional-looking document.

Word features a host of tools designed to improve your efficiency no matter what type of document you need to create, from prefabricated header and footer styles to building blocks for creating your own styles. The program's Research tools provide quick access to reference materials such as thesauri, dictionaries, and encyclopedias. You can even use Word to translate the text in your document into a different language.

In addition to enabling you to generate your own documents, Word 2010 also eases the process of sharing your documents with others. For example, the program's Track Changes feature enables you to easily pinpoint where edits have been made and by whom. And of course, by providing features to expedite blogging, Word enables you to share your writing with the world.

Quick Tips

Word offers a gallery of several predefined header and footer designs, called *building blocks*, that you can apply. Headers appear in the top page margin area, and footers appear at the bottom. Headers and footers are a great way to place repeating information on your document pages, such as a document title, page numbers, company name, and so on. Word's predefined headers and footers make it easy to insert the information.

Alternatively, you can create your own header/footer building blocks — for example, one that contains your name and contact information in

the color and font of your choice — and add that design to the gallery. That way, anytime you need to insert that particular header or footer, instead of reconstructing it, you can simply click it in the gallery.

In addition to creating header/footer building blocks, you can also create building blocks with other custom Office elements, such as cover pages, pull-quotes, and so on. Building blocks might also contain specific text or a graphic that you want to reuse throughout your Word documents.

Create a Header/ Footer Building Block

1 After designing the header or footer that you want to add to the header/footer gallery, select the text in the header/footer.

2 Click the Insert tab.

3 Click Header or Footer (depending on whether you created a header or footer).

4 Click Save Selection to Header Gallery or Save Selection to Footer Gallery.

The Create New Building Block dialog box opens.

5 Type a name for the header or footer.

6 Specify the gallery in which the header or footer should reside.

7 Select a category for the header or footer.

● Optionally, you can type a description of the header or footer.

8 Click OK.

The custom header/footer is added to the gallery.

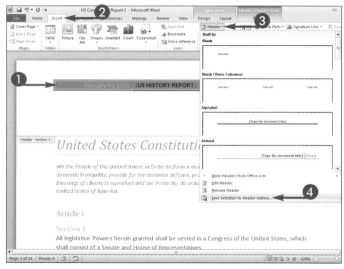

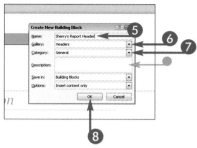

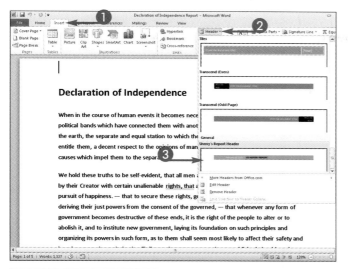

Apply a Header/Footer Building Block

1. With the document into which you want to insert the header or footer open, click the Insert tab.

2. Click Header or Footer.

3. Click the header or footer you want to add. (You might need to scroll down in the gallery to locate it.)

● The header or footer is inserted on the document page.

TIPS

Customize It!

If your document contains section breaks, you can apply different headers and footers to each section. Click in the section for which you want to create a unique header or footer, click Header or Footer in the Insert tab, and click Edit Header or Edit Footer. The Design tab appears in the Ribbon; click Link to Previous to deselect it. Then create the new header/footer or insert a header/footer building block from the gallery. (Repeat for each section in your document.) Designing separate headers and footers for even and odd pages is similar; just click the Different Odd & Even Pages check box (☐ changes to ☑) in the Design tab instead of clicking Link to Previous and add the different headers/footers as normal.

Apply It!

You can easily add headers or footers in Word 2010 just by clicking the Insert tab on the Ribbon and clicking the Header or Footer buttons in the Header & Footer tool group. Either button displays a list of pre-set headers or footers to choose from; you can you create your own from scratch by clicking Edit Header or Edit Footer.

Although Word offers several predefined Office elements, such as headers and footers, cover pages, pull-quotes, and so on, you can also create your own and add them to Word's gallery of choices. These elements, called *building blocks*, might contain specific text or a graphic you want to reuse — for example, your company logo or your name and contact information in the color and font of your choice.

You can share the building blocks you create by embedding them in a Word template, which

you can then distribute to others. Anytime someone applies the template you distribute to a document, the building blocks you embedded become available in that document.

To attach a template to a document, open the document, click the File tab, and click Options. In the Word Options dialog box, click Add-ins, click the Manage drop-down arrow, click Templates, and click Go. Finally, click Attach in the Templates and Add-ins dialog box, locate and select the template you want to attach, click Open, and click OK.

---

① Open the template to which you want to add a building block you have created.

② Select the text or graphic you want to include in the new building block.

③ Click the Insert tab.

④ In the Text group, click Quick Parts.

⑤ Click Save Selection to Quick Part Gallery.

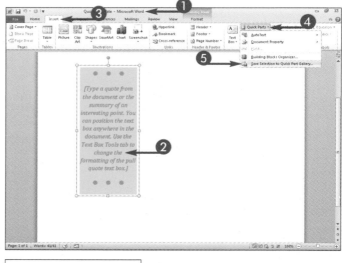

The Create New Building Block dialog box opens.

⑥ Type a name for the building block.

⑦ Specify the gallery in which the building block should reside.

⑧ Select a category for the building block.

⑨ Type a description of the building block.

● By default, the current template is listed here. To save the building block in another template, click here and choose another.

⑩ Click OK.

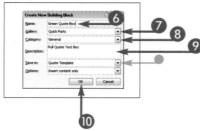

11 Save and close the template.

● The building block is added to the template. When the template is applied to a document, the block will be available from the gallery you specified.

Apply It!

To insert a building block that has been saved in a template into a document, attach the template to the document, click in the document in the spot where you want the building block to appear, click the Insert tab, click Quick Parts in the Insert group, and click the building block. If the building block does not appear in the gallery, click Building Blocks Organizer, locate and click the block you want to insert, and click Insert.

Important!

To include any paragraph formatting you have applied in the building block, ensure that the paragraph mark at the end of the paragraph is also selected. If no paragraph marks are visible, click the Home tab and, in the Paragraph group, click the Show/ Hide button (¶).

In today's global economy, being able to communicate with others who speak different languages is imperative. Fortunately, Word contains translation tools, including bilingual dictionaries and machine-translation functions, that enable you to quickly and easily translate words or phrases that you write in your native tongue into one of several other languages (and vice versa).

Word can translate text to and from many languages, including Arabic, Chinese, Dutch, English, French, German, Greek, Italian, Japanese, Korean, Portuguese, Russian, Spanish, and Swedish. (Note, however, that

your ability to translate text to and from all these languages may be limited by your computer's operating system.)

If you need to translate more than the occasional word or phrase and instead need to translate an entire document, you can use Word to access online translation services, some of which are fee-based.

Note that although translating text in this manner can convey the basics of the content, the full meaning and tone of the text may be lost. If it is imperative that the specifics of what the text contains be conveyed, human translation is recommended.

Translate a Word or Phrase

1. Right-click the word or phrase that you want to translate.

2. Click Translate.

● Word launches the Research pane, with the Translation options displayed.

3. Click here and choose the language you want to translate to.

● Word translates the selected text.

Translate a Document

1. With the document you want to translate open in Word, click the Review tab.

2. Click Translate.

3. Click Translate Document.

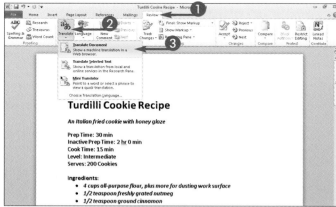

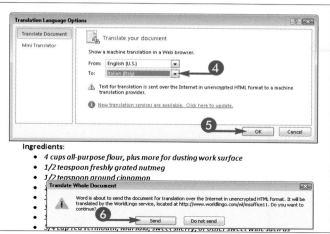

The Translation Language Options dialog box opens.

④ With the Translate Document tab selected, click the To drop-down arrow and choose a language.

⑤ Click OK.

⑥ Click Send.

● Word displays the translated text in your Web browser.

Note: You might find that only a portion of your document has been translated. In order for the rest of the document to be translated, you may need to pay a fee.

If you are new to the world of blogging, a *blog* is a sort of online journal. A blog might provide commentary on a topic as broad as food or politics, or as specific as the day-to-day activities of a single individual. Blogs can include text, images, links to other Web pages and blogs, and more.

Recent years have seen an explosion in the number of blogs on the Internet, with some estimates pegging the current number at more than 112,000,000. To accommodate this growing legion of bloggers, Microsoft has developed tools for composing and publishing

blogs to sites such as Windows Live Spaces and Blogger from within Word.

Composing blog posts within Word offers several advantages. First, you can use many of Word's formatting features, as well as its spelling- and grammar-checking capabilities on your blog entries. Second, you need not be connected to the Internet until you are ready to publish your piece.

To publish posts written in Word to your blog, you must first establish an account with a blogging site such as Blogger, and then register that account with Word.

① Click the File tab.

② Click New.

③ Double-click Blog post.

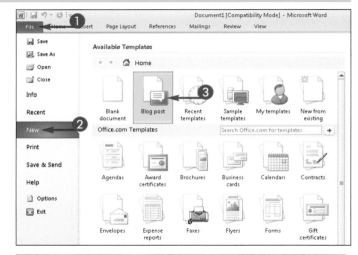

A Register a Blog Account prompt box appears if this is your first time creating a blog document.

④ Click Register Now to register your account with Word, or click Register Later if you want to complete the task after creating the blog. If you have already registered an account, skip to step 5.

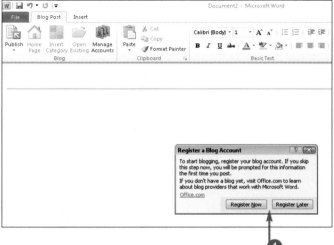

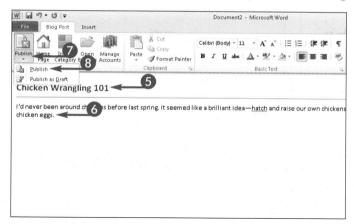

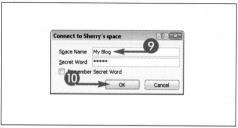

A blank blog post appears in the Word window.

⑤ Type a title for the post.

⑥ Type the text for your post, using Word's tools as needed to format and proofread the post.

⑦ Click Publish.

⑧ Click Publish or Publish as Draft.

A prompt box appears for you to log into your blog account.

⑨ Type in the appropriate logon information. Depending on your blog account, your logon information may vary.

⑩ Click OK to publish the blog.

Apply It!

If you are using Word to create a new blog post for the first time, Word prompts you to register your blog account. When it does, click Register an Account, click the Blog drop-down arrow, and choose your blog service provider. Click Next, enter the username and password for your blog account, click the Remember Password check box if you want Word to log you on automatically (☐ changes to ☑), and click OK.

Apply It!

Some blog providers automate the process of uploading photos to your blog; others require that you establish a separate account with a picture provider — that is, a site devoted solely to storing photos. To determine whether you need a picture provider account, check with your blog provider.

Navigating longer documents can be a bit daunting, especially when you are trying to locate a specific word or phrase. Word offers you several tools to help you search through a document. For simple word searches, the Navigation pane pops up and lets you search through a document, displaying any matches. You can use the pane's Search text box to enter the word or phrase you are looking for and immediately see any matches in the document.

The tried-and-true Find and Replace tool is the other go-to feature for searching through a document. You can use the Find portion of the tool to look for each occurrence of a word or phrase, and you can use the Replace portion of the tool to replace the word with different text. This makes quick work of finding a misspelled name and replacing it with the correct spelling, or searching a report for a particular price point and replacing it with a new price.

You can also use the Go To tab in the Find and Replace dialog box to jump to specific points in a document.

Finding Text

① Click the Home tab.

② Click the Find drop-down arrow.

③ Click Find.

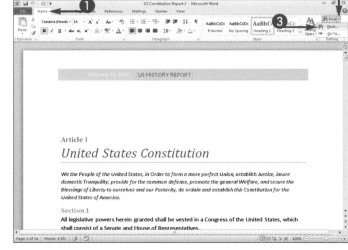

● The Navigation pane opens.

④ Type the word you want to look for in the Search text box.

● Word immediately highlights the first match in the document.

You can continue searching for more occurrences as needed.

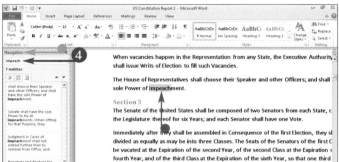

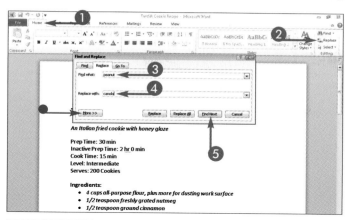

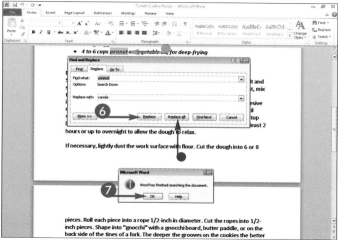

Finding and Replacing Text

① Click the Home tab.

② Click Replace.

The Find and Replace dialog box opens with the Replace tab displayed.

③ Type the word you want to look for in the Find What text box.

④ Type the replacement text in the Replace With text box.

● To view additional search criteria, click More and make your selections.

⑤ Click Find Next.

● Word highlights the first occurrence in the document.

⑥ Click Replace to replace the text.

● To replace all the occurrences, click Replace All.

⑦ When the search is complete, click OK.

More Options!

If you want to find a word and not replace it, just use the Find tab in the Find and Replace dialog box. It looks nearly identical to the Replace tab, only lacking the Replace With text box. To find a word, click the Home tab on the Ribbon and click Find to open the Navigation pane. You can type the word or phrase you are looking for in the Search box at the top of the pane; then press Enter to search for the first occurrence of the text.

More Options!

You can find a variety of tools for finding your way around longer documents. Learn more about navigating with bookmarks in the task "Jump Around Documents with Bookmarks" later in this chapter. You can also use the Navigation pane to navigate through longer documents by viewing thumbnails of your pages. See the task "Navigate Long Documents with the Navigation Pane."

If you are having trouble finding just the right word or phrase, you can use Word's thesaurus tool to find words with similar meanings (synonyms) as well as words with the opposite meaning (antonyms). Word even enables you to access thesauri in different languages. For example, if you are writing a document in French, you can use Word's French thesaurus just as you would use the English version when composing in English. In addition, Word includes a dictionary tool, which you can use to look up words of whose meanings you are not quite certain.

You access these tools from within Word's Research pane, from which you also access the program's translation tools and other reference-based features such as an encyclopedia, as well as research sites including HighBeam Research, the MSN Money Stock Quotes site, and the Thomson Gale Company Profiles site.

Another way to use the thesaurus and dictionary tools is to right-click the word for which you want to see synonyms or a definition. Word displays a context menu from which you can choose the desired option.

Find a Synonym

1. Right-click the word for which you want to find a synonym.

2. Click Synonyms.

   Word displays a list of synonyms.

3. Click the desired synonym.

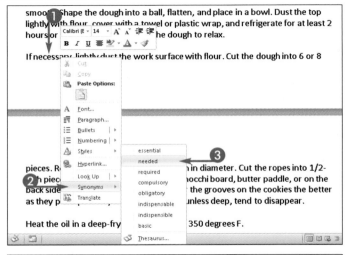

- Word replaces the original word with the synonym you selected.

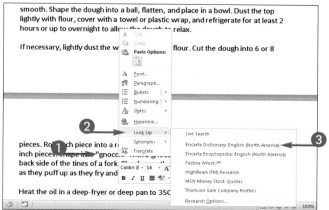

smooth. Shape the dough into a ball, flatten, and place in a bowl. Dust the top lightly with flour, cover with a towel or plastic wrap, and refrigerate for at least 2 hours or up to overnight to allow the dough to relax.

If necessary, lightly dust the w ... flour. Cut the dough into 6 or 8

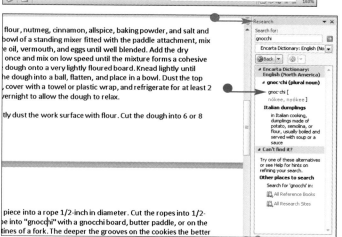

pieces. Ro ... ch piece into a r ... inch pieces ... "gnocc ... back side of the tines of a fork ... as they puff up as they fry and ...

Heat the oil in a deep-fryer or deep pan to 350

flour, nutmeg, cinnamon, allspice, baking powder, and salt and bowl of a standing mixer fitted with the paddle attachment, mix e oil, vermouth, and eggs until well blended. Add the dry once and mix on low speed until the mixture forms a cohesive dough onto a very lightly floured board. Knead lightly until he dough into a ball, flatten, and place in a bowl. Dust the top , cover with a towel or plastic wrap, and refrigerate for at least 2 vernight to allow the dough to relax.

tly dust the work surface with flour. Cut the dough into 6 or 8

piece into a rope 1/2-inch in diameter. Cut the ropes into 1/2-
ge into "gnocchi" with a gnocchi board, butter paddle, or on the
tines of a fork. The deeper the grooves on the cookies the better

Look Up a Word

① Right-click the word you want to look up.

② Click Look Up.

③ Click a resource.

● Word launches the Research pane and the resource you selected. In this example, the Encarta Dictionary (English) is activated.

● Word displays definitions of the word.

Apply It!
Another way to open Word's Research pane is to click the Research button in the Ribbon's Review tab.

Apply It!
Word's Research pane offers easy access to several online resources, such as the Encarta Encyclopedia, a free Web-based encyclopedia. You can change the reference source at any time in the Research pane. Click the drop-down arrow next to the source name beneath the Search box and choose another reference. If you do not see a source you want, you can use any of the links in the Research pane to access more resources online.

Another useful tool to help you navigate documents that span numerous pages is the ability to create bookmarks. A bookmark is rather like a physical bookmark you place in a book to save your place. A Word bookmark earmarks a specific location within a document. In essence, a bookmark identifies a location or selection of text in a document for future reference. For example, you might add a bookmark to a section in your document that you want to revise later, or you might use bookmarks to help you access an area of the document quickly.

You can assign a unique name to a bookmark, but the name must follow a few naming rules. Bookmark names must begin with a letter, and names can include numbers along with letter characters. However, no spaces are allowed in the bookmark name. If you do need to create a space, use an underscore character instead, such as Section_10.

To navigate to a bookmark, you can press Ctrl+G to open the Find and Replace dialog box to the Go To tab. Select Bookmark from the list, then choose the bookmark name you want to navigate to and click Go To.

Create a Bookmark

1. Navigate to the location where you want to add a bookmark and select the text.

2. Click the Insert tab on the Ribbon.

3. Click Bookmark.

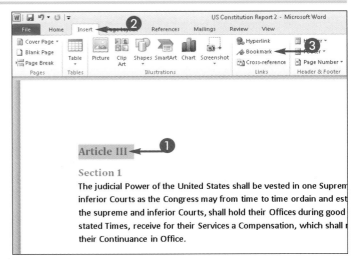

The Bookmark dialog box opens.

4. Type a name for the new bookmark.

5. Click Add to create the bookmark.

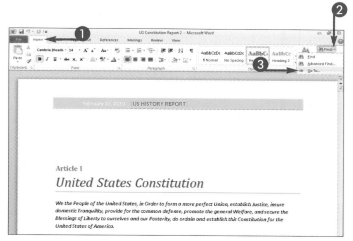

Navigate to a Bookmark

① Click the Home tab.

② Click the Find button's drop-down arrow.

③ Click Go To.

Note: *You can also press F5 or Ctrl+G.*

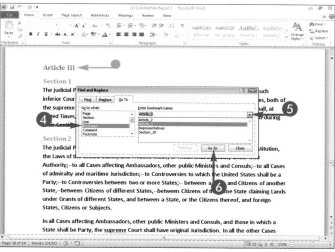

The Find and Replace dialog box opens to the Go To tab.

④ Click Bookmark.

⑤ Click the drop-down arrow and select the bookmark you want to navigate to.

⑥ Click Go To.

● Word displays the specified location in the document.

Remove It!
To remove a bookmark you no longer need, open the Bookmark dialog box, select the bookmark name from the list box, and click the Delete button.

More Options!
You can also mark a location instead of selected text as a bookmark. Just click the Location option at the bottom of the Bookmark dialog box when defining the bookmark (◯ changes to ◉). Keep in mind, however, that if you move the text, the bookmark stays.

You can use the new and improved Navigation pane to help you navigate your way around long documents. For example, if you are working on a long legal document or thesis paper, you can use the pane to quickly navigate to a page, a particular heading, or even a particular word or phrase.

The Navigation pane offers tools for browsing a document. One of the handiest browsing tools is to browse by headings. The Navigation pane lists the document's sections based on styles you assign, such as Heading 1, Heading 2, and so on. You can use the pane's list to quickly jump to a specific heading in your document.

You can also use the pane to browse through a document by viewing thumbnail images of all the pages. To view a page in its entirety, just click the thumbnail image.

The pane also lets you search through your document for words or phrases. This is covered in the task "Search Through a Document" earlier in this chapter.

① Click the View tab on the Ribbon.

② Click the Navigation Pane check box (☐ changes to ☑).

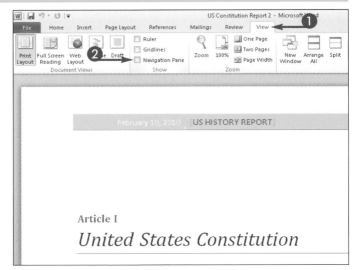

● Word displays the Navigation pane.

③ To browse headings, click the Browse the Headings tab.

④ Click the heading you want to navigate to in the document.

● Word immediately moves the document view to the designated heading.

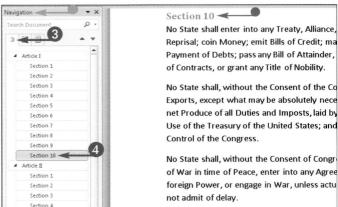

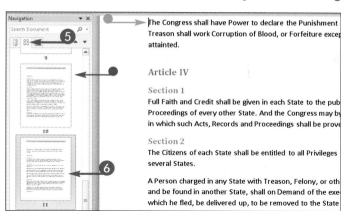

⑤ To browse by pages, click the Browse by Pages tab.

● Word displays pages as thumbnails in the pane.

⑥ Click the page you want to view.

Note: *You may need to scroll to the page you want to view.*

● Word immediately moves the document view to the selected page.

● To search for a word or phrase in the document, click the Browse the Results tab, type a word or phrase in the search box and press Enter.

Note: *See the task "Search Through a Document" to learn more about using the pane's search tool.*

⑦ Click here to close the pane when finished.

Remove It!

You can also close the pane by clicking the View tab and deselecting the Navigation Pane check box (☑ changes to ☐).

More Options!

You can resize the Navigation pane if you need to view more of the headings listed within. Simply move the mouse pointer to the right border of the pane, and then click and drag the pane to resize its width.

Do you find yourself typing the same long phrase or paragraph of text into a document over and over again? You can take away the tedium by saving the text as an AutoText entry. For example, if your company name is particularly long, you can simply add it to the AutoText Gallery and insert it as you need it.

Word's AutoText feature has been around for a long time, allowing users to speed up repetitious text-entry tasks. With Word 2010, AutoText is a part of the building blocks, a feature that lets you reuse chunks of data

throughout your documents. Building blocks, also known as Quick Parts, make it easy to insert preformatted text and graphics. AutoText is a part of this feature, offering its own gallery of stored snippets of text, such as salutations and closings for letters, lengthy legal disclaimers, contact information, and more.

When creating your own custom AutoText entries, you use the Create New Building Block dialog box, where you can assign a unique name for the text, and choose in which template you want to store the entry.

---

① Select the text you want to turn into an AutoText entry.

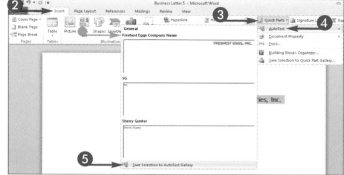

② Click the Insert tab.

③ Click Quick Parts.

④ Click AutoText.

● Word displays the AutoText Gallery.

⑤ Click Save Selection to AutoText Gallery to open the Create New Building Block dialog box.

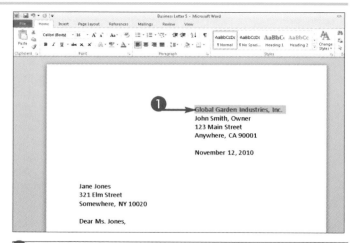

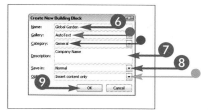

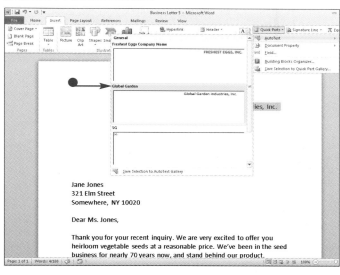

6 Click the Name box and type a name for the entry.

● By default, Word stores the entry in the AutoText Gallery, unless you specify another.

● AutoText entries are categorized as General by default.

7 Optionally, click the Description box and type a description of the entry.

8 To save the entry in the default template, leave Normal selected. To save it in another template, click here and specify the template.

● AutoText entries are typically inserted as content only. To insert your entry as its own paragraph or page, click here and make your selection.

9 Click OK.

● Word adds the entry to the AutoText Gallery.

Remove It!

To delete an AutoText entry you no longer need, display it in the AutoText Gallery, right-click it, and select the Organize and Delete command from the pop-up menu that appears. This opens the Building Blocks Organizer dialog box. With the entry highlighted in the dialog box's list box, click the Delete button to permanently remove the entry.

More Options!

If your Word tasks involve numerous AutoText entries related to a certain project or department, you can create a unique category for the entries, making it easier to find them listed in the Building Blocks Organizer dialog box. To create a new category, click the Category drop-down arrow in the Create New Building Block dialog box and click Create New Category. This opens a Create New Category dialog box where you can assign the new category a name. The next time you create an AutoText entry, you can assign the new category. You can also assign the new category to existing entries listed in the Building Blocks Organizer dialog box.

Word's AutoCorrect feature has long been a tool for automatically correcting misspelled words in your documents. You can also use it to help automate some of your typing tasks. AutoCorrect comes loaded with a long list of commonly misspelled words, and because the feature is turned on automatically, you may have already noticed it kicking in when mistyping words. For example, if you type "teh," AutoCorrect automatically corrects the spelling to "the."

If you are like most people, you probably have a few words not in the AutoCorrect list that you consistently misspell. You can add them to AutoCorrect's repertoire and count on Word to correct the problems as they arise.

In addition to misspellings, you can turn a phrase into an AutoCorrect entry. For example, if your company name is particularly long, you can simply type an abbreviation and Word offers to fill in the rest for you, saving you the time and effort of activating the AutoText Gallery where you normally store snippets of preset text.

---

① Click the File tab.

② Click Options.

The Word Options dialog box opens.

③ Click Proofing.

④ Click AutoCorrect Options.

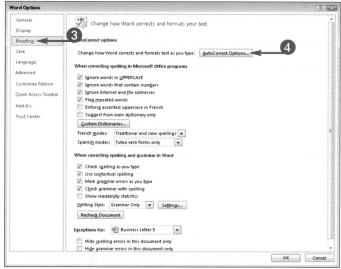

The AutoCorrect dialog box opens.

⑤ Click in the Replace box and type the misspelled word you want to add to the list.

⑥ Click in the With box and type the correct spelling of the word.

⑦ Click Add.

● AutoCorrect adds the word to the list.

⑧ Click OK.

⑨ Click OK to close the Word Options dialog box.

Did You Know?

To turn a long phrase into an AutoCorrect entry activated when you type the designated abbreviation, simply type the abbreviation in the Replace box in the AutoCorrect dialog box, and then type the full phrase in the With box. Click Add to add the entry to the listings.

Caution!

If you are having trouble adding a word in the With box in the AutoCorrect dialog box, click the Plain Text option (○ changes to ◉) and then try again.

Are you looking for a little drama to dress up your text? Word's drop caps feature might be just the thing you are looking for. You can use drop caps to quickly draw attention to the first letter in a paragraph. Commonly used in the printing business, a drop cap is the first letter in a paragraph that drops below the text line and extends into the second line of text, creating a large letter.

Throughout the history of printing, drop caps were used at the beginning of a chapter. You can use them in Word to the same effect.

You can use the Drop Cap dialog box to determine whether the letter drops within a paragraph or outside the paragraph margin. You can also change the drop cap's font, number of lines dropped, and even the distance between the drop cap and the rest of the paragraph text.

As with any formatting technique, it is good practice to use the drop cap feature sparingly. Too many on a page become quite distracting.

---

① Select the character you want to turn into a drop cap.

② Click the Insert tab on the Ribbon.

③ Click Drop Cap.

④ Click Drop Cap Options.

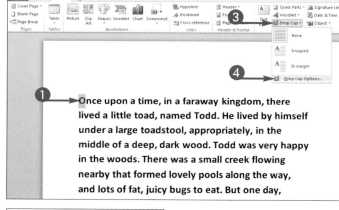

The Drop Cap dialog box opens.

⑤ Choose whether you want the position dropped or in the margin.

⑥ To choose a different font, click here and choose another.

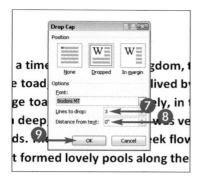

⓻ To change the number of lines dropped, type a new value here or use the spinner arrows to set a value.

⓼ To change the distance of the drop cap from the rest of the paragraph text, type a new value here or use the spinner arrows to set a value.

⓽ Click OK.

● Word applies the drop cap to the text.

O nce upon a time, in a faraway kingdom, there lived a little toad, named Todd. He lived by himself under a large toadstool, appropriately, in the middle of a deep, dark wood. Todd was very happy in the woods. There was a small creek flowing nearby that formed lovely pools along the way, and lots of fat, juicy bugs to eat. But one day, while hopping around the area, he ran into a stranger he had never seen in the woods before.

TIPS

Try This!
For a quick drop cap without any changes to the settings, just click the Drop Cap button on the Insert tab and click Dropped or In Margin to immediately assign the effect to the selected letter in the document. You can also just click anywhere in a paragraph and apply a drop cap to the first letter using this technique.

Remove It!
To remove a drop cap, select it or click the paragraph containing the drop cap and click the Drop Cap button again, this time choosing None from the menu that appears. You can also open the Drop Cap dialog box and select None from the position options.

As you are well aware, Word 2010 installs with a myriad of default settings in place for controlling everything from font and font size to margins as soon as you start the program. Although most of these settings work well for the average user, you may require different settings based on the type of work you do. Line spacing is an area in which individual document needs outweigh the defaults. By default, the line spacing is set to Multiple, which adds 1.15 points between each line of text. Happily, you can change the default line spacing to suit the way in which you work with Word. For example, if you produce a lot of

research and term papers, you may need to set the line spacing to Double, or if you are writing an article or book, you can change the setting to Single spacing.

Another spacing issue you may need to change is the default setting for paragraph spacing. By default, Word adds 10 points after a paragraph. This creates a gap of white space between paragraphs for you. Although this can be pleasing aesthetically, it does not work for all documents. You can change the spacing before and after paragraphs to suit your document needs.

① Click the Home tab on the Ribbon.

② Click the dialog box launcher in the Paragraph group on the Home tab.

Word opens the Paragraph dialog box.

③ To set new line spacing, click the Line Spacing drop-down arrow.

④ Set a new line spacing to keep as your default setting.

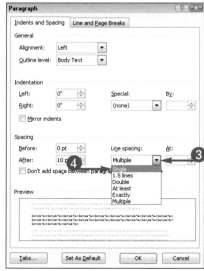

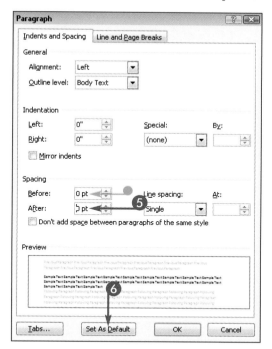

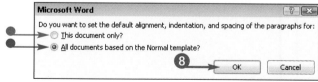

⑤ To set new paragraph spacing, click the After box and type a new value, or use the spinner arrows to change the value.

● Optionally, you can also set spacing to appear before each new paragraph, if needed.

⑥ Click the Set As Default button.

A prompt box appears asking how you want to save the changes.

⑦ Choose an option (○ changes to ◉):

● Click This Document Only if you want to keep the new defaults in place only for the current document. New settings will not affect new documents you create.

● Click All Documents Based on the Normal Template to keep the new default settings for all new documents you create in Word.

⑧ Click OK to save the new settings.

Did You Know?
Document settings are saved along with the Normal template, the template that starts every new file you create using the New command or the new file that appears every time you open Word. This default template, though blank in appearance, has all the default settings in place for font, font size, and paragraph settings. To learn more about setting a default font and font size, see Chapter 1.

More Options!
You can also set other new defaults in the Paragraph dialog box for alignment, indentations, and line and page breaks. Simply open the dialog box and make the changes, then click the Set As Default button to make the changes permanent to the current document or all future documents based on the Normal template.

With some documents you create in Word, you may find yourself needing a horizontal line placed on the page. One way to add a line is to draw one using Word's Shapes. This option lets you draw the line precisely where you want it and to the length you want, even adding arrows or other flourishes to either end of the line. While offering you a variety of formatting options for the line, this method takes a little longer to perform.

If you are looking for a more straightforward line, consider using this little-known technique — you can type characters on your keyboard and turn them into an instant horizontal line on your document page. You can choose from a solid line that is a ½ point thick, a dotted line, a double line, a thick line, a wavy line, or even a thick decorative line.

This technique works only when you add the horizontal line to a new line of text in your document.

① Click where you want to insert the line in your document.

② Type three dashes (---).

③ Press Enter.

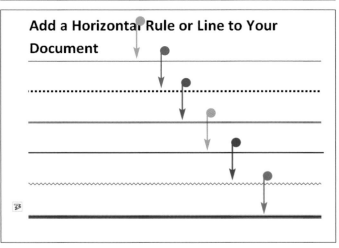

Add a Horizontal Rule or Line to Your Document

● Word inserts the line.

● To add a dashed line, type three asterisks (***) and press Enter.

● To add a double line, type three equal signs (===) and press Enter.

● To add a thick line, type three underscores (_ _ _) and press Enter.

● To add a wavy line, type three tildes (~~~) and press Enter.

● To add a thick, decorative line, type three pound signs (###) and press Enter.

When you use numbered lists in your Word document, you may sometimes need to interrupt the numbered list with a paragraph, and then resume the list. Word's SmartTags can help you pick up where you left off with the numbering. For example, perhaps you are explaining a procedure step by step, but need to add a paragraph clarifying a feature or exception to the steps, and then restart the numbered list to continue on. Ordinarily, you might think you must start a new list to set a new number sequence. Save your time and use this technique instead.

When you reapply the numbers again after the interruption of a paragraph, Word first assumes you want to start a brand new numbered list and promptly adds the number 1 to the list as usual. A SmartTag icon also appears next to the number, resembling a lightning bolt icon. You can activate the SmartTag and choose the Continue Numbering option to resume the numbering sequence. If you choose to ignore the SmartTag, you can simply start a brand new numbered list instead if you just keep typing.

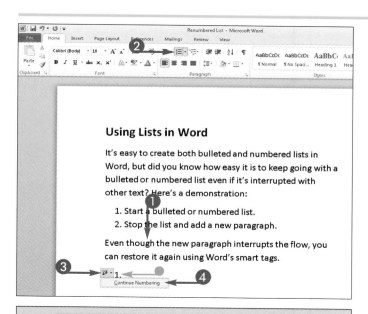

① Type your list and paragraph.

② Start the new numbered list on the next line by clicking the Numbering button on the Home tab.

● Word inserts the number 1 and displays a SmartTag icon.

③ Click the SmartTag.

④ Click Continue Numbering.

● Word changes the number to reflect where the previous list ended.

You can use partial or full borders to set off a paragraph within your document. For example, you can use a partial border to set off a pull-quote. A pull-quote is a sentence or two that you copy or extract from the document text to set off for visual and dramatic effect. Pull-quotes commonly appear in magazines and newspapers.

You can also set off an entire paragraph with a border, drawing attention to the text or message. For example, you can use a border to make the reader notice a paragraph of important facts and statistics, or a paragraph of important instructions or details.

For additional border formatting, you can access the Borders and Shading dialog box. You can choose from a variety of line styles and thicknesses, and control the color of the line borders. You can also change border color, set partial borders, or even apply a 3-D, shadow, or custom style. You can preview your border selections in the dialog box before applying them to the actual paragraph.

Add a Border

① Click inside of or select the paragraph to which you want to add a border.

② Click the Home tab.

③ Click the Borders drop-down arrow.

④ Click the border you want to apply.

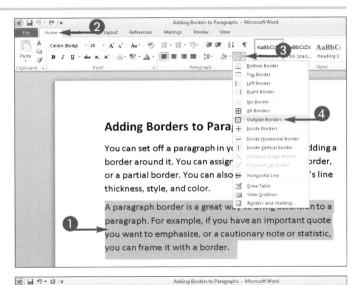

● Word applies the border.

● To apply background shading to the paragraph and border, click the Shading button and choose a color.

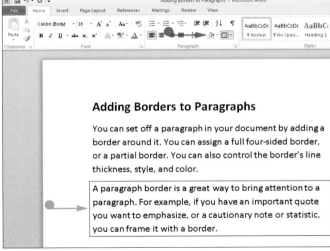

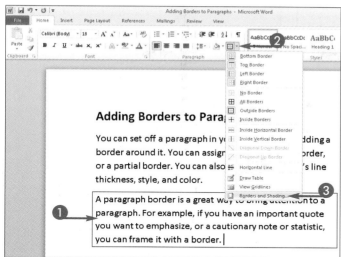

Format a Border

1 Click inside of or select the paragraph containing the border you want to edit.

2 Click the Borders drop-down arrow.

3 Click Borders and Shading.

The Borders and Shading dialog box opens.

4 Click the line style you want to apply.

5 Click here to change the line color.

6 Click here to set a new line thickness.

● The preview area lets you see what the formatting looks like before applying it.

○ You can click these buttons to create partial borders around the paragraph.

7 Click OK.

● Word applies the changes to the border.

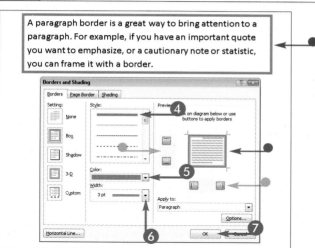

Did You Know?

You can add a border to an entire page in your document. You can use the Borders and Shading dialog box to set a page border, line style, color, width, or even apply an artsy border complete with graphical elements. Simply click the Page Border tab in the Borders and Shading dialog box. You can also add page borders using the Page Borders button on the Ribbon's Page Layout tab. This route opens the same Borders and Shading dialog box to the Page Border tab.

Remove It!

To delete a paragraph border you no longer want, select the paragraph, click the Borders drop-down arrow on the Home tab, and then click No Border from the menu.

If you work in an environment in which you share your Word documents with others, you can use the program's Track Changes feature to help you keep track of changes made to the file by you and by others.

When Track Changes is enabled, Word tracks edits such as formatting changes and text additions and deletions you or other users make to the file. Additions appear inline in the text; deletions appear either inline in the text or in balloons in the right margin, depending on the document view. For example, in Word, using Draft view displays deletions inline and

comments appear only when you move the mouse pointer over the text; using Print Layout view, however, displays deletions inline and comments appear in balloons in the right margin. If multiple people review the document, each person's changes appear in a different color to help you keep track of who made what edits.

When you review a document that has been edited with Track Changes on, Word flags each change that each user makes in the document, which you can then accept or reject.

① To enable Word's Track Changes feature, click the Review tab in the Ribbon.

② Click Track Changes.

Note: *If you click the Track Changes button drop-down arrow, you can access tracking options and change the username if you are not using your own computer to edit the file.*

③ Edit the document, adding and deleting text and changing the formatting as needed.

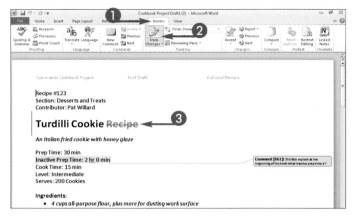

④ To begin reviewing changes to an edited document, click at the beginning of the document.

Note: *To turn off the Track Changes feature, click the Track Changes button a second time to disable it.*

⑤ Click Next in the Review tab.

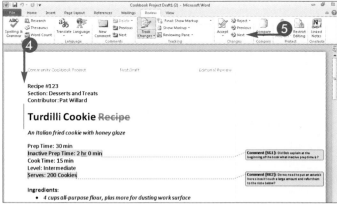

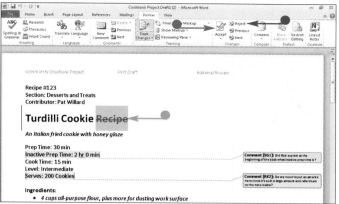

● Word highlights the first change in the document.

● To accept the change, click Accept in the Review tab.

● To reject the change, click Reject in the Review tab.

Note: *To accept all changes in the document, click the drop-down arrow under Accept and click Accept All Changes in Document.*

● Depending on which button you clicked, Word accepts (as shown here) or rejects the change.

● Word automatically highlights the next change in the document, which you can choose to accept or reject. You can continue accepting or rejecting changes as needed.

Did You Know?

By default, insertions appear as underlined text, and deletions appear either inline as strikethrough text, depending on the view. To change these and other settings, click the drop-down arrow beside Track Changes and choose Change Tracking Options. The Track Changes Options dialog box opens; change the settings as desired.

Try This!

You can click the Accept button's drop-down arrow and choose to accept all the changes in a document. You can also click the Reject button's drop-down arrow and choose to reject all the changes.

If you or someone else makes changes to a document without first enabling the Track Changes feature, but you want to determine exactly what edits were made, you can compare the edited document with the original.

When you compare an original document with an updated version, the result is a third file that flags the discrepancies between the two documents. (The two source documents — that is, the original and revised versions — remain unchanged.) These discrepancies look exactly like edits made with Track Changes enabled; that is, formatting changes and text additions and deletions become visible.

Additions and deletions appear inline in the text in Print Layout or Draft view. In Print Layout view, comments appear in balloons in the right margin. In Draft view, comments only appear when you move the mouse pointer over the text.

You review a file generated by comparing documents the same way you review a file that has been edited with Track Changes enabled. Word flags each change in the document, which you can then accept or reject.

---

1 With the original version of the document open, click the Review tab.

2 Click Compare.

3 Click Compare.

The Compare Documents dialog box appears.

4 Click here and choose the original version of the document you want to compare.

5 Click here and choose the revised version of the document.

Note: If the original or revised document does not appear in the list, click the Browse button ([image]) to the right of the Original Document or Revised Document field and choose the desired document from the Open dialog box that appears.

● To view additional comparison features, click More.

6 Click OK.

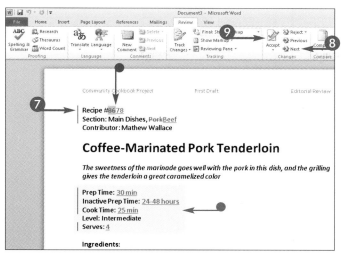

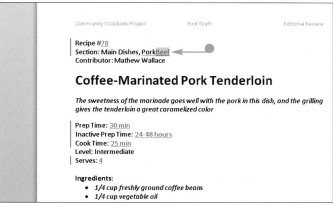

- Word compares the document by creating a new document file, flagging discrepancies such as text additions and deletions as well as formatting changes.

7 To begin reviewing the discrepancies, click at the beginning of the document.

8 Click Next on the Review tab.

- Word highlights the first discrepancy in the document.

9 Accept or reject the change. To accept the change, click Accept in the Review tab (as shown here). To reject the change, click Reject in the Review tab.

Note: To accept all changes in the document, click the down arrow under Accept and click Accept All Changes in Document.

- Depending on which button you clicked, Word accepts or rejects the change, and automatically highlights the next one in the document, which you can choose to accept or reject.

Did You Know?

To combine multiple revised files into a single document, click Compare on the Review tab and choose Combine. Select the original version of the document from the Original Document list, and select any of the reviewed versions from the Revised Document list. Click More and, under Show Changes In, click Original Document, and then click OK. Repeat for each revised version of the document.

More Options!

Another way to collaborate with others on a document is to use Word's Comments feature. To add a comment, select the text on which you want to comment, click New Comment in the Comments group of the Review tab, and type your comment in the balloon or field that appears.

You can insert filler text, also called dummy text or placeholder text, into a Word document. When creating a mock-up or layout design for a project in Word, such as a brochure or newsletter, you may need to insert some placeholder text. Filler text allows you to show how text fits into the layout, as well as demonstrate the font and size you plan to use later when you replace the placeholder text with the actual text.

You can use the RAND function to create filler text in Word. If you prefer Latin text instead of English, you can use the LOREM function

instead, such as =lorem(4,5). A function is a preset mathematical formula. Using the formula rules of Excel, all functions start with an equal sign, such as =rand(4,5). The numbers in parentheses determine the number of paragraphs and the number of sentences per paragraph. For example, =rand(4,5) creates four paragraphs with five sentences of dummy text in each paragraph. Your own design layout may require more or less paragraphs and sentences.

After inserting the filler text, you can apply formatting to the text.

---

① Click in the document where you want to insert filler text.

② Type **=rand(4,5)**.

To insert a different number of paragraphs, replace 4 with a different number.

To insert a different number of sentences, replace 5 with a different number.

③ Press Enter.

● Word inserts the text.

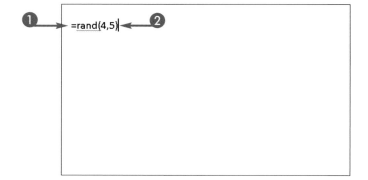

On the Insert tab, the galleries include items that are designed to coordinate with the overall look of your document. You can use these galleries to insert tables, headers, footers, lists, cover pages, and other document building blocks. When you create pictures, charts, or diagrams, they also coordinate with your current document look. You can easily change the formatting of selected text in the document text by choosing a look for the selected text from the Quick Styles gallery on the Home tab. You can also format text directly by using the other controls on the Home tab.

Most controls offer a choice of using the look from the current theme or using a format that you specify directly.

By default, Word 2010 automatically wraps a line of text to the next line once you reach the right margin of a document. However, this may result in an awkward break up of a multiword phrase or proper names. For example, if you type the name John Smith at the end of the line, Word may wrap the last name to the next line of text. Thankfully, you can apply a nonbreaking space to keep names and other multiword phrases together, and Word breaks before or after the phrase or name rather than in the middle.

Nonbreaking spaces, also called no-break spaces, are often crucial in certain types of reports and papers. You can use nonbreaking spaces to keep measurements together, such as 100 km, or version numbers intact, such as IE 8.9.

Nonbreaking spaces, like other nonprinting paragraph marks, do not appear visible in Print Layout view. If you want to see the spaces, you must turn on Word's Paragraph Marks; click the Show/Hide button (¶) on the Ribbon's Home tab.

together·the·olive·oil,·vermouth,·and·eggs·until·well·blended.·Add·the·dry· ingredients·all·at·once·and·mix·on·low·speed·until·the·mixture·forms·a·cohesive· mass.·Scrape·the·dough·onto·a·very·lightly·floured·board.·Knead·lightly·until· smooth.·Shape·the·dough·into·a·ball,·flatten,·and·place·in·a·bowl.·Dust·the·top· lightly·with·flour,·cover·with·a·towel·or·plastic·wrap,·and·refrigerate·for·at·least·2· hours·or·up·to·overnight·to·allow·the·dough·to·relax.·¬

Community·Cookbook·Project   →   First·Draft   →   Editorial·Review¶

1 Select the space after the first word in the phrase or name.

2 Press Ctrl+Shift+ Spacebar.

together·the·olive·oil,·vermouth,·and·eggs·until·well·blended.·Add·the·dry· ingredients·all·at·once·and·mix·on·low·speed·until·the·mixture·forms·a·cohesive· mass.·Scrape·the·dough·onto·a·very·lightly·floured·board.·Knead·lightly·until· smooth.·Shape·the·dough·into·a·ball,·flatten,·and·place·in·a·bowl.·Dust·the·top· lightly·with·flour,·cover·with·a·towel·or·plastic·wrap,·and·refrigerate·for·at·least· 2·hours·or·up·to·overnight·to·allow·the·dough·to·relax.·¬

Community·Cookbook·Project   →   First·Draft   →   Editorial·Review¶

● Word adds a nonbreaking space.

Charts and graphs are a great way to illustrate your data. Word 2010 includes several tools you can use to add charts and graphs to your documents. For example, you can use the SmartArt feature to quickly insert preset diagrams and simply insert your own text elements to describe a process, hierarchy, or other procedure. If you need a tried-and-true data-based chart, you can tap into the power of Excel's chart-building tools to create pie charts, bar charts, surface charts, and more, all linked and alongside Word.

If you have Excel 2010 installed, you can take advantage of the program's advanced charting capabilities. When you activate the charting feature, Excel opens with a new worksheet ready for you to replace the placeholder text with your own chart data. Using columns, rows, and cells, you enter the raw data to make the chart. Over in Word, the same placeholder chart appears in your document in its full chart form. Data you add in Excel is immediately added to the Word chart, too.

When you create a chart, Word displays additional charting tabs on the Ribbon that you can use to format the chart.

If you do not have Excel installed, the Microsoft Graph feature opens instead.

---

① **Click where you want to insert a chart and click the Insert tab.**

② **Click Chart.**

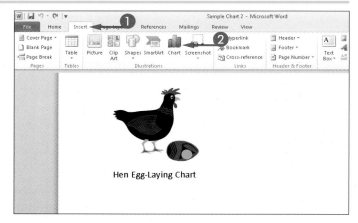

The Insert Chart dialog box opens.

③ **Click the category of chart you want to make.**

④ **Click the chart type.**

⑤ **Click OK.**

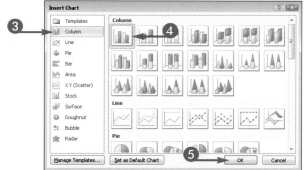

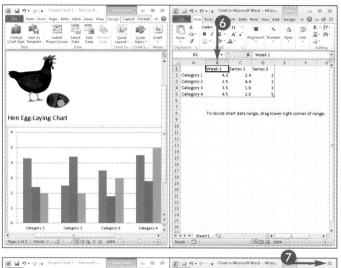

Excel opens and shares on-screen room with your Word document. A data sheet is ready to go in the worksheet, and a placeholder chart appears in the document.

6 Enter the data you want to chart using the worksheet cells.

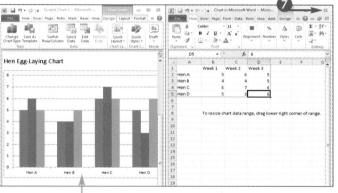

● The chart data is immediately updated in the Word document.

7 When finished entering your chart data, click Close to exit the Excel window.

Apply It!

To change your chart type, select the chart, click the Design tab under Chart Tools, and click the Change Chart Type button. This opens the Change Chart Type dialog box, which is exactly the same as the Insert Chart dialog box in step 3. Choose another chart type and click OK. The chart is immediately updated in the document. To delete a chart, select it in the document and press Delete.

More Options!

If you need to make changes to the chart data, you can reopen the datasheet in Excel and edit the cell data. Click the Design tab and click the Edit Data button. This reopens the Excel program window again with the chart data displayed. Simply edit the data and close Excel when you are finished. The chart is automatically updated in Word as you work.

Chapter 4

Utilizing Word's Document Building Tools

Other Word tools help you save time by generating special elements for your documents. One such special element is a bibliography, which lists the books, Web sites, and other sources used in the course of researching and writing your document. You simply add citations to the document that include the relevant information, and Word does the rest. Another special element you can generate automatically in Word is a table of contents that contains all the headings in your document.

To ensure that your document meets the strict standards of academic and professional environments, you can use Word to insert footnotes and endnotes. Word numbers these footnotes, automatically updating them as you add, delete, and move text in your document. This saves you the time and trouble of tracking these items yourself.

Finally, to help you make your documents look more professional, Word includes tools for creating a cover page, including several built-in designs from which you can choose. You can also add line numbers to your pages, or quickly insert cross-references to other parts of your document.

Quick Tips

If you are writing an academic paper, you will almost certainly be required to include a bibliography, a listing of all the books and other works cited in the paper. Word enables you to automatically generate a bibliography and format its entries using the style guide of your choice. Style guide options include American Psychological Association (APA), Modern Language Association (MLA), and The Chicago Manual of Style. To specify what style guide you want to use, click the References tab, click the Style drop-down arrow in the Citations & Bibliography group, and choose a style guide from the list that appears.

For Word to determine which entries should appear in the bibliography, you must cite sources in your document as you work. Word then collects the information from these citations to generate the bibliography. When you add a source to a document, Word saves it for use in subsequent documents, meaning that instead of reentering the information, you can search for the existing source.

Add a Citation

① Click at the end of the sentence or phrase that contains information you want to cite.

② Click the References tab.

③ Click Insert Citation.

④ Click Add New Source.

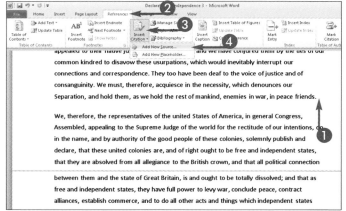

The Create Source dialog box opens.

⑤ Click here and select the type of source you want to cite.

Note: *The fields available in the Create Source dialog box depend on what you select in the Type of Source drop-down list.*

⑥ Type the author's name.

⑦ Type the source's title.

⑧ Type the year of publication.

⑨ Type the name of the city in which the source was published.

⑩ Type the name of the publisher.

⑪ Click OK.

● Word adds a citation to your document.

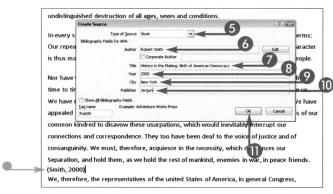

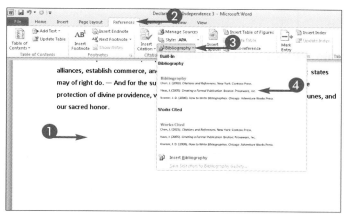

Generate the Bibliography

① Click the spot in the document where you want the bibliography to appear (typically at the end).

② Click the References tab.

③ Click Bibliography.

④ Click one of the gallery options to insert a predesigned bibliography into your document.

● Word inserts the bibliography.

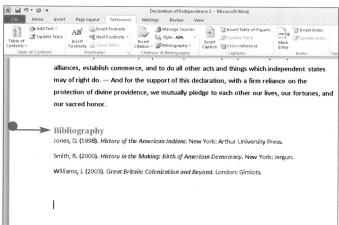

TIPS

Did You Know?

To reuse a source from another document, click Manage Sources in the Citations & Bibliography group. This opens the Source Manager dialog box. Under the Master List pane, click the citation you want to add to your current document, click Copy, and click Close.

More Options!

If you know you want to add a citation to your document, but you do not have all the necessary information at your fingertips, you can create a placeholder. Click Insert Citation in the Citations & Bibliography group on the Ribbon's References tab, choose Add New Placeholder, and type a name for the placeholder in the dialog box that appears. Later, you can add citation information to the placeholder by clicking Manage Sources in the Citations & Bibliography group of commands, clicking the placeholder under Current List, clicking Edit, and entering the necessary information.

You can use Word to insert footnotes and endnotes in your document. A footnote is an explanatory note, usually in a smaller font, inserted at the bottom of a page to cite the source of or further explain information that appears on that page. The information to which the footnote pertains is flagged, usually with a superscript numeral, but sometimes with a symbol, such as a dagger symbol. Endnotes are like footnotes, but they appear at the end of a section or document rather than at the bottom of a page.

When you insert footnotes or endnotes in a document, Word automatically numbers them

for you. As you add, delete, and move text in your document, any associated footnotes or endnotes are likewise added, deleted, or moved, as well as renumbered. You can also easily convert footnotes into endnotes, or vice versa.

To delete a footnote or endnote, but leave the text in the document to which it refers intact, select the superscript numeral or symbol flagging the footnote or endnote and press Delete on your keyboard. Word deletes the flag as well as the note.

One more thing: You must be in Print Layout view to add a footnote or endnote.

① Click in your document where you want to add the numeral or symbol indicating a footnote or endnote.

② Click the References tab.

③ Click Insert Footnote or Insert Endnote.

● A superscript numeral or symbol appears at the cursor location. In this example, a footnote is added.

④ Type the information you want to include in the footnote or endnote.

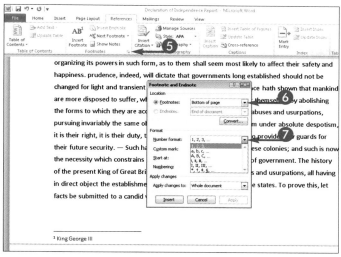

⑤ Click the dialog box launcher in the Footnotes group on the References tab.

The Footnote and Endnote dialog box appears.

⑥ Click here and select where on the page the footnote should appear.

⑦ Click here and select the desired number format.

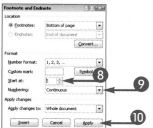

⑧ Click here and select the number, letter, or symbol that should appear first.

⑨ Click here and specify whether the numbering should be continuous, restart at the beginning of each section, or restart at the beginning of each page.

⑩ Click Apply to apply your changes.

Customize It!

If a footnote or endnote runs to a second page, you can add standard text, called a *continuation notice*, to it to indicate that it continues on the next page. To do so, first switch to Draft view, and then, in the References tab, click Show Notes in the Footnotes group. If prompted, specify whether you want to create a continuation notice for the footnotes or the endnotes in the document, click the Footnotes or Endnotes drop-down arrow and click Footnote Continuation Notice or Endnote Continuation Notice, and type the text you want to use in the notice.

Try This!

You can turn footnotes into endnotes, and endnotes into footnotes. To do this, click the Convert button located in the Footnote and Endnote dialog box. To open the dialog box, click the dialog box launcher (▣) in the Footnotes group on the References tab. Next, click the Convert button to open the Convert Notes dialog box where you can choose a conversion option.

Generate a Table of Contents

If your document requires a table of contents (TOC), you can use Word to generate one automatically. By default, a TOC generated in Word contains text formatted in one of Word's predefined heading styles. Word generates the TOC by searching for these styles, copying text that has been formatted with them, and pasting it into the TOC. The TOC itself is simply a preformatted table, listing the headings and page numbers for each.

If you used custom styles in your document to create headings rather than Word's built-in

styles, you can still generate a TOC; you simply indicate what styles Word should search for in your document when determining what the TOC should contain.

Regardless of whether you use Word's predefined heading styles to generate the TOC or you create a TOC that cites text formatted with custom styles, you can choose from Word's gallery of TOC styles to establish its look and feel.

Style Text as Headings

① Select text in your document that you want to style as a heading.

② Click the Home tab.

③ Click the More button.

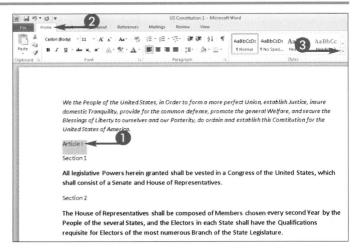

The Quick Style gallery appears.

④ Click the style you want to select.

● Word applies the style you chose to the selected text.

⑤ Repeat steps 3 and 4 to continue assigning styles throughout the document, as needed.

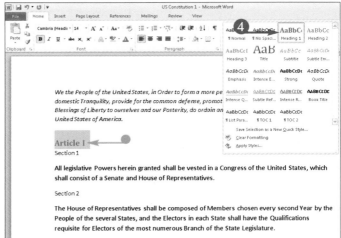

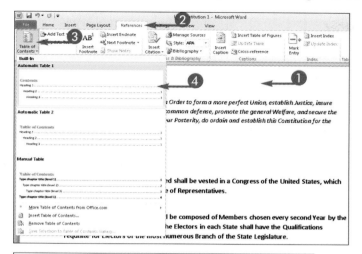

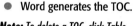

Contents

Generate a Table of Contents

1. Click the location in your document where you want to insert a TOC.
2. Click the References tab.
3. Click Table of Contents.
4. Choose the desired style.

● Word generates the TOC.

Note: *To delete a TOC, click Table of Contents in the References tab's Table of Contents group and click Remove Table of Contents.*

Customize It!

If you need to generate a TOC using custom styles rather than Word's predefined header styles, click Table of Contents on the References tab and choose Insert Table of Contents. The Table of Contents dialog box opens; click Options. In the Table of Contents Options dialog box, under Available Styles, locate the top-level heading style you applied to your document; then type **1** in the corresponding field to indicate that it should appear in the TOC as a level-1 heading. Repeat for additional heading styles, typing **2**, **3**, **4**, and so on to indicate their levels. Click OK to close the Table of Contents Options dialog box, and click OK again to close the Table of Contents dialog box.

Try This!

If you make changes to your document's headings, you can tell Word to update the table of contents. Just click the Update Table button on the Ribbon's References tab. This opens the Update Table of Contents dialog box where you can choose to update the entire table or just the page numbers.

To add a professional touch to your documents, you can add a cover page. For example, you might include a special cover page for an annual report that is sent to investors.

Word enables you to insert predefined cover pages from its Cover Page gallery. Alternatively, you can create your own cover page and save it to the gallery for future use.

Regardless of whether the cover page you add to your document is a predefined cover page

supplied by Word or a custom cover page you converted to a building block, the process of adding the cover page to your document is essentially the same.

Once a cover page is added to your document, you simply select the placeholder text and type over it with text of your own. You can also change the look and feel of the cover page just as you would any other page in Word — by using the program's various formatting tools.

Add a Cover Page

① Click the Insert tab.

② Click Cover Page.

③ Click the desired cover page.

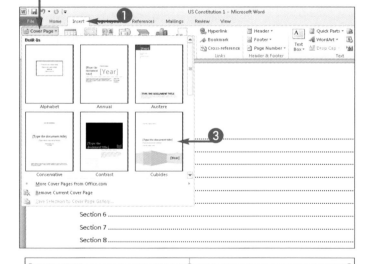

● Word inserts the cover page at the beginning of your document.

④ Select any placeholder text and type over it with text of your own.

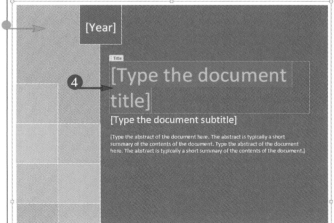

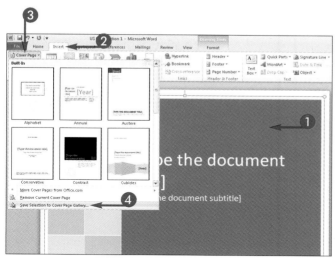

Save a Custom Cover Page to the Gallery

1. Create the cover page you want to add to the gallery and select it.

2. Click the Insert tab.

3. Click Cover Page.

4. Click Save Selection to Cover Page Gallery.

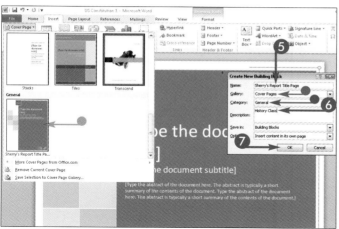

The Create New Building Block dialog box opens.

5. Type a name for the cover page.

● The new cover page is saved in the Cover Page gallery by default.

● The new cover page is assigned the General category by default.

6. Optionally, type a description for the cover page.

7. Click OK.

● Word adds the custom cover page to the Cover Page gallery.

TIPS

Customize It!

If your document contains page numbers along with a cover page, you probably want to omit the number from the cover page. Depending on whether the cover page you added was a predefined one that had a page number placeholder or one you created, you may need to manually remove the page number with a little help from the Page Setup dialog box. Click anywhere in the document, click the Page Layout tab, click the dialog box launcher ([⯐]) in the Page Setup group, and click the Layout tab in the dialog box that appears. Finally, click the Different First Page check box to select it and then click OK.

Remove It!

If you add a cover page to your document but later decide you want to remove it, click the Insert tab, click Cover Page, and click Remove Current Cover Page.

If your document requires an index, you can use Word to build one. Before Word can build an index, however, you must mark any words or phrases in your document that should appear in your index. When you do, Word adds a special XE (short for index entry) field to the document that includes the marked word or phrase, as well as any cross-reference information you care to add.

When you create an index, Word searches for the marked words and phrases, sorts them alphabetically, adds the appropriate page-number references, locates and removes

duplicate entries that cite the same page number, and then generates the index.

When you mark index entries, you have a few options. One is to mark a single word or phrase, which means it is listed once in the index for that particular spot you reference. Another option is to create entries for text that spans a range of pages, which means the index lists all the references. When you do the latter, you first select the text to which you want the entry to refer, and then create a bookmark for that text. When generating the index, Word refers to the bookmark information to determine the correct page range.

Mark a Word or Phrase for an Index

1. Select text you want to mark.

2. Click the References tab.

3. Click Mark Entry.

   The Mark Index Entry dialog box opens.

4. If the selected text does not appear as it should in the index, delete it and type the desired text. For example, if the entry is a person's name, type his or her last name first.

5. Click Current Page (◯ changes to ◉).

6. Click Mark to create an entry for the word or phrase on this page only, or click Mark All to create entries for all occurrences in the document.

● Word adds an XE field to your document and turns on paragraph marking.

Note: If you cannot see the XE field, click the Show/Hide button (¶), also known as Paragraph Marks, on the Ribbon's Home tab.

   The dialog box remains open so you can continue adding fields to the remainder of the document.

7. Click Close to exit the Mark Index Entry dialog box.

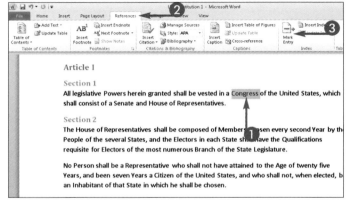

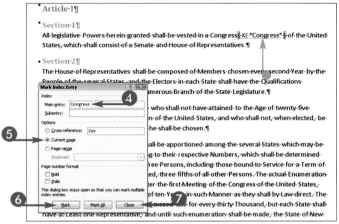

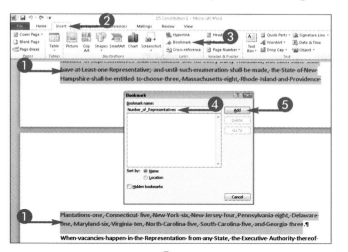

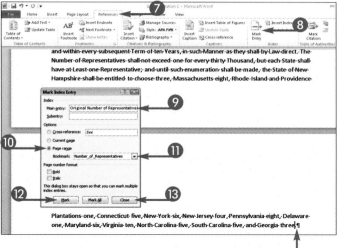

Mark a Word or Phrase that Spans a Range of Pages

1 Select the range of text to which the index entry should refer.

2 Click the Insert tab.

3 Click Bookmark.

The Bookmark dialog box opens.

4 Type a name for the bookmark.

5 Click Add.

6 Click at the end of the text you selected.

7 Click the References tab.

8 Click Mark Entry.

The Mark Index Entry dialog box opens.

9 Type the word or phrase that should appear in the index for this entry.

10 Click Page Range (◎ changes to ◉).

11 Click here and select the bookmark you just created.

12 Click Mark to add an XE field to your document.

13 When finished marking phrases, click Close to exit the dialog box.

TIPS

More Options!
If the text you selected should appear as a subentry rather than a main entry, type the entry under which the selected text should appear in the Main Entry field, and then type the selected text in the Subentry field. If the text should appear as a subentry and a main entry, add two XE fields — one for the main entry and one for the subentry. To include a third-level entry, type the subentry under which the third-level entry should appear, add a colon, and then type the third-level entry.

More Options!
To create index entries that refer to other entries, click Cross-reference in the Mark Index Entry dialog box and type the word or phrase to which this entry should refer.

After you have marked all the words and phrases in your document that you want to appear as index entries, you can create the index by either selecting one of Word's built-in index designs or creating a custom design.

If you make a change to your document — for example, adding more index entries, editing existing entries, or changing the text such that the page numbers in the existing index are no longer correct — you can update the index to reflect the change.

Note that to edit an existing index entry, you must find the XE field for the entry and change the text inside the field's quotation marks as needed. To change the contents of an XE field that appears multiple times in your document, click the Replace button in the Home tab, type the XE string you need to change in the Find What field (for example, XE "Winston Churchill"), type the replacement text in the Replace With field (for example, XE "Churchill, Winston"), and click Replace All.

Generate the Index

1 Click the spot in your document where you want to insert the index.

2 Click the References tab.

3 Click Insert Index.

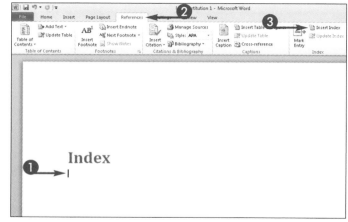

The Index dialog box opens.

4 Click Right Align Page Numbers (☐ changes to ☑).

5 Click here and select an index design.

● Preview the selected index design here.

6 Click Indented (◉ changes to ◉).

7 Click the Columns arrow buttons to change the number of columns per page the index will contain.

8 Click OK.

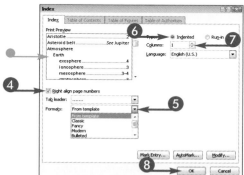

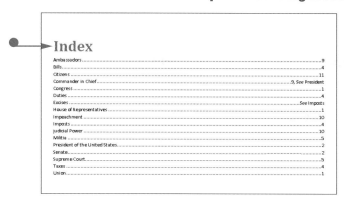

● Word generates the index.

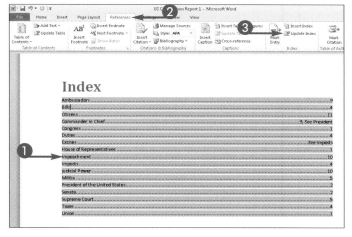

Update the Index

① After making changes to your document, click in the index.

Word automatically highlights the index table for you.

② Click the References tab.

③ Click Update Index and Word updates the index to reflect changes to the document that have occurred since the original index was generated.

TIPS

Customize It!

If you want your index to use a custom layout, click the Formats drop-down arrow in the Index dialog box, choose From Template, and click Modify. The Style dialog box opens; click the index style you want to change, and again click Modify. Finally, select the desired options in the Formatting section of the Modify Style dialog box. To add this custom index style to the template so that all documents you create with the template can use the style, click New Documents Based on this Template.

Remove It!

You delete an index entry by selecting the entire XE field, including the braces ({}) that surround it, and pressing Delete on your keyboard. Be sure to update the index after deleting any entries!

Suppose you want to insert text in one part of your document that refers the reader to a different part of the document for more information. To do so, you can insert a cross-reference. Cross-references can refer readers to text styled as a heading, to footnotes, to bookmarks, to captions, and to numbered paragraphs.

Before inserting a cross-reference, you will probably want to type some introductory text, such as "For more information, refer to." Then add the cross-reference after the text to complete the thought.

If the item to which a cross-reference refers is moved or changed, you can update the cross-reference to reflect the edit. To do so, select the cross-reference you want to update, right-click the selection, and click Update Field. To update all cross-references in the document, select the entire document rather than a single cross-reference.

Note that you can create cross-references only to items in the document that already exist. That is, you cannot create a cross-reference for a document element you have not yet created.

① Type any text you want to precede the cross-reference — for example, *For more information, see page*.

② Click the Insert tab.

③ Click Cross-reference.

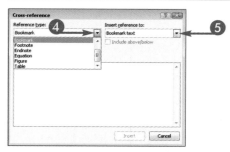

The Cross-Reference dialog box opens.

④ Click here and select the type of document element to which the cross-reference will refer.

⑤ Click here and select what type of information the cross-reference will contain.

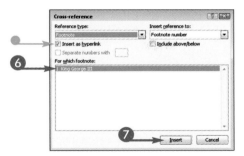

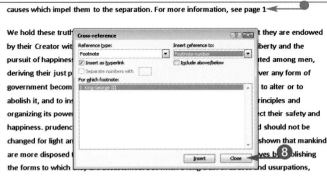

- Click Insert As Hyperlink (☐ changes to ☑) if you want readers to be able to jump directly to the item to which the cross-reference refers.

⑥ Select the specific item to which the cross-reference should refer.

⑦ Click Insert.

- Word inserts the cross-reference.

⑧ Click Close.

Note: To remove a cross reference, highlight it in the document and press Delete. The reference is immediately deleted.

causes which impel them to the separation. For more information, see page 1

We hold these truth... ...t they are endowed by their Creator wit... ...iberty and the pursuit of happines... ...ted among men, deriving their just p... ...ver any form of government becom... ...to alter or to abolish it, and to ins... ...rinciples and organizing its powe... ...ct their safety and happiness. prudenc... ...d should not be changed for light an... ...shown that mankind are more disposed t... ...ves by...lishing the forms to which t... ...nd usurpations, pursuing invariably the same object evinces a design to reduce them under absolute despotism, it is their right, it is their duty, to throw off such government, and to provide new guards for their future security. — Such has been the patient sufferance of these colonies; and such is now the necessity which constrains them to alter their former systems of government. The history of the present King of Great Britain[1] is a history of repeated injuries and usurpations, all having

---

TIPS

More Options!

In order to cross-reference figures or tables, you must use Word's captioning feature to create captions for these elements first. To learn more about adding captions in the Office programs, see the task "Add a Caption to a Graphic" in Chapter 14.

Did You Know?

Hyperlinks are another great way to cross-reference users to other parts of your document. Hyperlinks are links that, when clicked, jump the user to the designated spot. To add a hyperlink, select the text, click the Insert tab and click Hyperlink. This opens the Insert Hyperlink dialog box where you can specify a location to link to in the document based on heading styles or bookmarks.

Suppose you are working on a document that is particularly dense, and that will be reviewed by others in hard-copy form — for example, a lease agreement or contract, or something similar. To make it easier for others to reference portions of the document that require additional attention, you can add line numbers to the document.

The line numbers you add can be configured to restart at the top of each page or section in the document or to appear continuously throughout the document. You can also change the numbering increment — for example, entering an increment of 2 to include even numbers only.

Word does not include blank lines in the numbering, only lines in which text is entered. Headings, however, are included.

Note that line numbers are visible on-screen only in Print Layout view. You cannot view the numbers using any of the other view modes.

Add Line Numbers

① Click the Page Layout tab.

② Click Line Numbers.

③ Choose the desired numbering option.

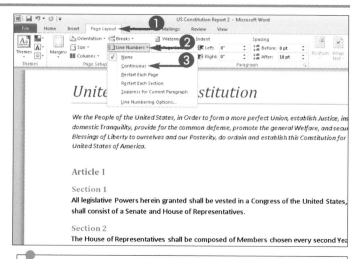

● Line numbers appear on the left side of the document.

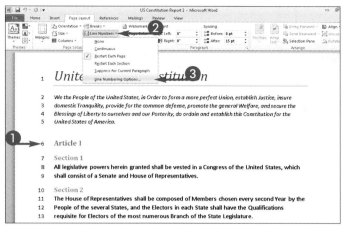

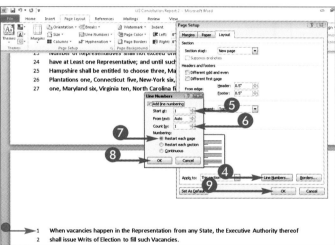

Change Numbering Increments

1 Add line numbers to your document.

2 Still in the Page Layout tab, click Line Numbers.

3 Click Line Numbering Options.

The Page Setup dialog box opens with the Layout tab shown.

4 Click Line Numbers.

The Line Numbers dialog box opens.

5 Click the Start At arrow buttons to start the numbering at a number other than 1.

6 Click the Count By arrow buttons to select an increment. For example, if you want the line numbers to be even numbers only, type **2**.

7 Specify whether the numbering should restart on each page, restart on each section, or appear continuously (◎ changes to ◉).

8 Click OK.

9 Click OK.

● Word changes the numbering increment. In this example, new numbering starts on the next page.

TIPS

Did You Know?

In addition to inserting line numbers in your document, you can also insert page numbers. Page numbers can appear in the document's header or footer area, or in the document's margins. To add page numbers, click the Insert tab and, in the Header & Footer group, click Page Number. Select where on the page you want the numbers to appear, as well as how you want the numbers to look. To change the page on which the numbering starts and other numbering options, click the Insert tab, click Page Number in the Header & Footer group, and click Format Page Numbers.

Remove It!

To remove line numbers, click the Page Layout tab, click Line Numbers, and choose None.

Chapter 5

Optimizing Excel

You can use Excel to perform a wide variety of number-crunching tasks on data, from the simplest calculation to the most complex formula. You can also use Excel to track and manage large quantities of data such as inventories, price lists, and more. You can even use Excel as a database, entering and sorting records.

Data you enter into Excel is stored in a workbook. Each workbook contains individual worksheets, which hold your data. By default, Excel workbooks have three worksheets, each identified by a tab at the bottom of the screen, but you can add or remove worksheets as needed.

A worksheet is a grid, formed by columns and rows. Columns are labeled with letters, whereas rows are numbered. Every

intersection of a column and row creates a cell. Cells are the receptacles for your Excel data. Every cell in an Excel worksheet has a unique name, also called an address or cell reference, which consists of the column letter and row number, with the column listed first. For example, cell A1 is the first cell in the worksheet. The next cell to the right is B1.

A group of related cells in a worksheet is called a range. Excel identifies a range by the anchor points in the upper left and lower right corners of the range, separated by a colon. For example, the range A1:B3 includes cells A1, A2, A3, B1, B2, and B3. Ranges are particularly useful when you begin creating formulas that reference groups of cells.

Quick Tips

By default, Excel opens a new, blank workbook every time you launch the program. This is fine and dandy if you want to start a new file each time you use Excel. But if you find yourself using the same spreadsheet every time you use Excel, you can tell the program to automatically open a particular workbook for you without being prompted.

To set up a workbook to open automatically, you can store the file in the XLSTART folder or create an alternate startup folder containing only the Excel file you want to launch. The XLSTART folder is created when you install

Excel on your computer, and the path to this folder varies depending on which operating system you are using. One way to find this folder path is to open the Trust Center to the Trusted Locations info. To make things easier, consider creating an alternate startup folder instead and save the workbook in the new folder. Once you have the required path and saved the file there, you can tell Excel to look for the workbook there every time you launch the program. You can also open more than one workbook at startup, if desired.

Create an Alternate Startup Folder

1. Open the workbook you want to launch at startup.

2. Click the File tab.

3. Click Save As.

   The Save As dialog box appears.

4. Navigate to the folder or drive where you want to add a new folder, if needed, and then click New Folder.

5. Excel adds a new folder; type a unique folder name and press Enter twice.

● Excel opens the new, empty folder.

6. Click Save to save the file to the new folder.

Designate a Startup File

1 Click the File tab.

2 Click Options.

The Excel Options dialog box appears.

3 Click Advanced.

4 Scroll down to the General settings.

5 In the At Startup, Open All Files In field, type the folder path to your alternate startup folder.

Note: *Be sure to type in the full folder path accurately or Excel cannot locate your file.*

6 Click OK.

The next time you open Excel, the designated file opens, too.

Note: *To remove a startup file, repeat these steps and delete the path found in the Excel Options dialog box.*

More Options!

If you use Excel every day, you can tell your computer to open the program automatically when you turn on your computer. You can place a shortcut to the Excel program in your Windows XP, Windows Vista, or Windows 7 Startup folder. Look up your system's Startup folder and place a shortcut to Excel in the folder.

Caution!

If you ever run into trouble with automatically launching a workbook, such as a system crash, you may have to visit the Advanced resources and enable the workbook startup again. Click the File tab and click Options to open the Excel Options dialog box. Click Advanced, and check the folder path in the General settings. If you accidentally moved the file, you may need to fix the designated path listed.

Automate Data Entry with AutoFill

Often, the data that needs to be entered into an Excel worksheet is part of a series or pattern. In that case, you can use Excel's AutoFill feature to automate data entry.

For example, you might type the word **Monday** in your spreadsheet, and then use AutoFill to automatically enter the remaining days of the week. Alternatively, you might type **January**, and then use AutoFill to enter the remaining months of the year.

In addition to automating data entry using predefined data lists such as the ones described in the preceding paragraph, you can create your own custom data lists for use with Excel's AutoFill feature. For example, you might create a custom list that includes the names of co-workers who work on your team, or a list of products you regularly stock.

Along with enabling you to enter predefined or custom text series, AutoFill allows you to automatically populate cells with a numerical series or pattern.

AutoFill a Text Series

1 Type the first entry in the text series.

2 Click and drag the fill handle that appears in the lower right corner of the active cell across or down the number of cells that you want to fill.

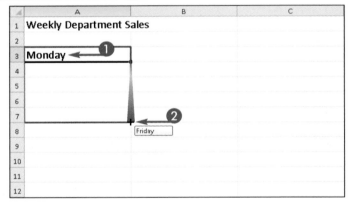

3 Release the mouse button and AutoFill fills in the text series.

● An Auto Fill Options button may appear, offering additional AutoFill options. For example, you can opt to copy the contents of the first cell into each cell rather than fill them with the series.

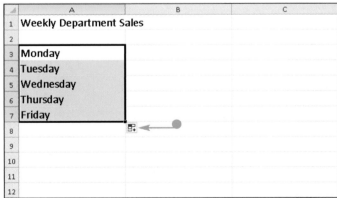

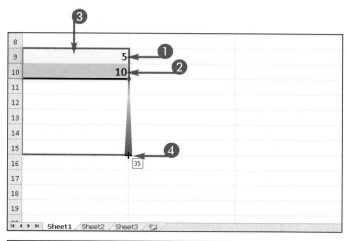

AutoFill a Number Series

① Type the first entry in the number series.

② In an adjacent cell, type the next entry in the number series.

③ Select both cells.

④ Click and drag the fill handle that appears in the lower right corner of the active cells across or down the number of cells you want to fill.

⑤ Release the mouse button and AutoFill fills in the number series.

● An Auto Fill Options button may appear, offering additional AutoFill options.

Customize It!

To add your own custom list to AutoFill's list library, first enter the contents of the list in your worksheet cells. Then do the following:

1. Select the cells containing the list you want to save.

2. Click the File tab.

3. Click Options to open the Excel Options dialog box.

4. Click Advanced.

5. Scroll down to the General group and click Edit Custom Lists.

6. In the Custom Lists dialog box, click Import. Excel adds the series to the custom lists. You can also create a new list by clicking Add and typing your list.

7. Click OK to close both dialog boxes.

Color-Code and Name Worksheet Tabs

A little-known organizing tip that most people never think about is formatting and naming the actual worksheet tabs. At the bottom of every worksheet, a tab marks the worksheet name and number in the stack. By default, the tabs are named Sheet1, Sheet2, and so on. The tabs themselves are very plain and nondescript. You can, however, use them to better organize your worksheet content.

For example you might color-code all the sheets related to the Sales Department in one color

and all the sheets related to the Marketing Department in another. This can help you tell in a glance the purpose of each sheet in the workbook. You can assign different colors to different sheets using colors from Excel's color palette.

You can also rename sheets to better describe their content. A sheet named "Quarterly Sales" easily identifies what it contains and differentiates it from a worksheet named "Yearly Sales."

Color-Code Sheet Tabs

① Right-click the tab you want to edit.

② Click Tab Color.

③ Click a color from the color palette.

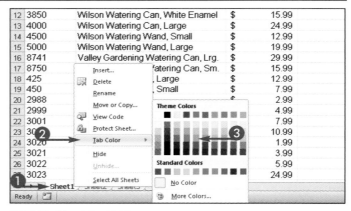

● Excel assigns the new color.

Note: *Click another tab to see the color change in the tab you edited.*

● Click Insert Worksheet to add new sheets, as needed.

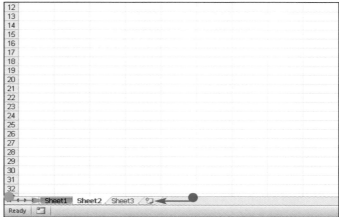

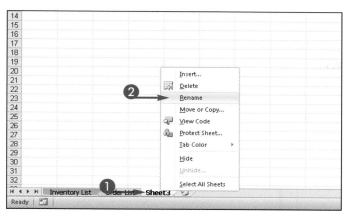

Name Sheet Tabs

1 Right-click the tab you want to edit.

2 Click Rename.

Note: *You can also double-click the tab name.*

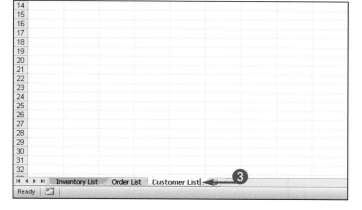

3 Type a new name.

4 Press Enter.

The name is assigned.

Remove It!

To remove color-coding from a worksheet tab, right-click it, click Tab Color on the pop-up menu, and then click No Color from the palette. This resets the tab to its original default status.

Try This!

If your workbook consists of dozens of sheets, you may tire of endlessly scrolling to find the one you want. Instead, try this trick: Right-click a scroll arrow to the left of the tab names. This displays a pop-up list of all the sheets in the workbook. Just click the one you want to view.

Keep Cells in View with a Watch Window

The longer your worksheet becomes, the more difficult it is to keep important cells and ranges in view as you scroll through your worksheet. You can use a Watch Window to monitor important cell data. A Watch Window displays the cell information no matter where you scroll in the worksheet.

For example, you may want to see the formula results in the cell at the very top of your worksheet while you make changes in the data referenced in the formula at the bottom of the worksheet. You can also use a Watch Window to view cells in other worksheets or in other linked workbooks.

After adding a Watch Window, you can resize the window or reposition it by dragging it elsewhere on-screen. The mini-window can also be docked, much like toolbars of previous incarnations of Excel, to the side or top of the sheet area. Just drag it to the edge of the worksheet; Excel immediately tries to dock it there in place.

You can also quickly visit the cell referenced in the Watch Window by simply double-clicking the cell reference.

---

① **Click the Formulas tab in the Ribbon.**

② **Click Watch Window.**

The Watch Window opens.

③ **Click Add Watch.**

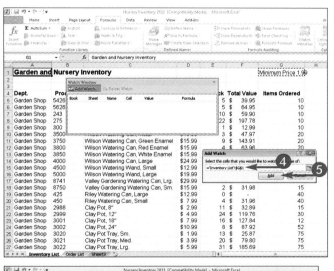

The Add Watch dialog box opens.

④ Select the cell or range in the worksheet you want to watch or type the cell reference.

⑤ Click Add.

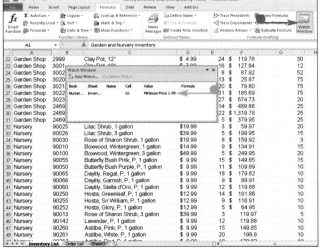

● Excel adds the cell(s) to the window, including any values or formulas within the cells.

You can now scroll in the worksheet and the Watch Window stays put.

● Click the Watch Window button again to toggle the feature off again.

TIPS

More Options!

You can add and remove watched cells in the Watch Window as needed. To add more cells, click the Add Watch button in the window and follow the steps in this task to add more cells to watch. To remove cells from the window, select the cell in the list area and then click the Delete Watch button.

Remove It!

When you no longer want to watch cells, you can close the Watch Window. Simply click the window's Close button (☒) in the upper right corner or click the Watch Window button on the Formulas tab. To open it again and keep watching the same referenced cell(s), just click the Watch Window button on the Formulas tab again.

Protect Cells from Unauthorized Changes

Excel offers several ways to protect data, but the differences between them can be a bit confusing. For optimal protection, you can protect your entire workbook file with a password which allows only authorized users access. With this scenario, you can control who opens the file or who has permission to make edits. This technique was described in Chapter 2.

You can also protect specific data within a spreadsheet. For example, if you share your workbook with a colleague, you may want to prevent changes in a cell or changes to workbook elements. You can choose to protect worksheet elements or protect the workbook structure, finding options for both on the Ribbon's Review tab.

Use the Protect Workbook feature to protect a workbook's structural elements, which include moving, deleting, hiding, or naming worksheets, adding new worksheets, or viewing hidden sheets. You can also use this feature to protect overall window structure, such as moving, resizing, or closing windows. Note that users can remove this level of workbook protection unless you assign a password.

You can use the Protect Sheet feature to prevent others from editing individual worksheet elements, such as cells, rows, columns, and formatting. Note that users can also turn off this protection feature unless you assign a password to the worksheet.

Protect Workbook Structure

1. Click the Review tab.
2. Click Protect Workbook.

   The Protect Structure and Windows dialog box opens.

3. Select which options you want to protect (☐ changes to ☑).
4. To allow users to view the workbook but not make changes, type a password.
5. Click OK.

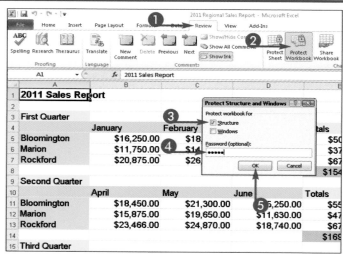

   The Confirm Password dialog box appears.

6. Retype the password exactly as you typed it in step 4.
7. Click OK.

   Excel assigns the password to the workbook. The next time you or any other user opens the workbook, features for deleting, moving, and renaming worksheets will be unavailable.

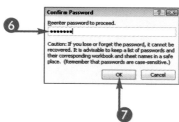

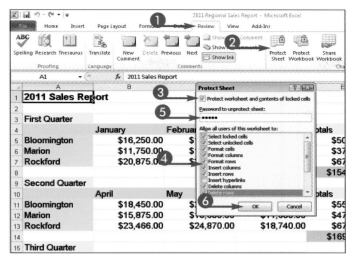

Protect Worksheet Elements

① Click the Review tab.

② Click Protect Sheet.

The Protect Sheet dialog box opens.

③ Make sure the Protect Worksheet and Contents of Locked Cells check box remains selected.

④ If you want users to be able to perform certain operations on the data in the worksheet, click the check box next to the desired operation (☐ changes to ☑).

⑤ To allow users to view the worksheet but not make changes, type a password.

⑥ Click OK.

Excel prompts you to retype the password.

⑦ Retype the password exactly as you typed it in step 5.

⑧ Click OK.

Excel assigns the password to the worksheet. The next time you or any other user opens the worksheet, only the features you selected will be available.

Caution!

The best passwords contain a mix of uppercase and lowercase letters, numbers, and symbols. Remembering your Excel passwords is critical. If you lose a password, you cannot make changes to a password-protected file. Consider writing the password down and keeping it in a safe place.

Remove It!

If you no longer want to password-protect a workbook or worksheet, you can easily remove the password protection. To unprotect a password-protected workbook, click the Review tab in the Ribbon and click Protect Workbook. The Unprotect Workbook dialog box appears; type the password and click OK. Unprotect a password-protected worksheet by right-clicking the sheet's tab and choosing Unprotect Sheet; in the Unprotect Sheet dialog box that opens, type the password and click OK.

Generate Random Numbers in Your Cells

You can use the RAND() function to generate random numbers in your worksheet cells. For example, you may want to generate random lottery numbers or fill your cells with random numbers for a template or as placeholder text. Depending on how you define the variables, you can generate a number between 0 and a maximum number that you specify. For example, if you define 100 as the maximum, the function randomly generates numbers between 0 and 100.

After assigning the function to one cell in your worksheet, you can use the fill handle to populate the other cells in the sheet with more

random numbers. The numbers you generate with the RAND() function take on the default numbering style for the cells. By default, Excel applies the General number format, with means that decimal numbers may appear.

To limit your random numbers to whole numbers, you can set the style to Number style and the decimal places to 0 using the Format Cells dialog box. You may want to do this before applying the function; from the Home tab, click the Number group's icon to open the Format Cells dialog box, select the Number category, and adjust the decimal places to suit your needs.

① Click inside the cell where you want to start the random numbering.

② Type **=RAND()*?**, replacing the ? with the maximum random number you want Excel to generate.

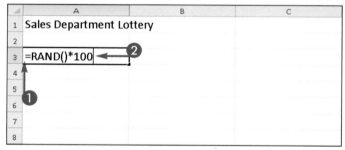

③ Press Enter.

● Excel generates a random number in the cell.

④ Click and drag the selected cell's fill handle across or down as many cells as you want to fill with random numbers.

Excel fills the cells when you release the mouse button.

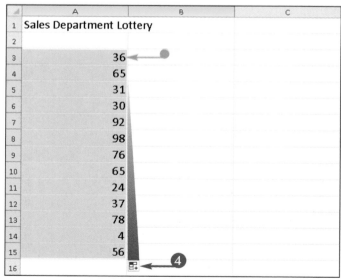

As you work with longer worksheets in Excel, it may become important to keep your column or row labels in view. The longer or wider your worksheet becomes, the more time you spend scrolling back to the top of the worksheet to see which heading is which. Excel has a freeze feature you can use to lock your row or column headings in place. You can freeze them into position so that they are always in view.

If you print out the worksheet, row and column headings appear as they normally do in

their respective positions on the worksheet. You can, however, instruct Excel to print column or row headings on every printed page using the Page Setup dialog box. In the Page Setup group on the Page Layout tab, click the Page Setup icon to open the Page Setup dialog box. Click the Sheet tab, and under the Print titles section you can specify the row or column heading cell range to repeat.

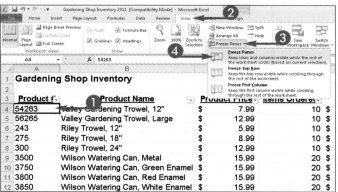

① Click the cell below the row you want to freeze or to the right of the column you want to freeze.

② Click the View tab.

③ Click Freeze Panes.

④ Click Freeze Panes.

● Excel adds a solid line in the worksheet to set off the frozen headings.

● When you scroll through the worksheet, the headings remain on-screen.

● To unfreeze the cells again, click Freeze Panes and choose Unfreeze Panes.

Insert a Comment in a Formula

You can add comments to your formulas to help explain the formula construction or purpose, or remind you to check something out about the formula. For example, you can add instructions about how to use the formula elsewhere in the worksheet.

Ordinarily, when you want to add a comment to your Excel worksheet, you use the comment text boxes. Comments can include anything from a note about a task to an explanation

about the data that a cell contains. To add a comment to a formula, you use the N() function instead of comment text boxes. The N() function enables you to add notes within the formula itself without affecting how the formula works.

The N() function is one of the many hundreds of functions available in Excel. To learn more about functions, check out the Excel Help feature.

---

① Click the cell containing the formula you want to edit.

② Click inside the Formula field where you want to insert a comment.

③ Type **+N("?")**, replacing the *?* with the comment text you want to add.

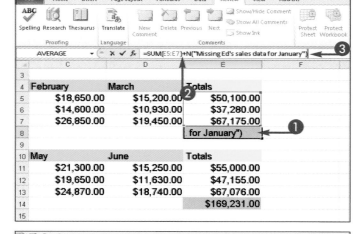

④ Press Enter.

● Excel adds the comment to the Formula field only, and the cell displays only the formula results.

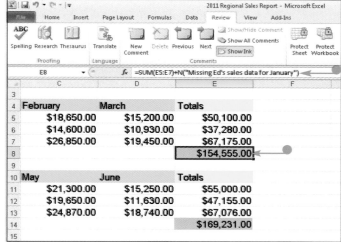

Join Text from Separate Cells

You can use the CONCATENATE function to join text from separate cells into a text string. For example, for a spreadsheet that lists the last, first, and middle names of a list of people in three separate columns, you can use the CONCATENATE function to join the names to print out or paste into another document.

When you use the CONCATENATE function, it is important to include spaces between the text strings to mimic spaces between names. In the formula, you can indicate spaces by entering actual spaces within quotes. If the

combined names require other punctuation, such as a comma, use a comma within the quotes between cell references. After establishing the formula for the first name in the list, copy the formula down the rows of the worksheet to join together the remaining names in the list.

You can use this same technique to join other types of text strings in Excel, such as product names and prices to print out for a customer, or dates and locations to give to a colleague.

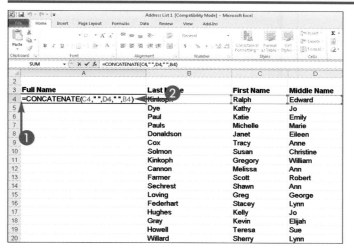

① Click inside the cell in which you want to display the text that you join together.

② Type **=CONCATENATE (?," ",?," ",?)**. Replace the *?* with cell references that contain the component names.

Note: *Do not forget to press the spacebar between the quotation marks to add space between the names you join.*

Note: *Be sure to write the cell references in the order in which you want them to join together.*

③ Press Enter.

● Excel combines the referenced cells into one cell.

Add a Calculator to the Quick Access Toolbar

You can add a digital version of a hand-held calculator to the Quick Access toolbar to that you can perform your own mathematical calculations. By activating the Calculator button, you can open a Calculator window and use the number pad buttons or the numeric keypad on your keyboard to enter calculations. You may find the Calculator window handy for a variety of calculating tasks. For example, if you need to add several numbers together before entering them into a worksheet cell,

you can use the Calculator window to quickly total the data.

To add the Calculator to the Quick Access toolbar, you must customize the toolbar with a little help from the Excel Options dialog box. The Calculator tool, when added, appears as a tiny calculator icon on the toolbar. As its own window, you can move it around, minimize it to the Windows taskbar, and close it when you no longer need it.

---

① Click the Customize Quick Access Toolbar button located at the end of the toolbar.

② Click More Commands.

Note: You can also add the Calculator tool to any Ribbon tab. See Chapter 1 to learn more about customizing the Ribbon.

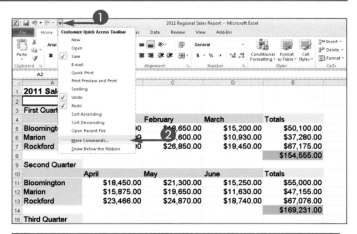

The Excel Options dialog box opens to the Quick Access Toolbar settings.

③ Click the category drop-down arrow.

④ Click Commands Not in the Ribbon.

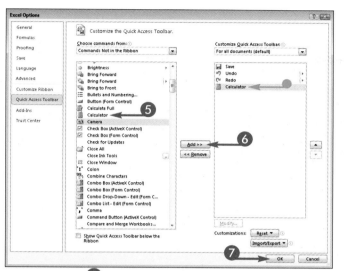

⑤ Scroll to and click the Calculator tool.

⑥ Click Add.

● Excel adds it to the toolbar list of commands.

⑦ Click OK.

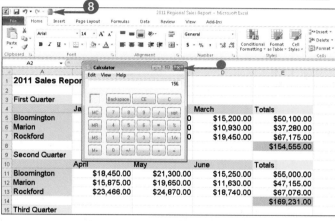

⑧ Click the tool button.

The Calculator window opens for you to perform calculations.

● Click here to close the window.

TIPS

Try This!

You can save yourself some repetitive typing time by simply copying and pasting a calculation result from the Calculator window to an Excel worksheet cell. With the Calculator window active, press Ctrl+C to copy the results to the Windows Clipboard. Next, click inside the cell where you want to paste the data and press Ctrl+V. Voila! The data appears in the cell.

Remove It!

You can remove the Calculator tool from the Quick Access toolbar just as easily as you placed it there. You can choose from two methods. One method is to reopen the Excel Options dialog box as shown in this task, click the Calculator's Custom name in the right list box, and click the Remove button in the center of the dialog box. Click OK and the icon is removed from the toolbar. Another method is to right-click the button and click Remove from Quick Access Toolbar.

Audit a Worksheet for Errors

If you see an error message, you should double-check your formula to ensure that you referenced the correct cells. One way to do so is to click the Smart Tag icon that Excel displays alongside any errors it detects; doing so opens a menu of options, including options for correcting the error. For example, you can click Help on This Error to find out more about the error message.

To help you with errors that arise when dealing with larger worksheets in Excel, you can use Excel's Formula Auditing tools to examine and correct formula errors. In particular, the Error Checking feature looks through your worksheet for errors and helps you find solutions.

Auditing tools can trace the path of your formula components and check each cell reference that contributes to the formula. When tracing the relationships between cells, you can display tracer lines to find *precedents* (that is, cells referred to in a formula) and *dependents* (cells that contain formula results).

Check Errors

1. Click the Formulas tab.

2. Click Error Checking.

● Excel displays the Error Checking dialog box and highlights the first cell containing an error.

● To find help with an error, you can click here.

● To ignore the error, click Ignore Error.

● You can click Previous and Next to scroll through all of the errors on the worksheet.

3. To fix the error, click Edit in Formula Bar.

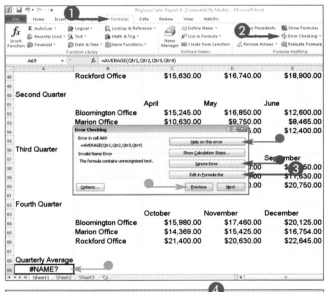

4. Make edits to the formula in the Formula bar.

In this example, a typo in the formula is corrected.

5. Click Resume.

When the error check is complete, a prompt box appears.

6. Click OK.

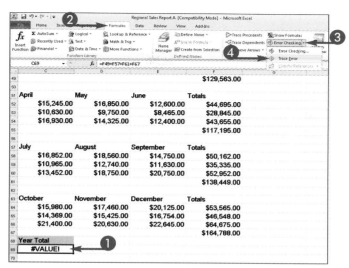

Trace Errors

① Click in the cell containing the formula, content, or error you want to trace.

② Click the Formulas tab.

③ Click the Error Checking drop-down arrow.

④ Click Trace Error.

● Excel displays trace lines from the current cell to any cells referenced in the formula.

● You can make changes to the cell contents or changes to the formula to correct the error.

⑤ Click Remove Arrows to turn off the trace lines.

TIPS

Did You Know?

You can click Evaluate Formula in the Formulas tab's Formula Auditing group to check over a formula or function step by step. Simply click the cell containing the formula you want to evaluate and click Evaluate Formula; Excel opens the Evaluate Formula dialog box, where you can evaluate each portion of the formula to check it for correct references and values.

Try This!

To quickly ascertain the relationships among various cells in your worksheet, click a cell, click the Formulas tab on the Ribbon, and click Trace Precedents or Trace Dependents in the Formula Auditing group. Excel displays trace lines from the current cell to related cells — that is, cells with formulas that reference it or vice versa.

Create Projections

You can use Excel to create projections in a manner similar to using the program's AutoFill feature. Excel offers a few options for creating projections. One is to determine a linear trend — that is, to add a step value (the difference between the first and next values in the series) to each subsequent value. Another is to assess a growth trend, in which the starting value is multiplied by the step value rather than added to the value in order to obtain the next value in the series, with the resulting product and

each subsequent product again being multiplied by the step value.

The easiest way to create a projection is to use Excel's automatic trending functionality. With it, you can simply right-click and drag to generate a projection. You can also create projections manually, entering a start value, a stop value, and the increment by which the trend should change. If your data is in chart form, you can still generate projections and even include a line in your chart to indicate the trend.

Determine a Linear Trend

1 Type the first known value.

2 In an adjacent cell, type the second known value.

3 Select both cells.

4 Position the mouse pointer over the fill handle that appears in the lower right corner of the active cells.

5 Right-click and drag across or down the number of cells you want to fill with linear trend data.

A context menu appears.

6 Click Linear Trend.

● Excel inserts the numbers that comprise the linear trend.

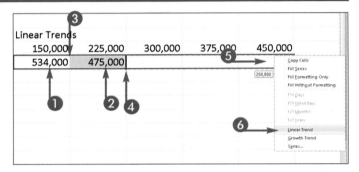

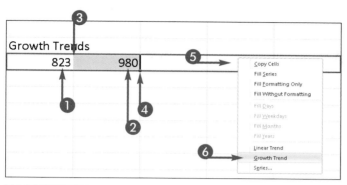

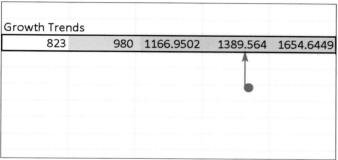

Determine a Growth Trend

① Type the first known value.

② In an adjacent cell, type the second known value.

③ Select both cells.

④ Position the mouse pointer over the fill handle that appears in the lower right corner of the active cells.

⑤ Right-click and drag across or down the number of cells you want to fill with growth trend data.

A context menu appears.

⑥ Click Growth Trend.

● Excel inserts the numbers that comprise the growth trend.

More Options!

Instead of automatically projecting linear and growth trends, you can project them manually. To do so, enter the first value in the series in a cell, and then select the cell. Next, click the Home tab and, in the Editing group, click Fill and select Series. Specify whether the series should cover columns or rows, enter the value by which the series should be increased, select Linear or Growth, select the value at which you want the series to stop, and click OK.

Did You Know?

You can use chart data to create projections, adding a trend line to your chart to represent the projection. For more information about creating charts in Excel and adding trend lines to those charts, see the Excel Help feature.

Establish What-If Scenarios

You can perform what-if speculations on your data. For example, you might do so to examine what would happen if you increased shipping fees or product prices. To perform these what-if speculations, you use Excel's Scenario Manager tool. Scenario Manager keeps track of what-if scenarios you run on a workbook, enabling you to revisit and make changes to the scenarios as needed.

It is a good practice to save a copy of the original workbook before using Scenario Manager to perform what-if scenarios on it. That way, you ensure that your data is not permanently replaced with the what-if data by accident. Alternatively, create a scenario that employs the original values; then, you can revert to that original scenario any time.

You can generate a report that summarizes what-if scenarios performed on a workbook. This report lists all inputs and results for each scenario.

To remove a scenario you no longer want, reopen the Scenario Manager dialog box, click the scenario you want to remove, and then click Delete.

1. Click the Data tab in the Ribbon.
2. Click the What-If Analysis drop-down arrow.
3. Click Scenario Manager.

   The Scenario Manager dialog box opens.

4. Click Add.

   The Add Scenario dialog box opens.

5. Type a name for the scenario.

6. If necessary, select the cells you want to change in the scenario or type their cell references.

7. Optionally, type any comments about the scenario here.

8. Click OK.

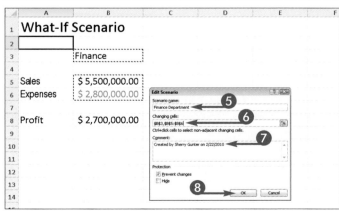

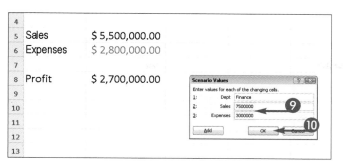

4		
5	Sales	$ 5,500,000.00
6	Expenses	$ 2,800,000.00
7		
8	Profit	$ 2,700,000.00
9		
10		
11		
12		
13		

The Scenario Values dialog box appears.

⑨ Type a new value for each cell you want to change in the scenario.

⑩ Click OK.

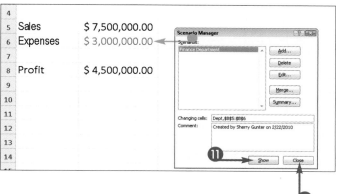

4		
5	Sales	$ 7,500,000.00
6	Expenses	$ 3,000,000.00
7		
8	Profit	$ 4,500,000.00
9		
10		
11		
12		
13		
14		

⑪ Click Show to view the scenario results in your worksheet.

● The results appear.

⑫ Click Close to close the Scenario Manager dialog box.

When you close the Scenario Manager, the last applied scenario remains in the worksheet.

TIPS

Try This!

To generate a summary report that compares the results of multiple scenarios either by listing them side by side or by arranging them in a pivot table, click the What If Analysis drop-down arrow in the Data tab's Data Tools group, click Scenario Manager, and then click Summary. In the dialog box that appears, click Scenario Summary or Scenario PivotTable Report and enter the references for cells whose values are changed by the scenario. Then click OK.

Apply It!

To view the results of a scenario, open the Scenario Manager dialog box as normal (click What If Analysis in the Data tab's Data Tools group and click Scenario Manager), click the scenario you want to view, and click Show.

Set Goals with Goal Seek

Where Excel's Scenario Manager enables you to run "what-if" speculations by tweaking various variables in your spreadsheet, Goal Seek does just the opposite: It enables you to set the desired result and work backward to determine what variables need to be tweaked to attain it. For example, suppose you are trying to calculate how much you can afford to spend each month on a new car. By entering the maximum amount you are willing to spend, Goal Seek can help you work backward to determine the maximum loan amount based

on such variables as interest rate, duration of loan, and so on.

You can use Goal Seek to solve single-variable equations of any kind. For example, although one of the most popular uses of Goal Seek is figuring out loan amounts and payments, as shown here, you can also use Goal Seek to help you figure out how much you need to sell to reach a sales goal (for example, to determine how many units must be sold to attain net earnings of $50,000).

---

① Click the Data tab on the Ribbon.

② Click the What-If Analysis drop-down arrow.

③ Click Goal Seek.

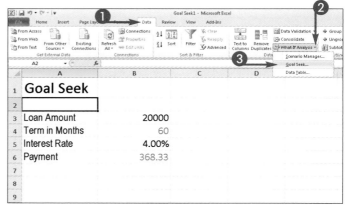

The Goal Seek dialog box opens.

④ Click the Set Cell field and type the reference or select the cell that contains the value or formula you want to resolve.

● In this example, the payment formula cell is referenced.

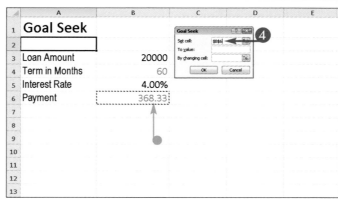

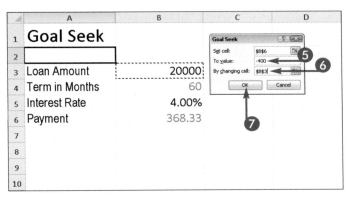

5 Type your goal value (here, a new car payment, written as a negative number because it represents a payment).

6 Select or type the cell whose value you want to change to attain the goal value (here, the price of the new car).

7 Click OK.

The Goal Seek Status dialog box opens.

● Goal Seek has determined how much the car can cost to reach the goal.

8 Click OK to close the dialog box.

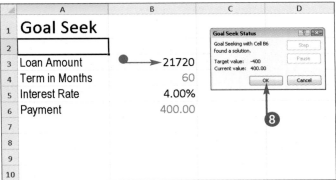

More Options!

You use Goal Seek when you want to produce a specific value by adjusting one input cell that influences the value. If you require adjustments to more than one input cell, use Excel's Solver tool instead. Solver is an add-in you can use for complex problems that use multiple variables. For more information about Solver, see the next task.

Try This!

If the Goal Seek dialog box is covering cells you need to select, click the Collapse Dialog button (■) on the right side of the Set Cell or By Changing Cell field to minimize the dialog box while you access cells. You can maximize the box again when you have selected your references. Look for this same collapsing/expanding button in other Excel dialog boxes to help you move them out of the way to view and select worksheet cells.

Define and Solve Problems with Solver

Goal Seek enables you to produce a specific value by adjusting one input cell that influences the value. In contrast, Excel's Solver tool enables you to produce a value using multiple variables.

To use Solver, you define the target cell along with the cells that Solver can modify to obtain a different value in the target cell. Solver then analyzes the formulas used to establish the value in the target cell and makes changes to the cells you specify to come up with different solutions. For example, if you are opening a new car dealership and have only $1,000,000.00 to spend on new cars, you can use Solver to help

you determine how many different kinds of cars you can purchase for your stock and meet that goal.

Solver is one of several add-in programs that come with Excel. In order to use Solver, you must first load the add-in. To do so, click the File tab and click Options. Click the Add-Ins entry along the left side of the Excel Options dialog box, click the Manage drop-down arrow along the bottom of the dialog box, click Excel Add-Ins, and click Go. Finally, in the Add-Ins dialog box, click the Solver Add-in check box and click OK.

---

① Click the Data tab.

② Click Solver.

Note: *If no Solver button appears on the Data tab, try unloading and reloading the Solver add-in. (To unload the add-in, deselect the Solver Add-in check box in the Add-Ins dialog box mentioned in the introduction to this task and click OK.)*

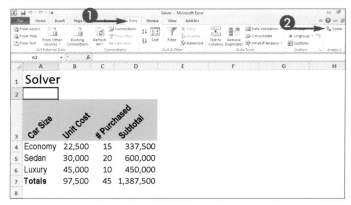

The Solver Parameters dialog box opens.

③ Select or type the reference for the target cell — that is, the cell that will contain the "goal" value (here, cell D7).

④ Click a To option.

⑤ Type the target value.

⑥ Click or type the references for each cell that Solver should adjust to attain the desired result.

Note: *To enter multiple noncontiguous cells, separate each cell reference with a comma.*

⑦ To enter constraints, click Add.

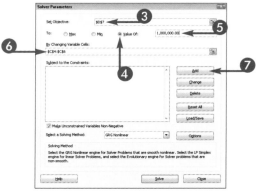

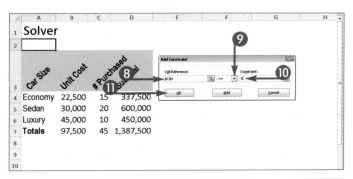

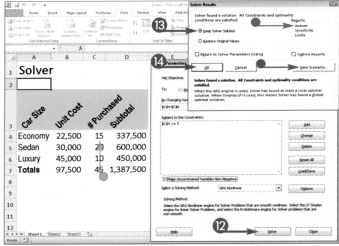

The Add Constraint dialog box opens.

⑧ Select or type the cell reference for the constraint.

⑨ Select an operator.

⑩ Specify a constraint value or cell reference.

In this example, the constraint is that at least five of the cars must be economy cars.

⑪ Click OK.

⑫ Click Solve.

The Solver Results dialog box opens.

● Excel makes changes to the designated target cell and any constraint cells you specified.

⑬ Select whether you want to save the solution or restore to the original values.

● If you click Keep Solver Solution, you can save the results as a report. To do so, click a report type.

● To save the changes as a scenario, click here.

⑭ Click OK to close the dialog box.

More Options!
You can set multiple constraints for the adjustable cells, the target cell, or any other cells related to the target cell to limit the solutions provided by Solver. To add more constraints, click the Add button in the Solver Parameters dialog box and define the constraints in the Add Constraint dialog box. To add more constraints within the Add Constraint dialog box, just click the Add button.

Create a Database Table

You can use an Excel worksheet to build a database table to manage large lists of data. A database table is simply a collection of related records, such as a phone directory, address list, inventory, and so on. After creating a database table, you can perform a variety of analysis, sorting, and filtering techniques on the data in the database table.

A database table is composed of fields, which break the table into manageable pieces. For example, a database table containing an address book will likely include fields with labels such as Name, Address, and Phone Number. You fill in these fields to create a *database record*. A database record might consist of the name, address, and phone number of a single individual.

Before you create a database table in Excel, take a bit of time to plan it out, deciding what kind of data you want the database table to store and how it should be organized. Otherwise, you may later discover that you have omitted important fields and have to reorganize your database table.

① **Add field labels to the top of the column table.**

② **Enter the first record in the row below the labels.**

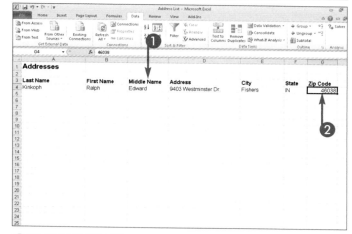

③ **Continue adding records to build your table.**

④ **Select the data you want to convert into a database table.**

⑤ **Click the Insert tab.**

⑥ **Click Table.**

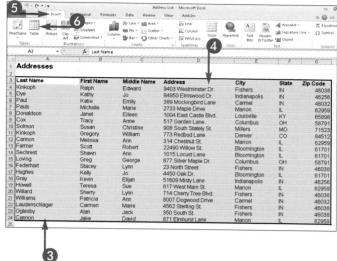

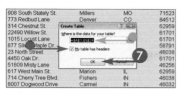

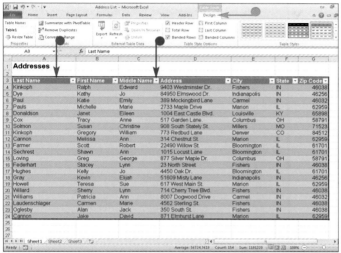

The Create Table dialog box opens.

● By default, the selected range appears here. If the range is not correct, you can select the correct cell references.

● Select this check box if it is necessary to include the headers in your table (☐ changes to ☑).

⑦ Click OK.

● Excel turns the data into a table, fills the cells of the table with table formatting, and displays filter drop-down arrows for each field.

● The Table Tools Design tab also appears on-screen.

● To filter a list, click here and select the data you want to filter out.

Did You Know?

Entering data into a table can be tedious. To speed up the task, you can use Excel's PickList feature, which is activated as soon as you create the first record in your database table and remembers the previous field entries so you can repeat them, if necessary:

1. Right-click a cell in a new record.
2. Click Pick From Drop-down List.
   A list of choices appears.
3. Click an entry to repeat it in the current cell.

Add and Edit Records Using Data Forms

If you have converted data in a spreadsheet into a database table, you can add information to that table using a data form instead of typing it directly into the cells in the worksheet. (For help converting data in Excel spreadsheets into database tables, refer to the preceding task.)

In Excel, data forms are special dialog boxes that contain all the fields in your table. For example, if your database table contains a Name field, an Address field, a City field, a State field, and a ZIP field, so too will the database table's data form dialog box. You can type the information for a database record into the dialog box rather than into the spreadsheet. (Note that you can also edit existing records from a data form dialog box.)

To access the command used to display the data form dialog box, you must first add it to the Quick Access toolbar. To do so, click the Customize Quick Access Toolbar button at the end of the toolbar, click More Commands, and, in the dialog box that appears, click the Choose Commands From drop-down arrow and choose Commands Not in the Ribbon. Then scroll down the list and click Form, click the Add button, and click OK.

---

① Click the first cell of any record in your database table.

② Click the Form button.

A data form dialog box opens displaying data from the record you selected in step 1.

③ Click New.

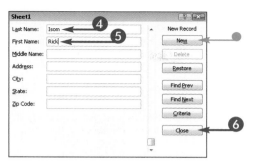

④ Type the data for the first field in the new record and press Tab.

⑤ Repeat step 4 to continue filling out the fields.

● To fill out another new record, click New.

⑥ When finished entering records, click Close.

● Excel adds the new record(s) to the database table.

	A	B	C	D
1	**Addresses**			
2				
3	**Last Name**	**First Name**	**Middle Name**	**Address**
4	Kinkoph	Ralph	Edward	9403 Westminster Dr.
5	Dye	Kathy	Jo	84950 Elmswood Dr.
6	Paul	Katie	Emily	389 Mockingbird Lane
7	Pauls	Michelle	Marie	2733 Maple Drive
8	Donaldson	Janet	Eileen	1004 East Castle Blvd.
9	Cox	Tracy	Anne	517 Garden Lane
10	Solmon	Susan	Christine	908 South Stately St.
11	Kinkoph	Gregory	William	773 Redbud Lane
12	Cannon	Melissa	Ann	314 Chestnut St.
13	Farmer	Scott	Robert	22490 Willow St.
14	Sechrest	Shawn	Ann	1015 Locust Lane
15	Loving	Greg	George	877 Silver Maple Dr.
16	Federhart	Stacey	Lynn	23 North Street
17	Hughes	Kelly	Jo	4450 Oak Dr.
18	Gray	Kevin	Elijah	51609 Misty Lane
19	Howell	Teresa	Sue	617 West Main St.
20	Willard	Sherry	Lynn	714 Cherry Tree Blvd.
21	Williams	Patricia	Ann	8007 Dogwood Drive
22	Laudenschlager	Carmen	Marie	4562 Sterling St.
23	Oglesby	Alan	Jack	350 South St.
24	Cannon	Jake	David	871 Elmhurst Lane
25	Isom	Rick	Eli	3245 Rangeline Rd.
26				

TIPS

Try This!

Click the Find Prev and Find Next buttons in the data form dialog box to navigate records in a database table. Edit records by typing over the existing values in the data form dialog box's fields.

Delete It!

To delete a record, click the first cell in any record in the table and open the data form dialog box. Then click the Find Prev or Find Next button as many times as necessary to locate the record you want to delete. Finally, click the Delete button in the dialog box, and click OK to confirm the deletion. Alternatively, select the row in the table that contains the record you want to delete and then press Delete. This deletes the row content. To remove the row entirely, right-click the row number and click Delete.

Sort and Filter Records

You can sort your database table to reorganize the information it contains. For example, you might want to sort a client table alphabetically by last name.

The easiest type of sort is a quick sort, which enables you to sort by a single criterion — for example, by last name. To perform a quick sort, simply click the drop-down arrow next to the name of the field by which you want to sort and click Sort A to Z (that is, ascending order) or Sort Z to A (that is, descending order). In the case of numbers, an ascending sort lists numbers from lowest to highest, and

a descending sort lists numbers from highest to lowest.

Another way to sort is to use the Sort dialog box. With it, you can sort by multiple fields. For example, if you have an employee table, you might want to sort by name, longevity, and salary.

Yet another option is to filter your records using Excel's AutoFilter tool. Unlike conducting a sort, which sorts the entire table, using AutoFilter selects certain records to display based on your criteria, while hiding the other records that do not match the criteria.

Sort with the Sort Dialog Box

① Click the leftmost header in your database table.

② Click the Data tab.

③ Click Sort.

The Sort dialog box opens.

④ Click here and select the field by which you want to sort.

⑤ Click here and select the desired criterion.

⑥ Click here and specify the desired sort order.

● To enter a second set of criteria, click Add Level.

⑦ Repeat steps 4 to 6 until all the necessary sort criteria have been added.

⑧ Click OK.

● Excel sorts the data based on the criteria you set.

Note: Click Undo (⟲) on the Quick Access toolbar to return the list to its original state.

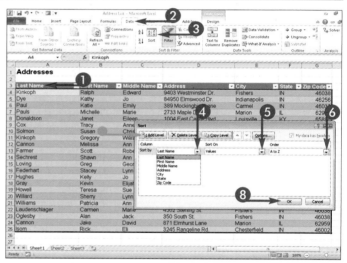

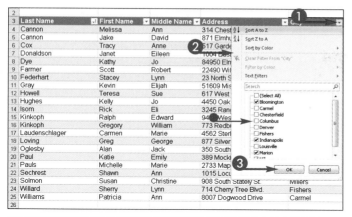

2					
3	Last Name	First Name	Middle Name	Address	City
4	Cannon	Melissa	Ann	314 Chestnut St.	
5	Cannon	Jake	David	871 Elmhurst Lane	
6	Cox	Tracy	Anne	617 Garden	
7	Donaldson	Janet	Eileen	1004 Dee	
8	Dye	Kathy	Jo	84950 Elm	
9	Farmer	Scott	Robert	22490 Will	
10	Federhart	Stacey	Lynn	23 North S	
11	Gray	Kevin	Elijah	51609 Mis	
12	Howell	Teresa	Sue	617 West	
13	Hughes	Kelly	Jo	4450 Oak	
14	Isom	Rick	Eli	3245 Ran	
15	Kinkoph	Ralph	Edward	94 Wes	
16	Kinkoph	Gregory	William	773 Redbi	
17	Laudenschlager	Carmen	Marie	4562 Sterl	
18	Loving	Greg	George	877 Silver	
19	Oglesby	Alan	Jack	350 South	
20	Paul	Katie	Emily	389 Mock	
21	Pauls	Michelle	Marie	2733 Map	
22	Sechrest	Shawn	Ann	1015 Locu	
23	Solmon	Susan	Christine	908 South Stately St.	Millers
24	Willard	Sherry	Lynn	714 Cherry Tree Blvd.	Fishers
25	Williams	Patricia	Ann	8007 Dogwood Drive	Carmel
26					

2					
3	Last Name	First Name	Middle Name	Address	City
5	Dye	Kathy	Jo	84950 Elmswood Dr.	Indianapolis
7	Pauls	Michelle	Marie	2733 Maple Drive	Marion
12	Cannon	Melissa	Ann	314 Chestnut St.	Marion
13	Farmer	Scott	Robert	22490 Willow St.	Bloomington
14	Sechrest	Shawn	Ann	1015 Locust Lane	Bloomington
17	Hughes	Kelly	Jo	4450 Oak Dr.	Bloomington
18	Gray	Kevin	Elijah	51609 Misty Lane	Indianapolis
19	Howell	Teresa	Sue	617 West Main St.	Marion
24	Cannon	Jake	David	871 Elmhurst Lane	Marion
25					
26					
27					
28					
29					
30					
31					
32					
33					
34					

Filter with AutoFilter

1 Click the drop-down arrow alongside the heading for the field you want to filter.

2 Click a Sort option, such as ascending or descending, or specify which filters to sort by.

● You can click to deselect any entries you want to omit (☑ changes to ☐) from the sort.

3 Click OK.

● Excel displays only those records whose entries were left checked.

Note: Click Undo to return the list to its original state.

More Options!
You can click the Advanced command on the Data tab to open the Advanced Filter dialog box. Here you can further customize the filter by selecting operators and values to apply on the filtered data.

Try This!
If you clear a filter but want to apply it again, click the Data tab and click the Reapply button in the Sort & Filter group.

Restrict Cell Entries with Data-Validation Rules

To ensure that the data entered into your database table is of a valid type, you can set up your database table to control exactly what kinds of data are allowed in the cells. This is handy if other people use your database table to enter records. You can make sure that they type the right kind of data in a cell by assigning a data-validation rule.

In addition to ensuring that the right types of characters are entered — for example, text or numbers — you can also set up data-validation

rules to, for example, restrict entries to a certain range of dates. You can also set up rules to limit data-entry choices by offering a drop-down list of options.

If users type the wrong data, such as text data instead of numerical data, Excel displays an error dialog box. You can configure Excel to include the text of your choosing in this dialog box — for example, instructions to the user with regard to what type of data can be entered.

---

① Select the range of cells to which you want to apply a data-validation rule.

② Click the Data tab.

③ Click the Data Validation drop-down arrow.

④ Click Data Validation.

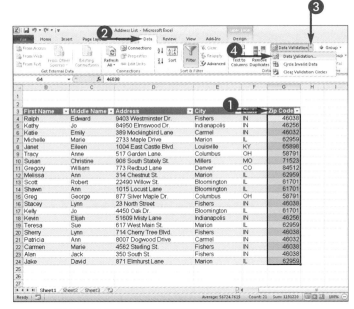

The Data Validation dialog box opens.

⑤ Click the Settings tab.

⑥ Click here and select the type of data you want entered into each cell in the selected range.

● Optionally, define data parameters.

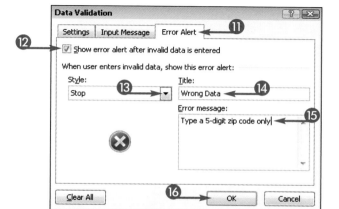

7 Click the Input Message tab.

8 Click the Show Input Message When Cell Is Selected check box (☐ changes to ☑).

9 Type a title for the input message.

10 Type the contents of the input message.

11 Click the Error Alert tab.

12 Click Show Error Alert After Invalid Data Is Entered (☐ changes to ☑).

13 Click here and select the type of icon that should appear in the Error Alert dialog box.

14 Type the text that you want to appear in the Error Alert dialog box's title bar.

15 Type the message that the Error Alert dialog box should convey.

16 Click OK.

Try This!

To create a drop-down list of options from which users can choose when entering data into your database table, click the Allow drop-down arrow in the Data Validation dialog box's Settings tab and choose List. Then, in the Source field, type the options you want to appear in the list, placing a comma between each entry. (Note that the width of the cell to which data validation is being applied determines the width of the drop-down list. To ensure that items in the list are not truncated, consider widening the column.)

Remove It!

To remove data validation, select the range containing the data validation rule and then reopen the Data Validation dialog box. Click Clear All; this turns off the data-validation rules.

Polishing Your Spreadsheet Data

Being able to crunch numbers or build database tables is of little use if your worksheet data is difficult or impossible for others to comprehend. Fortunately, you can mitigate this by liberally applying some of Excel's formatting tools. For example, you can apply themes to your workbooks to create a more polished and professional look, as well as add colors, patterns, and borders to cells to make them stand out. You can even use digital images as backgrounds in your worksheets.

To draw attention to cells that meet criteria you set, you can apply conditional formatting. For example, you might set a rule to highlight cells that contain values greater than, less than, equal to, or between a range of specified values. This enables you to detect problems, patterns, and trends at a glance.

Another way to display your data is in chart form. Whether you are depicting rising or falling sales or actual costs compared to projected costs, charts can make it easy for others to understand your data. By now, you are probably quite familiar with how easy it is to make a chart, but did you also know how easy it is to customize charts with various chart objects? You can also add mini-charts to your worksheet cells with the help of Excel's new Sparkline graphs.

To ensure that others can read the data in your worksheet's cells, you can fine-tune its appearance by adding gridlines, enabling Excel's text-wrapping feature (which automatically increases a cell's row height to make room for the data it contains), and changing text orientation within the cells. This chapter introduces you to a variety of tasks designed to help you make your data look great and print great so you can convey your information with ease and clarity.

Quick Tips

Apply Workbook Themes

Tired of applying formatting to your worksheet data? You can use Excel's Themes Gallery to apply a combination of preset formatting settings to your spreadsheet to create an instant, professional looking spreadsheet.

To use themes to their fullest, you must apply styles to your worksheet, such as a heading style to any column headings or a title style to the worksheet title. Applying styles is easy, just select the cell to which you want to apply the style, click the Home tab, click the Cell Styles button in the Styles group, and choose a style.

If you want the worksheet to display the theme's background color, you must apply a background color beforehand. Select the cells to which the color should be applied, click the Home tab, click the drop-down arrow next to the Fill Color button, and choose a color.

You can modify a theme you have applied using the Colors, Fonts, and Effects buttons in the Page Layout tab's Themes group and then save the modified theme for reuse.

Apply a Theme

1. Click the Page Layout tab.
2. Click Themes.

● Excel displays the Themes Gallery.

3. Click the theme you want to apply.

● Excel applies the theme to the worksheet.

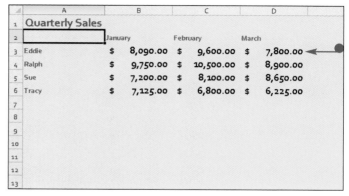

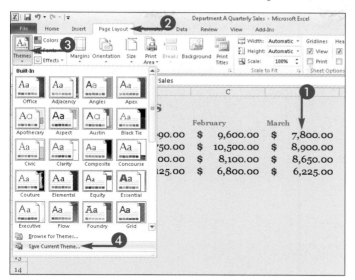

Save a Theme

1. Modify the theme you want to save.

   In this example, the font, size, and color are modified.

2. Click the Page Layout tab.

3. Click Themes.

4. Click Save Current Theme.

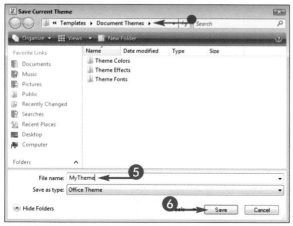

The Save Current Theme dialog box opens.

- Themes are stored in a default location among the other Office themes and templates.

5. Type a unique name for the theme.

6. Click Save to save the theme.

Did You Know?

You can find more themes to use with your Office 2010 programs online. Themes are just templates with ready-made formatting for the design appearance of a spreadsheet or other Office document. Although the Themes Gallery in Excel displays a wide variety of themes, you may be looking for something more stylized. Check out the Microsoft Office Web site (http://office2010.microsoft.com) and browse for more themes you can download and use.

Remove It!

If you create a custom theme and decide you no longer want it in your library, you can easily remove it. Display the Themes Gallery on the Page Layout tab and right-click the custom theme name. Next, click the Delete command. This opens the Microsoft Excel prompt box asking if you want to delete the theme. Click Yes and the theme is removed.

Change Gridline Color

Gridlines are an essential element of every Excel worksheet you display. Gridlines are key to helping you maintain order and keeping your data-entry tasks organized and easy to perform. Gridlines help you keep your contents lined up properly in their respective cells.

By default, the gridlines appear as faint bluish-gray lines that define column and row borders and the cells contained within. Depending on how busy your worksheet becomes as you enter more and more data, it is not always easy

to see the gridlines. Thankfully, you can customize the worksheet and substitute another color setting for gridlines.

You can change the gridline color by accessing the Excel Options dialog box and the Advanced options. If, after assigning a new color, you prefer to return to the default setting, simply revisit the dialog box settings and switch back to Automatic as your color choice for the gridlines.

---

① Click the File tab.

② Click Options.

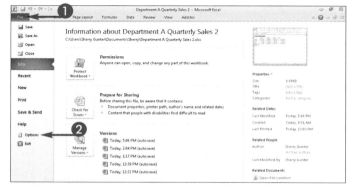

The Excel Options dialog box appears.

③ Click Advanced.

④ Scroll down to the Display Options for This Worksheet section.

⑤ Click the Gridline Color button.

⑥ Click a new color.

⑦ Click OK.

● The color is assigned to the current worksheet.

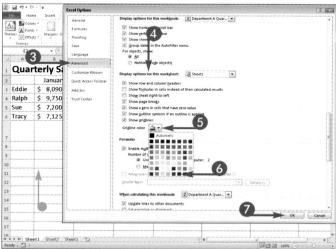

Gridlines make it easier to read a worksheet. By default, gridlines appear on-screen, but not in printed versions of your worksheet. If you plan to print your worksheet, you might want to set up Excel to print it with the gridlines displayed. Doing so makes the printed worksheet a bit easier to read — although be aware that printing with gridlines takes a bit longer than printing without them.

You can apply two methods to activate gridline printing. You can click the Print check box (☐ changes to ☑) on the Page Layout tab under the Gridlines settings, or you can use

Excel's Page Setup dialog box to activate gridline printing. In addition to specifying that gridlines be printed, you can also choose other print-related options in Excel in the Page Setup dialog box.

When you are finally ready to print the worksheet, you can use the Print settings available in Backstage view; click the File tab and click Print to display all the printing options and the command for printing the workbook. You can also see a preview of what your printed gridlines will look like.

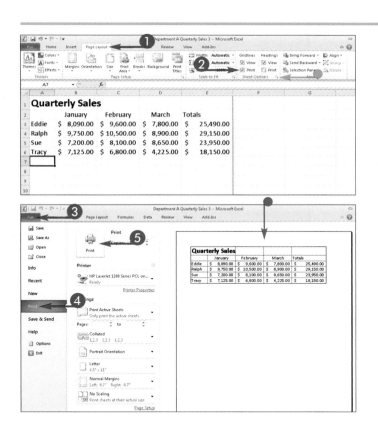

① Click the Page Layout tab.

② In the Sheet Options group under Gridlines, click Print (☐ changes to ☑).

● If you want Excel to print gridlines and you want to alter other print settings, click the Sheet Options icon to display the Page Setup dialog box.

③ Click the File tab.

④ Click Print.

● You can preview the printed gridlines and cells here.

⑤ Click Print to print out the worksheet.

Add Emphasis with Borders

You can add borders to your worksheet cells to help define the contents or more clearly separate the data from surrounding cells. You can apply a border to all four sides of a cell or range of cells or to just one, two, or three sides. Any borders you add to the sheet print out along with worksheet data.

One way to add borders is to select the cell or cells around which you want to apply a border, click the Home tab, click the drop-down arrow next to the Borders button, and click a border style in the list that appears.

If your border requires a bit more formatting than that, you can open the Format Cells dialog box and set all of the border formatting in one convenient location. In addition to specifying which and how many sides of the cell or cells should sport a border, you can choose a line style and color. (Color options include Theme Colors, which mesh with whatever theme is currently applied to the worksheet, as well as a wider range of standard colors.)

① Select a cell or range of cells.

② Click the Home tab.

③ Click the Font group's dialog box launcher.

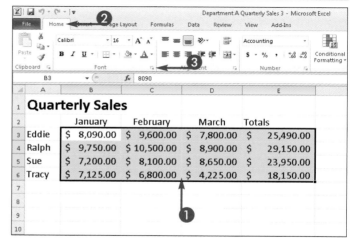

The Format Cells dialog box appears.

④ Click the Border tab.

⑤ Click a line style.

⑥ Click here and select a line color from the color palette that appears.

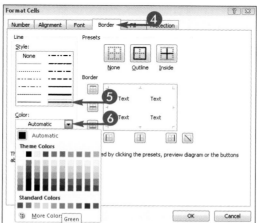

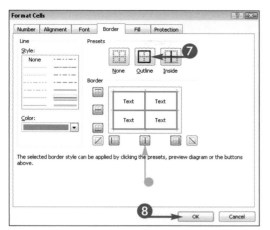

⑦ Click the type of border you want to apply.

● To customize different sides of the cells, click the corresponding border button to toggle the border section on or off.

⑧ Click OK.

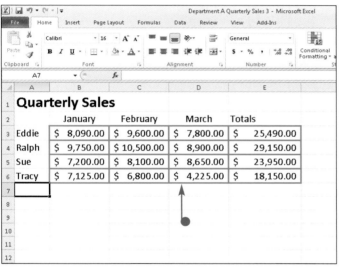

● Excel applies the border. In this example, a green inner and outer border is applied.

Remove It!

Anytime you want to remove a border from a cell or group of cells, start by selecting the cells and then clicking the Borders drop-down arrow on the Home tab. From the menu that appears, click the No Border option. This removes all borders associated with the cell or cells.

Add a Background Color, Pattern, or Image

You can add a background color or pattern to the cells in your worksheet to make it more visually appealing. Excel offers a variety of preset colors and patterns from which you can choose to create just the right look for your worksheet data.

The easiest way to apply a quick background color or shading to selected cells is to apply a fill color. Just click the Fill Color button on the Home tab. For more fill options, including patterns, you can open the Format Cells dialog box to customize the fill. Anytime you choose

a background color you need to be careful not to choose a color that makes it difficult to read the cell data.

In addition to adding a color or pattern to cells to serve as a background for your worksheet, you can also add a photo or other digital image. For example, if your worksheet documents sales, you might add a picture of a product. As with fill color, you need to choose an image that does not clash with the cell data or render it illegible. If it does conflict, you might need to change the color of the worksheet data.

Add a Fill Pattern

1. Select the cells to which you want to apply a background color or pattern.

2. Click the Home tab.

3. Click the Font group's dialog box launcher.

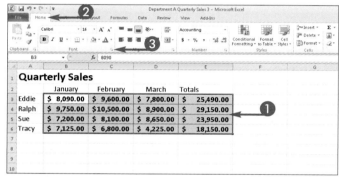

The Format Cells dialog box opens.

4. Click the Fill tab.

● To apply a background color, click the desired color in the palette.

● To assign a gradient fill effect, click Fill Effects and customize the settings.

5. Click here and then select the desired pattern color.

6. Click here and then select a pattern.

7. Click OK.

● Excel applies the selected background pattern.

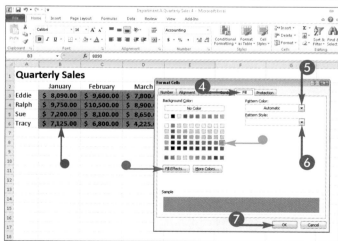

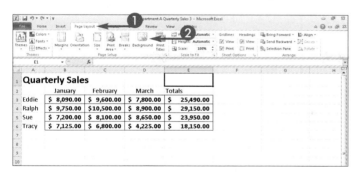

Add a Background Image

① Click the Page Layout tab.

② Click Background.

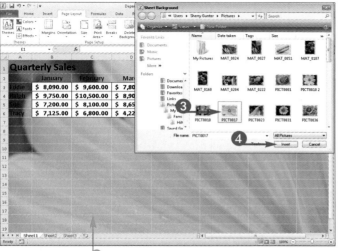

The Sheet Background dialog box opens.

③ Locate and click the image you want to apply to the background.

④ Click Insert.

● Excel applies the selected background image.

TIPS

Try This!

Even if you do not have a color printer, you can take advantage of the various shades of gray to add background colors to your worksheet cells. You can also experiment with the palette of solid colors to create varying degrees of background shading in grayscale tones.

Remove It!

To remove all of the formatting in a cell, including background colors or patterns, select the cell, click the Home tab, and then click Cell Styles. In the gallery of styles that appears, click Normal. This removes all the formatting that has been applied. To delete a background image, click Delete Background in the Page Layout tab.

Color-Code Your Data with Conditional Formatting

You can use Excel's conditional formatting functionality to assign certain formatting only when the value of the cell meets a specified condition. This enables you to detect problems, patterns, and trends at a glance.

Excel offers several predefined rules for conditional formatting. For example, you can set a rule to highlight cells that contain values greater than, less than, equal to, or between a range of specified values; specific text or dates; duplicate values; the top ten or bottom ten values; above-average or below-average values; and more.

You can format cells that meet conditions you set by changing the font or cell background. You can also apply data bars, where the length of the bar represents the value in the cell; color scales, which enable you to compare cells in a range using a gradation of color; and icon sets, which enable you to classify data into categories with each category represented by a particular icon.

If none of the predefined rules suits your needs, you can modify or create a new one.

---

① Select the cell or range to which you want to apply conditional formatting.

② Click the Home tab.

③ Click Conditional Formatting.

④ Click the desired rule category (here, Highlight Cells Rules).

⑤ Click the desired rule (here, Less Than).

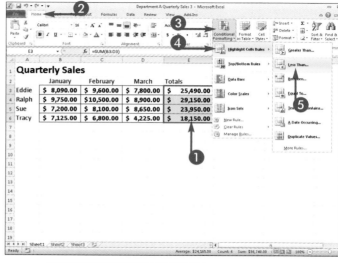

A dialog box appears, enabling you to specify the desired conditions.

Note: Depending on the rule you selected, the dialog box settings will vary.

⑥ Enter the values or text for the condition. In this example, the cell is formatted if its value is less than 20,000.

⑦ Click here and select a format to apply.

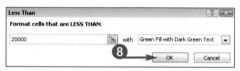

8 Click OK.

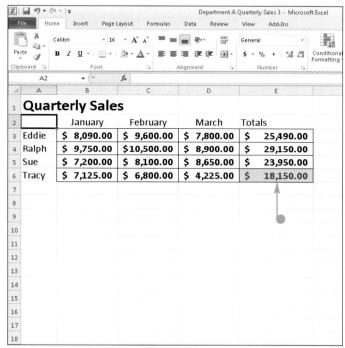

● Excel applies the conditional formatting to any cells that meet the established conditions. In this example, the value is less than 20,000.

Try This!

To quickly locate cells to which a conditional formatting rule has been applied, click any cell in the sheet, click the Home tab, click Find & Select, and click Conditional Formatting. To find only those cells with the same conditional formatting, click a cell to which said formatting has been applied, click Find & Select, choose Go To Special, click Conditional Formats, and click Same under Data Validation.

Remove It!

To remove conditional formatting from a worksheet, click the Home tab, click Conditional Formatting, point to Clear Rules, and then click Clear Rules from Entire Sheet. To remove conditional formatting from certain cells only, select the cells, click the Home tab, click Conditional Formatting, point to Clear Rules, and then click Clear Rules from Selected Cells.

Creating charts is a popular task in Excel; however, not many users go beyond adding just a basic chart. One way that charts make data easier to interpret and understand is through the use of chart objects. These include legends, which convey what each data series in your chart represents; the chart title, which looks like a headline for your chart (as outlined here); the plot area, which is the background area of your chart; the value axis, which is the axis listing values for the data series; the value axis title, which is a headline identifying the value axis; the category axis, which lists the categories for the data series; the category axis title, which is a headline identifying the category axis; and the data series, which is the data plotted on the chart.

If the predefined chart style you applied to your data series does not include a particular chart object, you can add it manually from the Layout tab.

Whether an object in your chart appears by default or was applied manually, you can format it to suit your needs — for example, change the font or color of the object.

① Click the chart to which you want to add a chart object.

② Click the Layout tab.

③ Click the desired chart object type in the Labels or Axes group.

④ Click the object you want to add.

● Excel adds the object. In this example, a chart title object is added to the chart.

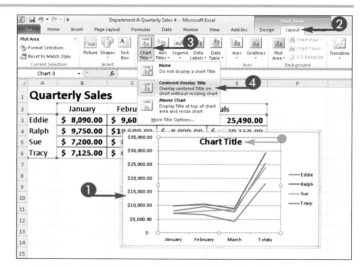

⑤ If necessary, type the text you want to appear in the object (here, "Quarterly Sales").

⑥ To format the object, click it to select it.

⑦ Click the Format tab.

⑧ Click Format Selection.

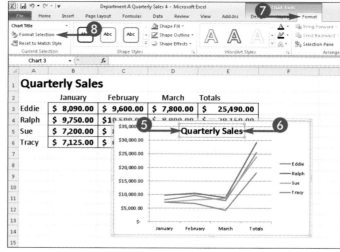

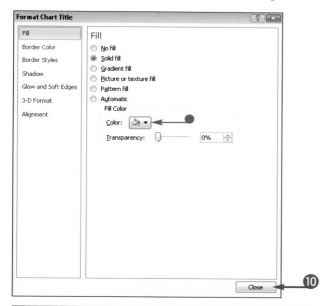

A format dialog box appears. Depending on the chart object you want to edit, the options offered will vary.

⑨ Make the desired changes to the chart object.

● In this example, a fill color is applied to the object.

⑩ Click Close.

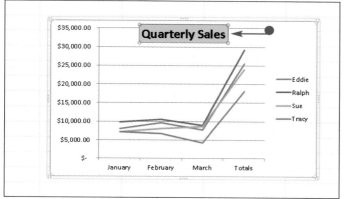

● Excel applies your changes to the chart.

TIPS

Did You Know?

If you find you use a particular chart type often, you can set it as the default type. To do so, open the Insert Chart dialog box by clicking the dialog box launcher (▣) in the Charts group on the Insert tab; then click the Set As Default Chart button. Thereafter, when you open the Insert Chart dialog box, that chart subtype is selected by default.

Try This!

To move the chart to the desired location in a sheet, click an empty area in the window containing the chart and drag the chart to the preferred spot. Alternatively, move the chart to its own sheet by clicking Move Chart on the Design tab and clicking New Sheet.

Reveal Trends with Trendlines

You are not limited to using charts to illustrate existing data; you can also chart forecasts using trendlines, which are used primarily in line, area, bar, and scatter charts. A *trendline* is a graphic representation of a trend in a data series.

For example, suppose you have created a chart showing your monthly household expenditures for the preceding year. You can add a trendline to your chart to show the projected expenditures for upcoming months. You can also add trendlines to show the general trend (that is,

upward or downward) of the existing data series, or add a line to represent a moving average. A moving average is a sequence of averages computed from parts of a data series. Moving averages are helpful for smoothing the fluctuations in data to more clearly reveal the general pattern or trend.

Excel enables you to format various aspects of the trendline, such as its color, width, and so on.

---

① Click the chart to which you want to apply a trendline.

② Click the Layout tab.

③ Click Trendline in the Analysis group.

④ Click the desired trendline type.

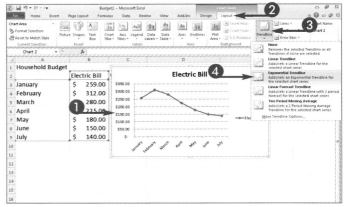

● Excel applies the trendline.

⑤ To change the look of the trendline, click it.

⑥ Click Format Selection.

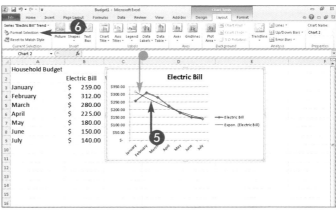

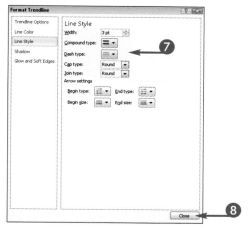

The Format Trendline dialog box appears.

⑦ Make the desired changes to the trendline.

⑧ Click Close.

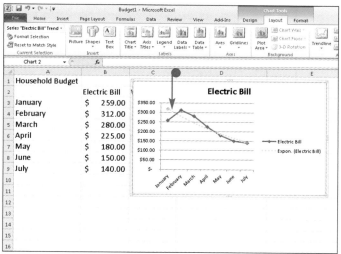

● Excel applies the format changes to the trendline.

In this example, the line width, style, and color are modified.

Customize It!

You can customize your trendline by changing the various input parameters. For example, if you opted for a moving average trendline (see step 4), you can change the number of periods averaged to determine line placement. You can make this and other changes to the trendline from the Trendline Options screen of the Format Trendline dialog box. (Open the dialog box by right-clicking an existing trendline and clicking Format Trendline, or by clicking Trendline in the Layout tab and clicking More Trendline Options.)

New to Excel 2010, you can use Sparklines to illustrate data trends at a glance. Sparklines are mini-charts you can insert inside worksheet cells that let you view data that represents change for a particular row or column of entries. Unlike regular charts you create in Excel, Sparklines fit inside a single cell and quickly sum up information into a tiny visual glimpse. In previous versions of Excel, you needed a third-party add-in program to create Sparklines. Now this functionality is readily available to Excel 2010.

Sparklines present trends and variations in measurement, such as the ups and downs of stocks or varying degrees of temperature, just to give a few examples.

In order to utilize Sparklines, you need data that can be measured with three chart types: line, column, and high-low. When you activate the Sparkline tool, the Create Sparklines dialog box opens and you can specify the data range you want to chart and a location range in which to place the Sparkline chart.

---

① Click the Insert tab.

② Click the type of Sparkline you want to use.

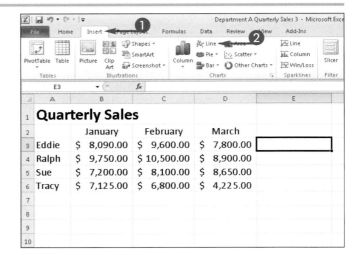

The Create Sparklines dialog box appears.

③ Click the Data Range box and drag across the worksheet range you want to chart. In this example, cells B3:D3.

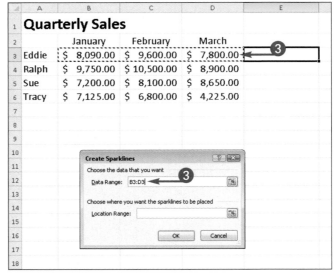

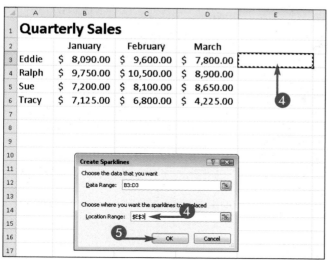

4 Click the Location Range box and drag across the worksheet range where you want to place the Sparkline. In this example, cell E3.

5 Click OK.

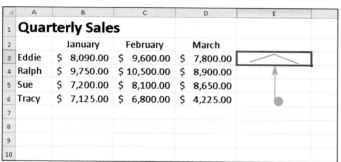

● Excel inserts the Sparkline in the cell.

Did You Know?

Sparklines were named by their inventor, Edward Tufte, for "small, high-resolution graphics embedded in a context of words, numbers, and images," also described as "intense, simple, word-sized graphics." They were created specifically to bring meaning and context to reported numbers by embedding them into what they describe.

Customize It!

When you insert a Sparkline, Excel displays the Sparkline Tools Design tab, which offers tools for formatting the chart type, what elements appear, and a style for the chart. You can even alter the color of the chart.

You may run into situations where the text you need to enter is wider than the cell meant to hold it, especially if your worksheet contains cells with lengthy text. By default, when the amount of data in a cell exceeds the cell's width, the data remains on one line. If the cells to the right of the cell in question are empty, this poses no problem because the data simply stretches across subsequent cells.

If, however, the cells to the right contain data, those cells will obscure any text that spans beyond the cell in question. To view the data in its entirety, you must click the cell that contains the data and look at the Formula bar.

If you want to be able to see the data in its entirety within the cell, you can turn on Excel's Wrap Text feature. When you do, data in the cell wraps to the next line, with the height of the row containing the cell increasing to make room.

① Click to select the cell or cells that you want to edit.

② Click the Home tab.

③ Click the Wrap Text button.

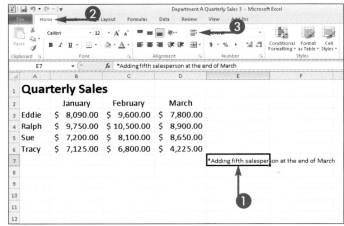

● Excel applies text-wrapping to the selected cell(s).

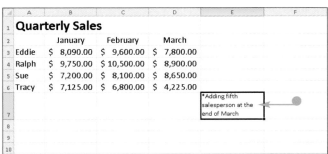

Change Cell Text Orientation

You can add visual interest to your worksheet text by changing the text orientation, such as angling the text upwards or downwards in the cell. You might use this technique to make a long column heading take up less horizontal space on the worksheet. This can often prevent Excel from spreading the data to a second document page for printing. Angling the column headings is also a great way to make the text visually appealing.

Using the Orientation tool, you can rotate text to a diagonal angle or orient the text straight up or down in a cell. For a quick orientation assignment, simply click the Orientation button and choose the desired setting. For more control over the effect, open the Format Cells dialog box and set an exact degree of rotation, as shown in this task.

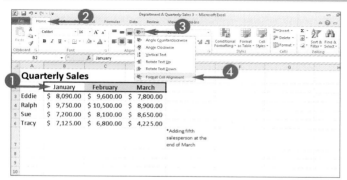

① Select the cell or range you want to edit.

② Click the Home tab.

③ Click the Orientation button.

④ Click Format Cell Alignment.

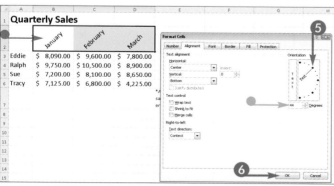

The Format Cells dialog box opens to the Alignment tab.

⑤ Click an orientation setting.

● You can also enter an exact value in the Degrees box or click the spinner arrows to set a value.

⑥ Click OK.

● Excel applies the new orientation.

By default, Excel aligns all printed data to the left and top margins of the page when you print it out, unless you specify otherwise. You may find that some of your worksheets look better if you center the data on the printed page. You can use the Page Setup dialog box to determine how you want the printed data to align on the page.

You can select the Horizontally option to center data between the left and right margins,

or the Vertically option to center the data between the top and bottom margins. You can also apply both centering alignments to the same page at the same time.

In addition, you can also use the Page Setup dialog box to control other margin aspects for the printed page, such as setting exact margin values or margins for header or footer text.

---

① Click the Page Layout tab.

② Click the Page Setup group's dialog box launcher.

The Page Setup dialog box appears.

③ Click the Margins tab.

④ Click a centering option (☐ changes to ☑).

⑤ Click OK.

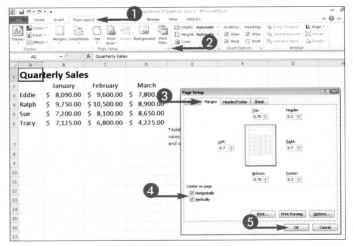

● The new setting is applied when you print the worksheet. In this example, the data is centered both horizontally and vertically.

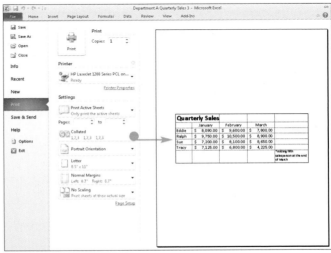

Another way to make your worksheets more visually appealing is by centering title text, such as a range heading, across several columns. Ordinarily, when you want to center text across several worksheet cells, you must use the Merge Cells command. This command creates one large cell to contain the title text. However, if you need to cut or copy the rows or columns that intersect with the merged cell, Excel does not allow you to do so. You may

also find it difficult to perform a sort on a list that contains a merged cell.

Fortunately, there is another technique that centers your title text without combining worksheet cells. Using the Center Across Selection option in the Format Cells dialog box, you can achieve the same appearance as if you merged the cells. This technique leaves intersecting rows and columns safe for cutting and copying later.

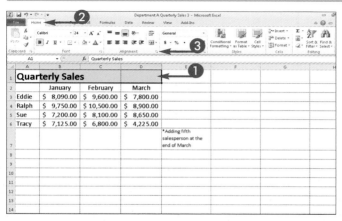

1 Click the cell containing the text you want to center and the cells you want to span.

2 Click the Home tab.

3 Click the Alignment group's dialog box launcher.

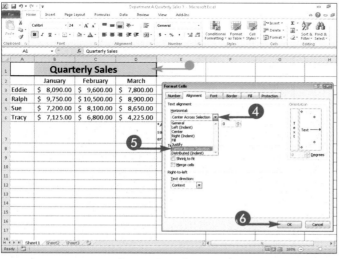

The Format Cells dialog box opens to the Alignment tab.

4 Click the Horizontal drop-down arrow.

5 Click Center Across Selection.

6 Click OK.

● Excel centers the text.

Increasing PowerPoint's Potential

You can use PowerPoint to create presentations to convey all kinds of messages to an audience. For example, you might employ PowerPoint to present an idea to a prospective client, explain a concept or procedure to employees, or teach a class about a new subject. Your presentation can include words, graphics, media clips, charts, tables, and more.

When creating a presentation, you build an outline, with each first-level heading in the outline serving as the title of an individual slide. Second-level headings appear as bullet points; third-level headings appear as sub-bullets; and so on.

Once your presentation is set up, you can set a time length for the display of each slide, add narration, and insert action

buttons and hyperlinks to link to other content. If, for example, you want the presentation to play back in a booth at a trade show, you can set it up to run automatically, such that it requires no external input or management. If, on the other hand, you are the presenter, you can print out speaker notes for your use during the show. To help your audience better follow along, you can also print handouts, which contain the slides in your presentation.

If you intend to deliver your presentation using a different computer, you can copy the presentation to a CD. You can also place your presentation on the Web, enabling you to widen your audience substantially.

Quick Tips

Convert a Word Document into a Presentation

Perhaps you have invested significant time generating a document in Word, and your boss asks you to give a presentation about that document. Instead of retyping the information from the document and reproducing it all over again in PowerPoint, you can import it. This can really save you time and effort.

When you import a Word document into PowerPoint, PowerPoint translates any text in the Word document that is represented in Word's Outline view into a PowerPoint

outline. Any heading in the document styled with Word's Heading 1 style appears as a slide title atop a new slide. Second-level headings become bullet points, third-level headings become second-level bullet points, and so on. Normal-style text between the headings is omitted.

You can edit a presentation generated from a Word document just as you would any other presentation: by selecting the slide you want to edit and making the necessary changes.

---

① Click the File tab.

② Click Open.

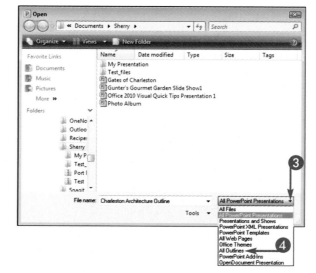

The Open dialog box appears.

③ Click the file types drop-down arrow.

④ Click All Outlines.

⑤ Navigate to and select the Word file you want to use.

⑥ Click Open.

● PowerPoint imports the Word document, adding all first-level headings as slide titles, second-level headings as bullets, and so on.

Caution!

Before importing a Word document, make sure the appropriate headings are applied. You can use Word's Outlining feature to create easy outlines using heading styles, such as Heading 1, Heading 2, Body text, and so on. To switch to Outline view, click the View tab on the Ribbon and click Outline. This opens the Outlining tab where you can use the tools to create an outline for a presentation.

Organize a Presentation into Sections

Giant presentations can be cumbersome and difficult to navigate when creating content and organizing slides. Thankfully, PowerPoint 2010 offers a new tool to make handling larger presentations easier by assigning sections. You can easily keep track of a group of slides that share the same section, or hand off a section to a colleague for collaboration. You can even use sections to help you systematize topics for a brand-new presentation.

Sections are labeled as such in the Slides pane of Normal view as well as in Slide Sorter view.

When you add a new section, PowerPoint assigns a default section name which you can then replace with something more meaningful.

You can expand and collapse the sections in the Slides pane in Normal view to help you view just the slides you want to work with, and you can move sections up and down in the slide order. To organize your slides, simply move them from one section or another by dragging them in the Slides pane or Slide Sorter view. You can also remove sections you no longer need.

---

① Click where you want to insert a section in the Slides pane.

② Click the Home tab.

③ Click Section.

④ Click Add Section.

● PowerPoint inserts a new section.

⑤ Right-click the section name.

⑥ Click Rename Section.

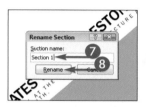

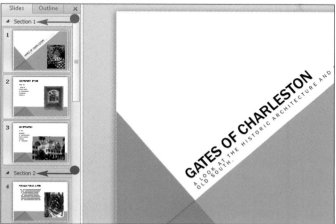

The Rename Section dialog box opens.

⑦ Type a name for the section.

⑧ Click Rename.

● PowerPoint renames the section.

● You can add more sections to your presentation as needed.

Try This!

To move a section to another spot in the presentation, right-click its name and chose Move Section Up or Move Section Down. You can also drag and drop section names in Slide Sorter view to move sections. Simply click and drag the section title to a new location in the presentation. All the accompanying slides move with the section head.

Remove It!

PowerPoint offers you several ways to handle removing a section in a presentation. To remove a section only, but leave the slides intact where they are, right-click the section name and choose Remove Section. To remove the section along with its associated slides, choose the Remove Section & Slides option. To take out all the sections in a presentation, leaving all the slides in place, choose Remove All Sections.

Send a Presentation to Reviewers

If your presentation involves a group effort, you likely need to share it with others before delivering it to your audience. An easy way to do so is to e-mail the presentation.

One way to e-mail a presentation is to simply send the presentation file as an attachment from within your e-mail program. If you prefer, however, you may be able to send the file from within PowerPoint, assuming you use a compatible e-mail program, such as Outlook.

When others review your presentation, they can use PowerPoint's comment features to provide feedback quickly and easily. With these tools, reviewers can insert, edit, and delete comments, as well as opt to show or hide edits. These tools are available from the Comments group under the PowerPoint Ribbon's Review tab.

Before sharing your presentation with others, consider running a spell check. To do so, click the Spelling button in the Review tab's Proofing group.

① **With the presentation you want to share open in PowerPoint, click the File tab.**

② **Click Save & Send.**

③ **Click Send Using E-mail.**

④ **Click Send as Attachment.**

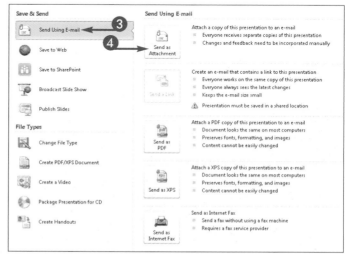

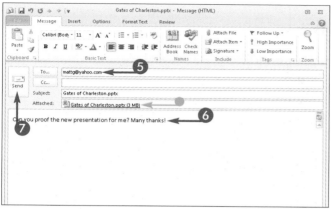

● Your default e-mail program opens. In this example, Microsoft Outlook 2010 opens and displays a new message window with the PowerPoint presentation file already attached.

⑤ Type your message recipient.

⑥ Type the message text.

⑦ Click Send.

The message and attachment are sent and you are returned to the PowerPoint program window.

Try This!

You can also send a presentation as a file attachment in the PDF or XPS formats, two popular formats that are easy to view if someone does not have PowerPoint installed. When you click Save & Send in Backstage view and click the Send Using E-mail option, you are presented with options for sending the file as a PDF or XPS copy. With either format, the presentation looks pretty much like it does in PowerPoint, with the fonts and formatting preserved.

Try This!

If you save your presentation in a shared location, such as a shared folder or workgroup location, you can use PowerPoint's Send a Link command to offer a link to the file in an e-mail rather than send the entire presentation as a file attachment. To activate this command, click the File tab, click Save & Send, click Send Using E-mail, and then click the Send a Link button. This button is operable only if the presentation has been saved to a shared location.

Reuse a Slide from Another Presentation

Suppose you are working on a new presentation and you want to include information covered in an existing presentation. Instead of re-creating the content all over again, you can insert the relevant slide from the existing presentation into the new one.

This is a great timesaver if, for example, you have created a slide with a highly detailed chart, table, or diagram, because it saves you the trouble of reentering data and reformatting the object on the slide. When you insert a slide from a different presentation, the slide automatically adopts the colors, fonts, graphics,

and other formatting attributes of the new presentation (although you can opt to keep the original formatting if you prefer).

To reuse a slide from another presentation, you first locate the presentation containing the slide you want to reuse. This presentation might reside on your computer's hard drive, on a CD you insert in your CD drive, on a network to which your computer is attached, or in a Slide Library on a SharePoint Server. PowerPoint then displays the slides in the selected presentation in the Reuse Slides task pane.

---

① In either Normal or Slide Sorter view, select the slide after which you want to insert the new slide.

② Click the Home tab.

③ Click the New Slide drop-down arrow.

④ Click Reuse Slides.

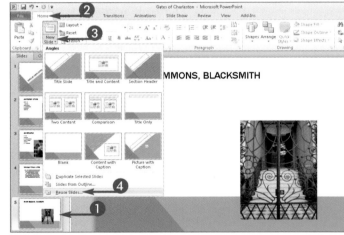

● The Reuse Slides pane opens.

⑤ Click the Browse button.

⑥ Click Browse File.

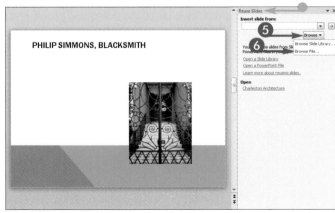

The Browse dialog box opens.

⑦ Navigate to and select the PowerPoint file you want to use.

⑧ Click Open.

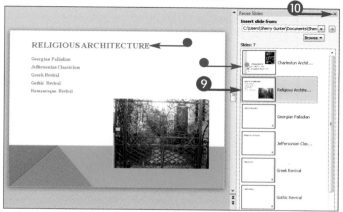

● The presentation's slides are listed in the Reuse Slides pane.

⑨ Click the slide you want to reuse.

● PowerPoint immediately inserts it into the presentation.

⑩ Click the pane's Close button to exit the Reuse Slides pane.

Try This!

To get a better look at the slides in the Reuse Slides task pane, position the mouse pointer over the slide thumbnail rather than the slide title. When you do, an enlarged version of the thumbnail pops up, providing enhanced visibility and readability.

Apply It!

If the slide you are looking for is not in the presentation you selected in the Browse dialog box, click the Browse button in the Reuse Slides task pane and choose Browse File to redisplay the Browse dialog box. Then locate and select the correct presentation file to reveal the presentation's slides in the Reuse Slides task pane.

Rehearse Timings

When delivering a presentation, you typically advance the slides manually by clicking the mouse button. You can, however, set up your presentation to advance the slides automatically. That way, you are free to move as you speak instead of being tethered to your laptop throughout the presentation.

If you opt for automatic slide advancement, you must rehearse the timing of your presentation to ensure that the slides advance at the correct time. To do so, use the Rehearse Timings feature to record the amount of time you need for each slide. PowerPoint then uses the times you record during the presentation

to determine when to advance from one slide to the next.

Note that the Rehearse Timings feature also works well for creating a self-running presentation — that is, a presentation that runs without narration (for example, in a kiosk at a trade show).

As far as slide timing goes, a good rule of thumb is to allow for enough time for your audience to read and view the contents, and if you are speaking along with the presentation, allow enough time to cover all of the necessary points you want to make.

---

① With the slide show you want to rehearse open in PowerPoint, click the Slide Show tab.

② Click Rehearse Timings.

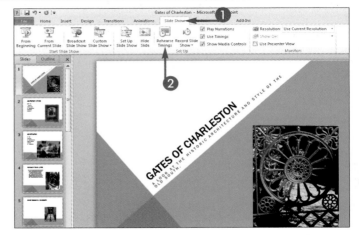

PowerPoint switches to full-screen view and displays the Recording toolbar.

③ Rehearse your speech for the current slide.

● You can click the Pause button to pause the timer at any time.

● The timer for the current slide appears here.

● You can click the Repeat button to restart the timer for the current slide.

● The timer for the overall presentation time appears here.

④ When you are finished speaking or rehearsing with the first slide, click the Next button or the spacebar.

⑤ Repeat steps 3 and 4 for each remaining slide in the presentation.

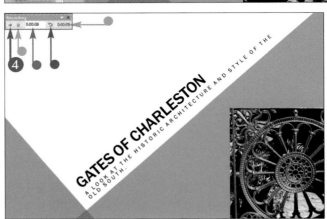

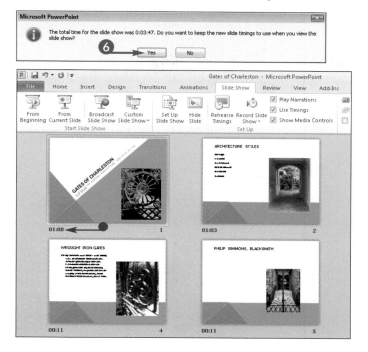

When you click the Next button after rehearsing the last slide, PowerPoint informs you of the total time for the presentation and asks whether you want to keep the new slide timings you created.

⑥ Click Yes if you are satisfied with the slide timings. If you want to change the slide timings, click No and make the desired changes to the presentation.

● PowerPoint displays the slides in the show in Slide Sorter view, with the timing for each slide noted.

Try This!

You can apply transition effects to your PowerPoint presentations. When you do, PowerPoint plays a special effect when advancing from one slide to the next. For example, you can choose a wipe transition effect, where the next slide appears to wipe the current slide from the screen. You can also apply sound effects for transitions, and establish how quickly the transition should occur. You access these settings from the Transitions tab's Transition to This Slide and Timing groups.

More Options!

If you decide you want to advance the slides manually rather than use the timings you set, simply disable the timings by deselecting the Use Timings check box in the Slide Show tab's Set Up group (☑ changes to ☐).

If you do not intend to present your PowerPoint show live — for example, if you will show it at a kiosk or over the Web — you might want to record a narration that talks the viewer through your key points. When a presentation uses a recorded narration, it advances to the next slide automatically at the end of the previous slide's narration.

Before you record your narration, take time to jot down just what you want to say when each slide appears. When recording the narration, speak slowly, and be sure to enunciate.

Most computers today have a built-in microphone you can use, or you can plug in additional microphones. Be sure to check out what is available on your system (Control Panel) and make sure the microphone is functioning properly before recording.

PowerPoint has combined the Rehearse Timings feature with the Record Narration feature so you can do both at the same time when recording narration. You can use the Recording toolbar that appears during your recording session to pause the show, redo the narration again, and keep track of how long the slide is in view as well as the overall length of the presentation.

---

① Click the Slide Show tab.

② Click Record Slide Show.

③ Click Start Recording from Beginning.

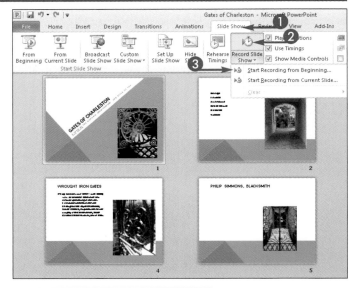

The Record Slide Show dialog box opens.

● To include slide and animation timings along with your recorded narration, leave this check box selected.

④ Click Start Recording.

PowerPoint switches to full-screen view and displays the Recording toolbar.

⑤ Speak your narration into your microphone, pressing the spacebar or the Next button on the toolbar to advance to the next slide as needed.

● You can click the Pause button to pause the timer at any time.

● You can click the Repeat button to restart the timer for the current slide.

⑥ To play back your slide show and listen to the narration, you can switch to Normal view and click the audio clip icon on the slide.

● PowerPoint displays a playback bar and the Audio Tools on the Ribbon.

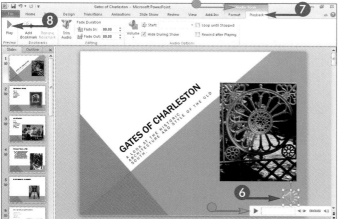

⑦ Click the Playback tab.

⑧ Click Play.

Note: *You can also click the Play button (▶) on the playback bar that appears when you position the mouse pointer over the audio icon.*

Remove It!

To clear the narration from a slide, select the slide and click the Slide Show tab. Click the Record Slide Show button, click Clear, and then click Clear Narration on Current Slide. To remove narration for the entire presentation, choose Clear Narration on All Slides. The Clear menu also lets you remove all slide timings, too.

More Options!

You can tinker with the audio options for your narration using the controls in the Playback tab. Click an audio icon on the slide in Normal view to display the Audio Tools on the Ribbon, and then click the Playback tab. Here you will find options for trimming an audio clip, adding fade in or fade out effects, adjusting volume, and more.

Insert Action Buttons

You can insert action buttons onto your slides to create interactivity. Action buttons enable you to quickly jump to related content while delivering a slide show. You might insert an action button that leads to another slide in your presentation, another presentation altogether, a Word document, a program, or a Web page. Alternatively, clicking an action button might result in the playing back of a sound file. (Note that the item to which the action button is linked must reside on the computer you are using to conduct your presentation. If the item is a Web page, then the computer must be connected to the Internet.)

PowerPoint offers several predesigned action buttons from which to choose; alternatively, you can create your own custom button. After you select the button type, you then choose what action will occur when the button is clicked during a show.

Action buttons are especially handy for self-running presentations (that is, presentations that do not use a presenter, which are often played back at a booth or kiosk). They enable the audience to access additional materials or simply navigate the presentation.

① Click the Insert tab.

② Click Shapes.

③ Among the Action Buttons group, click a button you want to use for your action.

In this example, an informational button is selected.

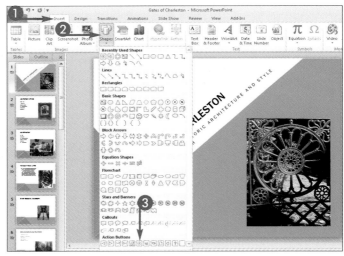

The mouse pointer turns into a cross hairs.

④ Click in the slide and drag diagonally to insert the action button.

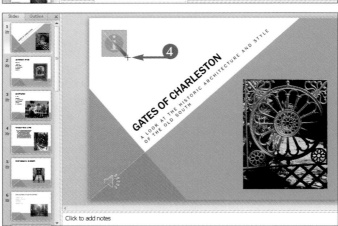

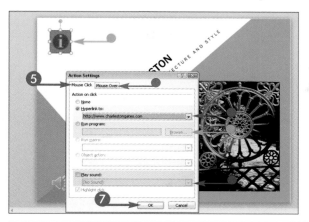

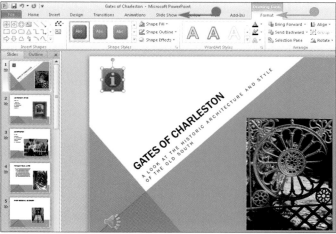

- PowerPoint inserts the action button and displays the Action Settings dialog box.

⑤ Click the Mouse Click tab.

- To engage the action button when the mouse is positioned over the button instead of clicked, choose the Mouse Over tab instead and set the action options.

⑥ Click the action you want to associate with the button.

- Click Hyperlink To to link the action button to another slide in your presentation.

- To link to an external item, click Run Program; click Browse to select the target item.

- To play a sound, click Play Sound and select the sound file.

⑦ Click OK.

PowerPoint assigns the action to the button.

- To test the button, run the slide show; click Slide Show or click the Slide Show tab and click From Current Slide.

- To apply formatting to the new button, click the Format tab and make your changes to the button's appearance.

Try This!

PowerPoint installs with a variety of preset sound clips you can use with your slides. Click the Play Sound drop-down arrow to view a list of sound effects ranging from applause to a cash register sound. The clips are short in length and are especially handy if you want to try out your action button and see what it does. At the bottom of the drop-down list, you can select Other Sound to open the Add Audio dialog box and add sound files you have stored on your computer.

Apply It!

To edit your action, click the button and click the Insert tab. Then click the Action button in the Links group of tools. This opens the Action Settings dialog box where you can edit the action, changing the action or target associated with the action.

Insert a Hyperlink

In addition to inserting action buttons, you can insert hyperlinks directly into your slides. These are similar to action buttons in that clicking them enables you to direct the viewer to another slide in your presentation, another presentation altogether, a Word document, a program, a Web page, or a sound file. Like action buttons, hyperlinks are especially handy for self-running presentations.

Unlike action buttons, however, hyperlinks do not clutter up your slide. Instead, you can use

the text on your slide as a hyperlink. Then, the user need only click the text to engage the link.

Note that you can remove the hyperlink from text in a slide by selecting the text and clicking the Hyperlink button in the Insert tab. Then, in the dialog box that appears, click Remove Link.

The item to which the hyperlink is linked must be stored on the computer on which you are giving your presentation or, if the item is a Web page, the computer must be connected to the Internet.

---

① Select the text you want to convert to a hyperlink.

② Click the Insert tab.

③ Click Hyperlink.

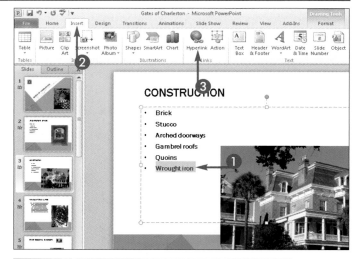

The Insert Hyperlink dialog box appears.

④ Click the kind of link you want to insert.

In this example, Existing File or Web Page is selected.

Depending on what you select in step 4, different options appear in the dialog box.

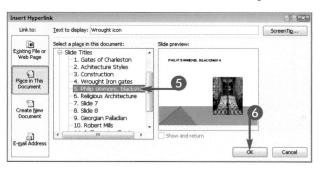

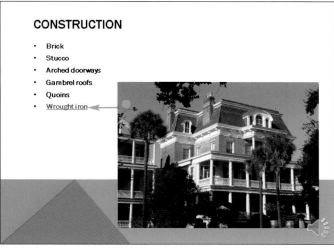

⑤ Locate and select the target item.

In this example, the target is another slide in the presentation.

⑥ Click OK.

● PowerPoint places the link in your slide.

When you run the slide show, you can click the text to follow the link.

TIPS

Try This!

To help you remember where the link leads, you can add a ScreenTip. To do so, click the ScreenTip button in the Insert Hyperlink dialog box and type some descriptive text in the dialog box that appears. Then, when you mouse over the link during a presentation, PowerPoint displays the ScreenTip.

Caution!

When linking to a Web site, you need to know the site's address, or URL. You can type the URL in the Address box that appears at the bottom of the Insert Hyperlink dialog box. Be sure to include the full address, including the http:// prefix, such as http://www.mysite.com.

Add an Equation

You can use the new Equation Editor to quickly insert common mathematical equations and expressions into your PowerPoint slides. You can also use it to create your own custom equations and expressions. Microsoft's Equation Editor was part of Word 2007 and Excel 2007, but it is now a part of the Office 2010 suite, including PowerPoint. Equation Editor is actually a separate program; it lets you construct equations or expressions without leaving the PowerPoint slide.

You can access the Equation Editor through the Insert tab on the Ribbon. When you activate the Equation Editor, a tab of Equation tools appear on the Ribbon, including operators and symbols, and equation structures.

When you add an equation, PowerPoint creates a text box for the equation on the slide. Like any other slide object you add, you can reposition the text box, resize, and format it.

---

① Click the Insert tab.

② Click Equation.

● If you click the drop-down arrow, you can choose a preset equation to add.

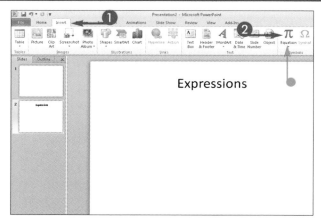

● An equation placeholder text box appears on the slide.

● The Equation Tools Design tab appears on the Ribbon.

③ Type your desired equation.

● You can use the tools on the tab to help you construct your expression or equation.

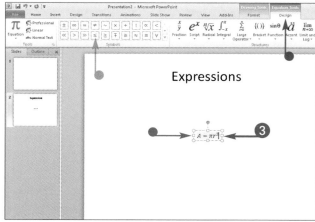

Create a Self-Running Presentation

If your presentation is destined for playback at, for example, a booth at a trade show, you can set it up to be a self-running show, with no presenter required. Alternatively, you might burn a self-running presentation to CD and send it to prospective clients. Self-running presentations are perfect in classroom situations, public venues, and as office training modules.

Your self-running presentation can include hyperlinks or action buttons to enable your audience to navigate the presentation;

alternatively, you can set up the show to advance from slide to slide automatically. You can also include voice narration in your self-running presentation. (Follow the steps in the task "Record Narration" earlier in this chapter.) If you want, you can set up your show to *loop* — that is, run over and over again from beginning to end. This is handy if your presentation is running at a trade show booth or kiosk. You set up a presentation to be self-running from the Set Up Show dialog box.

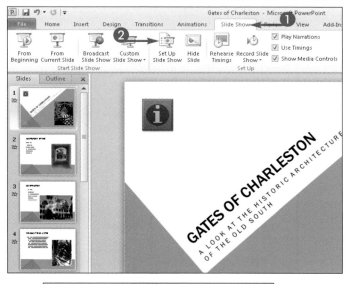

① With your presentation open, click the Slide Show tab.

② Click Set Up Slide Show.

The Set Up Show dialog box opens.

③ Click the Browsed at a Kiosk option.

● When you select Browsed at a Kiosk, PowerPoint automatically loops your presentation continuously.

● If you recorded narration for the presentation, make sure the Show Without Narration check box is unchecked.

● If you set timings for your slides, click Using Timings, If Present.

● If you want your viewer to navigate the show manually, click Manually.

④ Click OK.

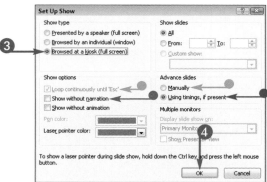

Write on a Slide During a Presentation

Have you ever given a slide show presentation and wished you could actually write or draw on the slide? You can! PowerPoint lets you draw freehand on your screen during a presentation by turning the mouse into a drawing tool. For example, you might use the highlighter tool to highlight text on a slide, or use the pen tool to annotate an important point or to jot down ideas contributed by your audience. Both tools let you draw or write freehand on the slide.

In addition to writing or highlighting, you can also control the color of your pen or highlighter tool. The color palette lets you pick a color that works best on your slide. For example, a red pen is not easy to view against a red slide background, so you might want to choose another, more visible color instead.

At the end of the presentation you can choose to keep the ink annotations or discard them all.

① While running a presentation, right-click a slide.

② Click Pointer Options.

③ Select a pen type, such as Pen or Highlighter.

④ Click and drag to draw or write with the pen.

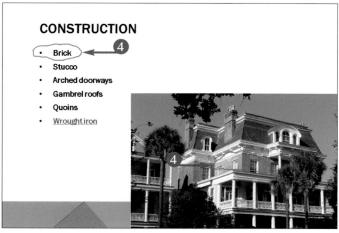

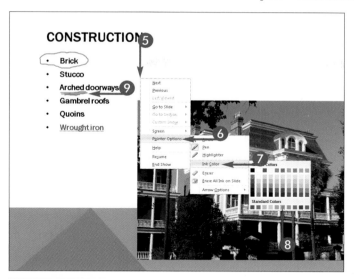

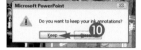

⑤ To change the pen or highlighter color, right-click the slide again.

⑥ Click Pointer Options.

⑦ Click Ink Color.

⑧ Click a color from the palette.

⑨ Write on the screen to view the new color.

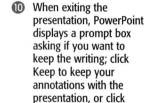

⑩ When exiting the presentation, PowerPoint displays a prompt box asking if you want to keep the writing; click Keep to keep your annotations with the presentation, or click Discard to lose them all.

TIPS

Remove It!
To rid a slide of any drawing or writing you have added with the pen or highlighter, simply right-click and click Pointer Options again. To erase only individual elements, choose the Eraser command and then drag over the writing you want to erase. To erase all the writing on a slide, click Erase All Ink on Slide.

More Options!
In addition to a pen or highlighter, you can also turn your mouse pointer into a laser pointer during the slide show. Press and hold Ctrl on the keyboard and then press and hold the mouse pointer. This turns the pointer into a red laser icon. You can also use this technique in Reading view.

Create Speaker Notes

When giving a presentation, having a cheat sheet with additional facts, or with answers to questions the audience may ask, is handy. To create just such a cheat sheet, you can enter notes into PowerPoint slides, and then print them out. When you print out the notes you enter, the printout includes a small version of the slide to which the notes refer. You can preview your notes before printing using the Notes Page view.

If you need more room for typing in your slide notes in Normal view, you can resize the Notes pane. Just position your mouse pointer over

the top border of the notes area until the pointer becomes a double-sided arrow pointer ($\updownarrow$ changes to $\updownarrow$). Click and drag the border to a taller height to enlarge the notes area.

If you want, you can use PowerPoint's Notes Master to control how printouts of your notes are laid out. For example, you can use the Notes Master to change where the image of the slide appears, as well as to add placeholders for headers, footers, the date, or slide numbers. To use the Notes Master, switch to Notes Master view (click Notes Master in the View tab).

---

❶ In Normal view, click a slide in the Slides pane to which you want to add notes.

❷ Click the Notes pane and type any notes you want to include.

Note: *You can repeat steps 1 and 2 for other slides to which you want to add notes.*

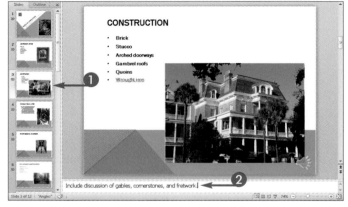

❸ Click the View tab.

❹ Click Notes Page.

❺ Click and drag the Zoom bar to zoom in and see your note text for each slide.

To help your audience follow along as you perform your presentation, as well as provide a place for them to take notes for future reference, you can print presentation handouts. These handouts can contain one, three, five, six, or nine slides per page. (Printing several slides per page can help you save paper when printing handouts for a lengthy presentation.)

When selecting handout orientation, you can choose Horizontal or Vertical to indicate how the slides should be oriented on the printout. Choosing Vertical prints slides in order down the left column, continuing in order down the right column.

You can use PowerPoint's Handout Master to control how your presentation handouts are laid out. For example, you can use the Handout Master to change where the images of the slides appear, as well as add placeholders for headers, footers, the date, slide numbers, a company logo, and so on. To use the Handout Master, switch to Handout Master view (click Handout Master in the View tab). Then use the various tools available on the Handout Master tab to add or remove placeholders, change the fonts or colors used, and so on.

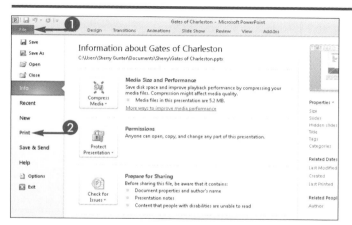

① Click the File tab.

② Click Print.

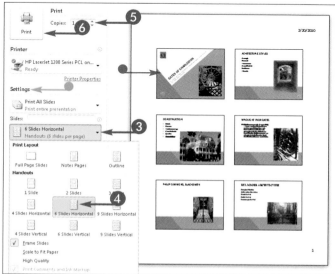

● Backstage view displays the Print settings.

③ Under Settings, click here.

④ Click the number of slides that should appear on each page.

● The preview area shows what the printed page will look like.

⑤ Specify how many copies you want to print.

⑥ Click Print.

PowerPoint prints the handouts.

If your presentation includes a lot of embedded media files, such as soundtracks, narration, video and movie clips, you may end up with a presentation that consumes a great deal of file space. Media clips are notorious consumers of file size. Thankfully, PowerPoint 2010 offers a tool to help you save disk space. You can compress your media files and even improve playback quality.

The Compress Media feature keeps track of your overall file size, and you can view this notation using the Info tab in Backstage view. You can choose from three quality settings: Presentation Quality, Internet Quality, and

Low Quality. Choose Presentation Quality if you want to maintain high quality yet save some space. Choose Internet Quality to emulate streaming media found on the Internet. Choose Low Quality if you are sending the presentation as a file attachment.

After the compression process is completed, the Info screen displays information about what quality setting you applied. If the compression results were not to your liking, you can click the Compress Media button and choose Undo, and then try another quality setting.

① Click the File tab.

② Click Info.

● Overall media space consumption is listed here.

③ Click Compress Media.

④ Click a quality setting.

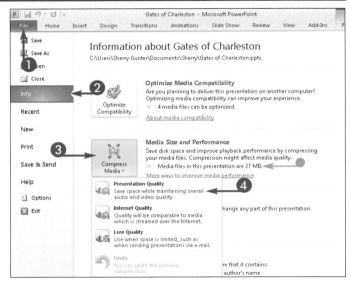

● The Compress Media dialog box appears and displays compression progress.

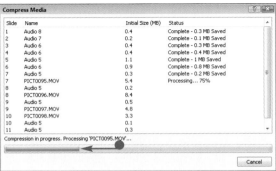

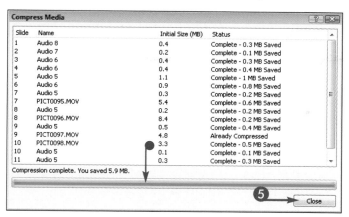

● When the compression is complete, view how much disk space you have saved here.

⑤ Click Close.

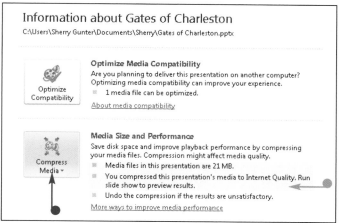

● The Media Size and Performance area lists the type of compression you used.

● Click Compress Media and click Undo if you want to undo the compression.

More Options!

If your presentation is full of digital images instead of media files, you can use PowerPoint's Compress Pictures option to help cut down on file size. Select a picture in a slide to display the Picture Tools Format tab, and then click the Compress Pictures button. The Compress Pictures dialog box opens and you can choose a compression option and a target output. For example, you can discard cropped areas of your pictures to save space, and optimize the pictures for e-mailing or printing.

More Options!

You can also use the Optimize Media Compatibility feature to help ensure your files play back properly on other computers. To bypass problems encountered by end users who are unable to play your media clips properly because of missing decoders, activate the Optimize Media Compatibility feature. Click the File tab, click Info, and then click Optimize Compatibility.

Turn a Presentation into a Video

PowerPoint has always offered users a variety of ways to share their presentations, such as sending them via e-mail, uploading them onto the Internet, or packaging them onto CDs for distribution. With PowerPoint 2010, you can now turn your slide show into a video.

Previously you had to use a special program to accomplish such a conversion. Most people have access to video players today, including through such devices as iPods and iPhones. You can easily turn your presentation into a Windows media video file (WMV). If you want to use another file format, you need a third-party utility to do so.

Using the Create Video feature, you can turn your presentation into a video file that includes all of your assigned transitions, narration, slide timings, and animations. You can choose from three quality settings ranging from larger to smaller in overall file size. Choose Computer & HD Displays to maintain the highest quality setting appropriate for monitors, projectors, or high definition television. Choose Internet & DVD quality if you plan to save the file to a DVD or the Internet. To prepare the presentation for a mobile device, choose the Portable Devices setting.

---

1. Click the File tab.
2. Click Save & Send.
3. Click Create a Video.
4. Click here and choose a quality setting.

5. Click here and choose whether you want to include recorded timings and narrations or not.

Note: By default, PowerPoint assigns a five second default time to slides without preset timings; you can change the timing here to increase or decrease the time.

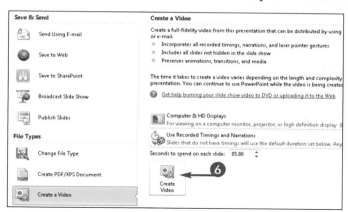

⑥ Click Create Video.

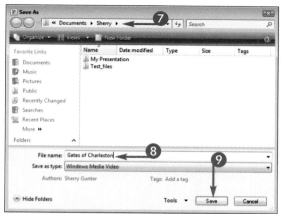

The Save As dialog box appears.

⑦ Navigate to the folder or drive where you want to store the file.

⑧ Type a name for the file.

⑨ Click Save.

PowerPoint creates the video file.

Note: Depending on your presentation, the conversion process for turning a slide show into a video file can take several hours. You may prefer to set this process up to occur overnight so the video file is done and ready for use in the morning.

Note: To play a video, navigate to the folder where you saved the file and double-click the file name.

More Options!

You may prefer to save your presentation to a DVD so that anyone with a standard DVD or disc player can watch it. Start by saving the presentation as a video file as outlined in this task. Then open Windows DVD Maker, click Add Items, and select your newly created video file. Click the Add button, choose your burner, pop in a DVD, and burn the file to the disc. Windows DVD Maker is included in Windows Vista Home Premium and Windows 7 (Home Premium, Professional, and Ultimate editions).

Did You Know?

Just what parts of a presentation are not included in a video file? PowerPoint does not include any media clips you inserted into your slides from previous PowerPoint versions. Any QuickTime media clips are not included, no macros are included, and no OLE or ActiveX controls are stored either. Items definitely included are sounds, narration, animations, transitions, and slide timings.

If you know you will give your presentation using a computer other than your own, you can copy it onto a CD. Then, you can simply insert the CD containing your presentation into whatever computer is available and run it from there.

When you copy your presentation to CD, the computer also copies any files to which that presentation links by default. For example, if you set up an action button in your presentation

to launch a program or document when clicked, the computer also saves the target program or document on the CD with your presentation.

In the event the computer on which you plan to run your presentation does not have PowerPoint installed, PowerPoint includes a copy of PowerPoint Viewer when you burn a presentation to CD. You can then use the CD to install PowerPoint Viewer on the machine on which the presentation will run.

---

① Insert a blank CD in your computer's CD drive.

② With the presentation you want to copy to CD open in PowerPoint, click the File tab.

③ Click Save & Send.

④ Click Package Presentation for CD.

⑤ Click Package for CD.

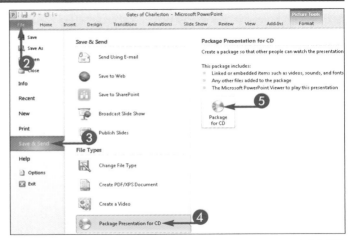

The Package for CD dialog box opens.

⑥ Type a name for the CD.

● To add more presentations to the CD, click Add. In the dialog box that appears, locate and select the presentation you want to add and click Open.

● To copy the presentation to a different folder on your computer or to a location on a network, click Copy to Folder and select the desired folder in the dialog box that appears.

⑦ To copy the presentation to CD, click Copy to CD.

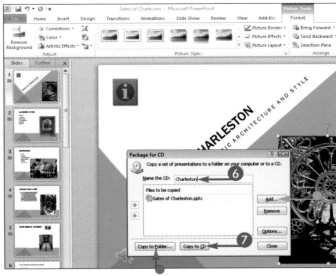

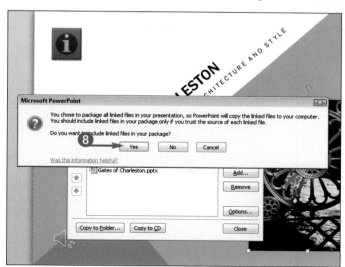

PowerPoint asks whether you want to include linked files on the CD.

⑧ Click Yes.

PowerPoint copies your presentation to CD and displays a progress bar to let you know how the process is going.

More Options!

Instead of saving the entire presentation to a CD, you can choose to save it to a special folder on your computer. To copy the presentation to a different folder on your computer or to a location on a network, click the Copy to Folder button in the Package for CD dialog box and select the desired folder in the Copy to Folder dialog box that appears. Click OK to start the copying. If you leave the Open Folder When Complete check box selected, the folder opens when you finish and you can view the file.

Another new way to share your PowerPoint 2010 presentation is to store it to the new Windows Live SkyDrive. Part of Windows Live, SkyDrive offers you free server storage space you can use to store Office 2010 documents, presentations, pictures, and more. After placing a presentation online, you can access it from any computer using an Internet connection. This handy feature makes it easy to share a presentation with friends or colleagues anywhere.

In order to use SkyDrive, you must sign up for a Windows Live account in with Microsoft. If you do not have a Windows Live account yet, visit the www.home.live.com Web site and follow the links for creating your own Windows Live ID.

When saving to SkyDrive, you can store your presentation in a personal folder or in a public folder where everyone can view it. SkyDrive offers up to 25GB of storage. Every folder you create on SkyDrive has a unique address, which means you can save the link in other files and e-mails.

① Click the File tab.

② Click Save & Send.

③ Click Save to Web.

④ Click Sign In.

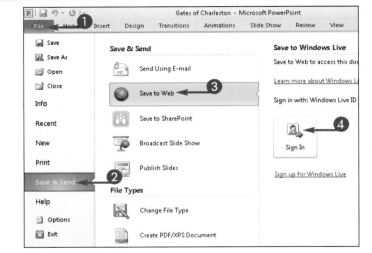

⑤ Sign into Windows Live using your Windows Live credentials (e-mail address and password).

⑥ Click OK.

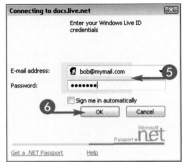

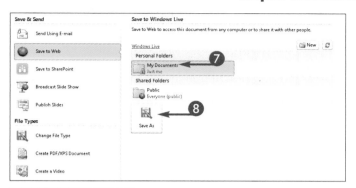

⑦ Click the folder you want to save to, such as the My Documents folder.

⑧ Click Save As.

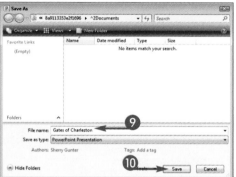

The Save As dialog box opens.

⑨ Type a name for the file or use the default file name.

⑩ Click Save.

The file is uploaded to the specified SkyDrive folder.

Apply It!

In order to see where your presentation is stored on SkyDrive, you must open your Web browser and log onto your Windows Live account and navigate to the SkyDrive page. Using your Web browser, navigate to http://skydrive.live. com and click the My Documents folder or the folder in which you stored the file.

More Options!

If you set up a Windows Live ID and a SkyDrive connection, you can add more than just PowerPoint presentations. You can add files and folders to your account, upload photos, and customize a profile. On the Web site, click the Profile link to create a profile or change settings for your account. To return to the SkyDrive page at any time and view your folders and documents, click the SkyDrive link on the Profile page or click the More link at the top navigation bar and click SkyDrive.

Broadcast a Presentation

New to PowerPoint 2010, you can broadcast a presentation to multiple participants. Similar to a live meeting broadcast, you can use the PowerPoint Broadcast Service to present a slide show, live and synchronized, to friends or colleagues regardless of their location. Simply send them a link provided by the feature and start the show when you are ready to present it. Best of all, the invitees do not need to have PowerPoint 2010 installed in order to view the show. They can use their default browsers to view the presentation.

You need a Windows Live account in order to use this service. If you are not logged on, you need to sign in first to use the service. If you do not have a Windows Live account, use your browser to navigate to www.home.live.com and follow the instructions for creating an account.

When you send out a link to recipients, they can share the link with others. Because the link is public, anyone with the link can view the show.

---

① Click the File tab.

② Click Save & Send.

③ Click Broadcast Slide Show.

④ Click Broadcast Slide Show.

Note: *You can also click the Broadcast Slide Show button on the Slide Show tab to start the process.*

The Broadcast Slide Show dialog box appears.

⑤ Click Start Broadcast.

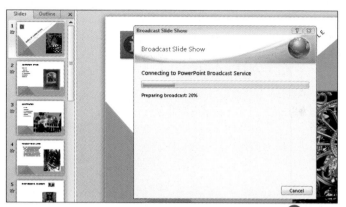

PowerPoint connects you to the broadcast service and prepares your presentation.

Note: *If you are not already logged onto your Windows Live account, you are prompted to do so before preparing the presentation.*

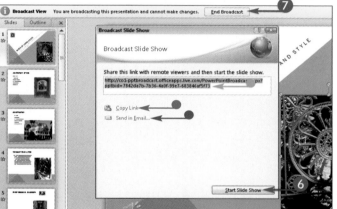

● When you are ready to give the presentation, share the link shown here with your friends or colleagues.

● Click here if you want to copy the link.

● You can click here to send the link in an e-mail.

⑥ When you are ready to start the show, click Start Slide Show.

⑦ When finished, click End Broadcast.

More Options!

If you are a SharePoint user, you can also save your PowerPoint presentation to a SharePoint site, which allows you to collaborate with others in your workgroup. SharePoint uses the same broadcasting tools described in this task to upload a presentation file to a designated spot on the Web. To save your presentation to a SharePoint site, click the File tab, click Save & Send, and then click the Save to SharePoint option. You can browse for a location, and then click Save As to start the process.

Enhancing Your Presentations

Whatever your presentation's message, PowerPoint is designed to enable you to convey it in the most interesting way possible. To that end, the program offers countless features for enhancing your presentation visually.

When you create a presentation, PowerPoint enables you to select from several predesigned slide layouts. A slide's layout determines how the title, text, graphics, and other visual elements are positioned in a slide. You are not compelled to use existing layouts all the time. You can create your own custom layouts and save them to reuse in other presentations.

In addition to selecting the slide layout, you can apply themes to your slides. A theme is a set of colors, fonts, placeholder positions, graphic elements, backgrounds, effects, and other formatting attributes. PowerPoint installs with a variety of premade themes that help you to streamline the look and feel of your presentation. You can also customize an existing theme, as well as

save the custom work as a new theme to add to the library.

Of course, you are not limited to including text-based content in your slides. PowerPoint enables you to insert any number of objects, such as images, video, sound, and SmartArt graphics. Introduced in Office 2007, SmartArt graphics are ideal for creating organizational charts and illustrating other concepts and processes. In Office 2010, Microsoft has added more graphics to the library.

For added interest, you can animate slide objects — for example, you might set up your slide show to fly in an image from the upper left portion of the screen, landing it in the bottom right corner. In moderate doses, animation can go a long way toward keeping your audience engaged.

If your presentation focuses more on images than on text, you can use PowerPoint's special Photo Album feature to create a unique photo album presentation. This feature provides editing tools for arranging your images just so.

Quick Tips

PowerPoint installs with a myriad of layouts; however, if none of the standard layouts available in PowerPoint's Layout gallery quite suits your needs, you can create a new layout from scratch. You create a new layout from within Slide Master view and give it a unique name. (You can learn more about this view in the next task.) When you create a new layout, you add the necessary text- and object-specific placeholders.

Whether working with a predefined layout or a custom one, you can edit the placeholders in a slide's layout. For example, you can resize a placeholder, move it to another location on your slide, or delete it entirely. You can also add as many placeholders to a slide as you need. You

can determine exactly what kind of placeholder to add, such as a text box, clip art, chart, or multimedia item. Anytime you add a placeholder element, you can control the size for the content it holds just by defining its dimensions by "drawing" the placeholder on the slide. To do this, you drag the placeholder box to the size you want when inserting the item.

After you have created your custom layout, PowerPoint adds it to the Layout gallery, and you can reuse it throughout your presentation. You can also save the entire presentation as a template to make the custom layout available in new presentations you create using the template.

---

① **Click the View tab.**

② **Click Slide Master.**

● **The Slide Master tab appears in the Ribbon and is selected by default.**

③ **Click Insert Layout.**

● **PowerPoint adds a new default slide to the list.**

④ **Customize the layout as needed.**

● **Remove any unwanted default placeholders by clicking the border or bounding box of the placeholder and pressing Delete on your keyboard.**

Note: *To move a placeholder, position your mouse pointer over the placeholder's bounding box (that is, the box surrounding the placeholder). The mouse pointer changes to a four-headed arrow ( ); click and drag to relocate the placeholder.*

● **To add a placeholder, click the Insert Placeholder drop-down arrow, click the type of placeholder you want to insert, and then drag to draw the placeholder in the slide.**

⑤ **Click Rename.**

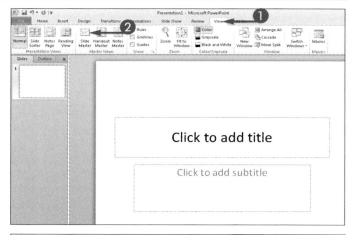

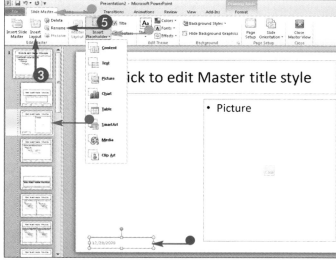

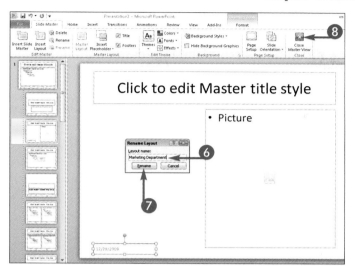

The Rename Layout dialog box opens.

6 Type a unique name for the layout.

7 Click Rename.

8 Click Close Master View.

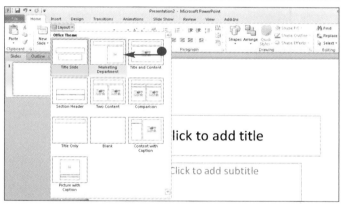

● The new layout is now listed in the New Slide and Layout galleries.

Try This!

To resize a placeholder, first click in the placeholder, and then position your mouse pointer over a sizing handle on the placeholder. The mouse pointer changes to a two-headed arrow (↗); click and drag inward or outward to change the size of the placeholder. (Note: To preserve the aspect ratio of the placeholder — that is, the ratio of the height and width — press and hold Shift and drag one of the corner-sizing handles.)

Apply It!

To save a presentation as a template, simply select PowerPoint Template from the Save As Type drop-down menu in the Save As dialog box (click the File tab and click Save As). You can apply the template as a new presentation at any time by clicking the File tab, New, and selecting the template file from the My Templates folder.

Insert a Custom Slide Master

You can insert your own custom slide masters into a PowerPoint presentation. By definition, a *slide master* determines the type of content and positioning of the various placeholders in the slide. Much like a template for controlling a Word document, a PowerPoint slide master is a template upon which all the presentation's slides are based — a pattern, if you will, for all the slides you add to the presentation. Slide masters are a great way to save time formatting and create a unifying look for a long presentation. It makes sure any additional slides you add always share the same look and feel.

You can customize a slide master to suit your presentation needs. Each slide master you add includes a subset of corresponding layouts. When you apply a theme to a presentation, that theme includes predefined slide masters. If you make a change to a slide master, such as increasing the font size for slide titles or adding a footer or graphic, that change is applied to every slide in the presentation.

You work with the slide master in Slide Master view. You can use the specialized tools on this Ribbon tab to delete, create, preserve, or rename masters, or change the placeholders contained in the master layout.

① With the presentation for which you want to create a custom slide master open in PowerPoint, click the View tab.

② Click Slide Master.

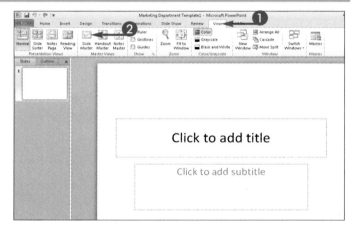

The Slide Master tab appears in the Ribbon and is selected by default.

③ Click Insert Slide Master.

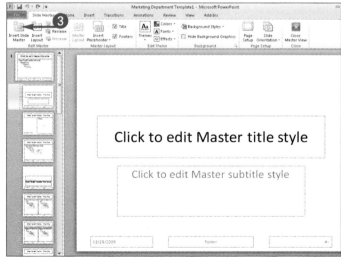

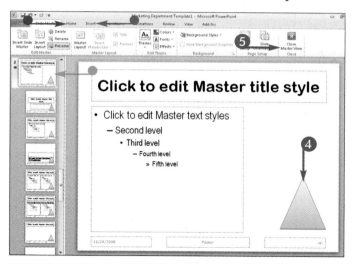

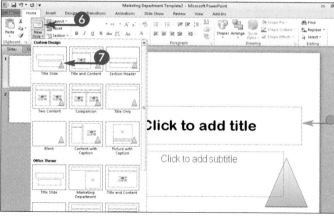

● A new slide master appears along with a subset of layouts.

④ Edit the slide master as needed.

● You can use the Insert tab to insert elements such as footers, a date, slide numbers, graphics, or what have you.

● You can use the Home tab to apply formatting to the various slide elements.

⑤ When you finish customizing the new slide master, click the Close Master View button on the Slide Master tab.

Note: *Be sure to save the presentation as a template file to use the custom slide master in other presentations you create.*

⑥ To apply a slide using the new slide master, click the New Slide button on the Home tab.

⑦ Click a slide.

● PowerPoint displays a slide based on the new slide master.

Try This!

In addition to inserting footers, images, and other items into slide masters, you can also insert placeholders. A placeholder reserves space in a slide for a particular type of element, such as a picture. You can then replace the placeholder with the specific picture you want to use. In this way, you can use a different picture on each slide, even though the same master is applied. To insert a placeholder, click the Slide Master tab, click Insert Placeholder, and choose the type of placeholder you want to insert.

Did You Know?

PowerPoint uses four different master slides for your presentations. As you have already learned, the Slide Master is the boss of all the other slides you add to your presentation, with the exception of the Title Master. The Title Slide Master is the layout template for the Title page only. The Notes Master and Handout Master control Notes pages and Handout pages. You can create a custom master for each type.

Streamline Your Presentation with Themes

Although you can manually format the slides in your presentation one by one — applying backgrounds, fonts, colors, graphics, and so on — an easier way to streamline the look and feel of the slides in your presentation is to apply a theme. Doing so applies specific colors, fonts, placeholder positions, graphic elements, backgrounds, effects, and other formatting to the slides in the presentation in one quick, easy operation. PowerPoint installs with a large library of ready-to-go themes you can apply. The theme's slide masters determine the

positioning of the placeholders and objects for the current theme, saving you time and effort doing it all yourself.

You can apply one theme to all the slides in a presentation to lend a consistent, professional look. Alternatively, you can apply different themes to certain slides. Note that if you do opt to apply a different theme to certain slides, be sure it complements the design used on other slides. Otherwise, the transition from one theme to another as you move from slide to slide can be jarring to viewers.

① With the presentation to which you want to apply a theme open in PowerPoint, click the Design tab.

② Click the More button to display the Themes gallery.

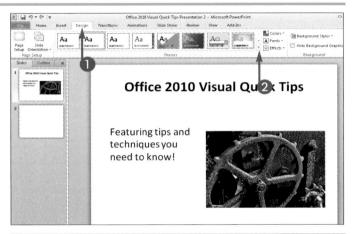

③ Move your mouse pointer to a theme thumbnail.

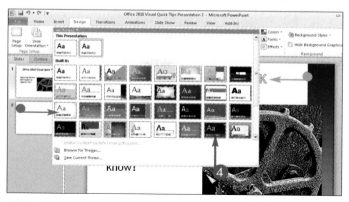

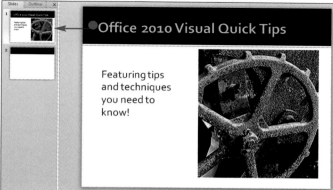

- With Live Preview, you can preview any design theme you position the mouse pointer over in the Slide pane.

- Theme thumbnails display their associated color palettes along with the applied theme formatting.

④ When you find a theme you want to apply, click its thumbnail.

- PowerPoint applies the theme to all the slides in the presentation.

Did You Know?

Generally, dark-colored backgrounds with light-colored text work better in darker spaces, such as hotel conference rooms. Lighter backgrounds are easier to read in brighter, smaller spaces, such as small meeting rooms. Be warned: People may grow weary of looking at bright colors such as oranges or reds for an extended period of time.

Try This!

As mentioned, you can apply different themes to certain slides. To do so, switch to Slide Sorter view and select the slides to which you want to apply the different theme. (Press and hold Ctrl as you click to select noncontiguous slides in the presentation.) Then open the Themes gallery, right-click the theme you want to apply to the selected slides, and choose Apply to Selected Slides.

If you apply a theme to your presentation, but decide that you would prefer to use different colors or fonts with that theme, you can easily change them by selecting a different color theme or font theme. A *color theme* controls the colors automatically applied to text and objects such as tables and SmartArt diagrams. The *font theme* dictates the font formatting for all text.

Changing the color theme or font theme can give your presentation an entirely fresh look, even as other theme attributes are retained.

Choosing different color and font themes can also help make your presentation more attractive — not to mention readable — when it appears on-screen or in printout form.

In addition to applying a new predefined color theme or font theme to your presentation, you can also create your own custom color and font themes.

You can apply a different color theme to selected slides in your presentation or to the entire show. The font theme, however, must be applied to the presentation in its entirety.

Apply a New Color Theme

1. With the presentation whose theme you want to change open in PowerPoint, click the Design tab.

2. Click Colors.

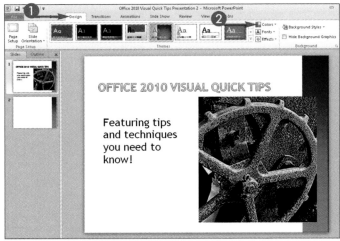

- A gallery of color themes appears.

3. Choose the color theme you want to apply.

- PowerPoint applies the color theme.

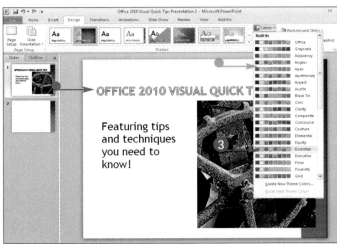

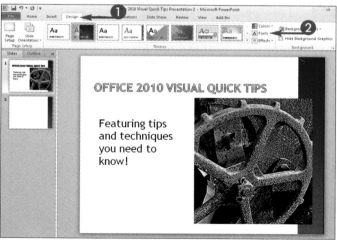

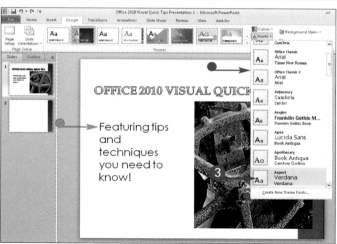

Apply a New Font Theme

① With the presentation whose theme you want to change open in PowerPoint, click the Design tab.

② Click Fonts.

● A gallery of font themes appears.

③ Choose the font theme you want to apply.

● PowerPoint applies the font theme you chose.

TIPS

Try This!

You can create your own custom color theme or font theme by clicking Colors or Fonts and clicking Create New Theme Colors/Create New Theme Fonts. In the dialog box that appears, select the desired colors or font, type a name for the custom color or font theme, and click Save. You can then apply the custom color or font theme just as you would a built-in one.

More Options!

You may have more themes available in other places on your computer. Click the More button in the Themes group to display the full gallery, and then click the Browse for Themes command. You can browse for themes on your own computer using the Choose Theme or Themed Document dialog box. You can also check Microsoft's Office Web site for more themes you can download and use with PowerPoint.

Save a Custom Theme

If you opt to apply formatting to your slides manually, or if you customize an existing theme, you can save your formatting choices as a new theme. Doing so enables you to apply the same formatting settings to other presentations in the same way you would apply any other theme.

If you want, you can make the theme you save — or any other theme, for that matter — the default theme. PowerPoint then automatically applies that theme to any

new presentations you create. To make a theme the default theme, click the Design tab, click the More button, right-click the theme you want to set as the default, and choose Set as Default Theme.

In addition to saving themes you create for reuse, you can save presentations you create as templates on which subsequent presentations can be based. The template file includes both the presentation design (that is, the theme) and content, such as bulleted lists.

---

① With the presentation whose theme you want to save open in PowerPoint, click the Design tab.

② Click the More button to display the Themes gallery.

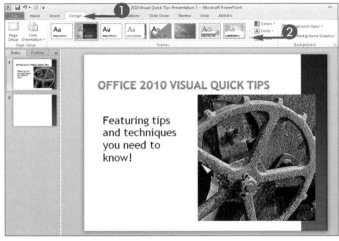

③ Click Save Current Theme.

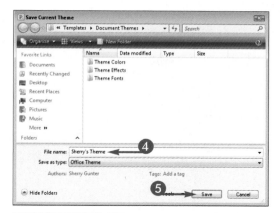

The Save Current Theme dialog box appears.

④ Type a file name.

Note: *Do not change the folder in which the theme is saved. Using the default location ensures that the custom theme appears in the Themes gallery.*

⑤ Click Save.

● PowerPoint adds the theme to the gallery in a special section labeled Custom.

● You can position your mouse pointer over a thumbnail to reveal its name.

More Options!
You can share your themes with others. Themes are saved in the Document Themes folder by default as .thmx file types. You can copy and share the theme files with other users who can store them in their own Document Themes folder or locate the shared theme through the Browse for Themes command (click the Themes group More button and then click Browse for Themes).

Try This!
In addition to saving themes you create, you can also save a presentation as a template. To save a presentation as a template, click the File tab, click Save As, type a name for the template, click the Save As Type drop-down arrow, choose PowerPoint Template, and click Save.

Add a Picture to Your Presentation

Adding graphic elements, such as clip art or your own personal photos or other images (for example, a company logo) can enhance the slide's appearance and give it some visual impact. This is especially helpful because most people are typically visually oriented by nature. Graphic elements can be placed anywhere on your slide.

After you insert a picture into your slide, you can move and resize it as needed. To move a picture, click it in the slide, rest your mouse pointer over the box surrounding it, click, and drag it to the desired location. Resize a picture by clicking it, and then clicking and dragging any of the resizing handles that appear around the border of the picture. Depending on the picture type, you can also rotate and flip pictures. To rotate a picture, click the object to select it, and then drag its rotation handle, the green circle located at the top middle of the picture.

To otherwise edit a picture — for example, to change the image's brightness, contrast, or color tone, crop it, apply a picture style, add a border, and so on — click the picture to select it, click the Format tab, and use any of the various tools that appear. To learn more tips and techniques for working with graphics in Office 2010, see Chapter 14.

Insert Clip Art

❶ With the slide to which you want to add clip art open in Normal view, click the Insert tab.

❷ Click Clip Art.

The Clip Art task pane appears.

❸ Type a search keyword or phrase.

● Click here and select what type of files you want your search to return.

❹ Click Go.

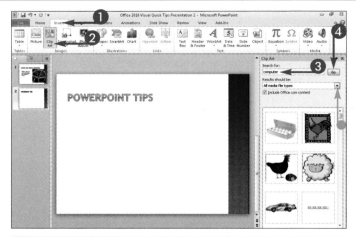

● The Clip Art task pane displays any matching search results.

● Scroll to locate the picture you want.

❺ Click the picture.

● PowerPoint inserts it into the slide. You can move or resize the clip art as needed.

❻ Click to close the Clip Art task pane.

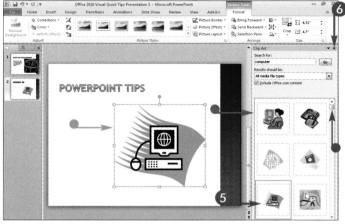

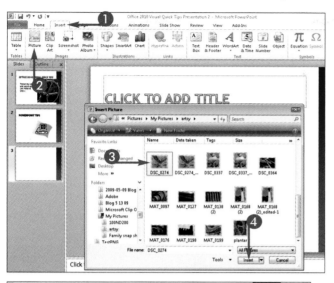

Insert a Picture

1. With the slide to which you want to add a picture open in Normal view, click the Insert tab.

2. Click Picture.

   The Insert Picture dialog box opens.

3. Navigate to and select the picture file you want to insert.

4. Click Insert.

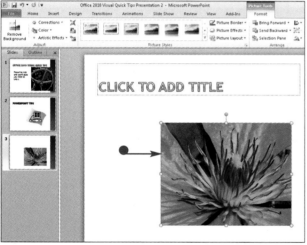

● PowerPoint inserts the image. You can resize or move the picture as needed.

Did You Know?

To find all kinds of formatting options for your picture or clip art graphic, just open the Format Picture dialog box. Right-click the graphic object and click Format Picture. In the Format Picture dialog box, you can find commands listed under a variety of tabs, such as Picture Corrections, Artistic Effects, and Position.

Try This!

You can double-click a clip art object or picture to quickly bring the Picture Tools Format tab in view on the Ribbon, offering you all kinds of commands for formatting the graphic.

Insert a SmartArt Graphic

You can insert a SmartArt graphic or diagram to illustrate a process, hierarchy, cycle, or relationship. For example, a diagram can show the workflow in a procedure or the hierarchy in an organization, as illustrated in this task. Using SmartArt graphics, you can create designer-quality graphics that beautifully convey your message with a few clicks of the mouse. PowerPoint offers dozens of SmartArt graphic layouts. Simply insert the graphic you want to use and add any necessary text.

When you insert a SmartArt graphic into your presentation, it has the same visual characteristics (that is, the color, style, and so on) of other content in the presentation. You can, however, change the style or color of the SmartArt graphic, or add effects such as glow or 3-D. You can even animate your SmartArt graphic. To remove any formatting changes you make to a SmartArt graphic, click the Design tab and click Reset Graphic.

You can also find the SmartArt feature in Word and Excel.

---

1 Click the Insert tab.

2 Click SmartArt.

   If your slide layout has a content placeholder, you can click the Insert SmartArt Graphic icon instead.

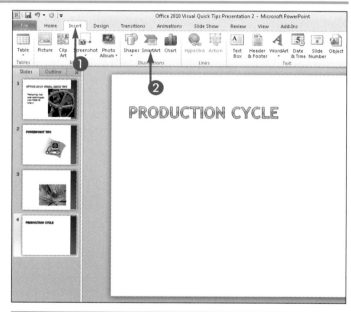

The Choose a SmartArt Graphic dialog box appears.

3 Click a diagram style.

4 Click a specific diagram layout.

5 Click OK.

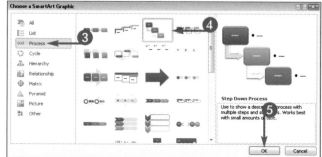

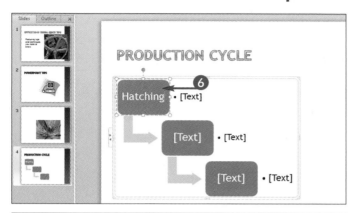

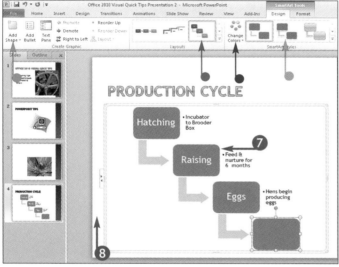

The dialog box closes and the diagram appears on the slide, ready for editing.

⑥ Click in a shape in the diagram and type the desired text.

● To add more shapes to the diagram, click the shape and click Add Shape, choosing where the new shape should appear.

● Click an option in the Layouts group to change the layout of the SmartArt graphic.

● Click Change Colors to choose a different set of colors for the SmartArt diagram.

● Choose a new style for the SmartArt graphic from the SmartArt Styles group.

⑦ Repeat step 6 for the remaining diagram elements.

⑧ Click outside the diagram to finish creating it.

TIPS

Did You Know?
PowerPoint automatically resizes the text you type to fit the SmartArt diagram. You do not need to adjust the font size yourself. The more text you type, the smaller it is. You can apply formatting to any of the SmartArt text; select it and position the mouse pointer over the mini toolbar and select from the formatting controls, or use the formatting controls on the Home tab or on the SmartArt Tools tabs.

Try This!
If your slide already contains the text you want to appear in your SmartArt graphic, you can convert it. To do so, click in the placeholder that contains the text you want to convert to a SmartArt graphic. Then click the Home tab and, in the Paragraph group, click Convert to SmartArt Graphic. (Alternatively, right-click the placeholder that contains the text you want to convert and choose Convert to SmartArt.) A gallery of SmartArt graphic layouts appears; click the one you want to use.

To enhance your presentation, you can add video or movie clips to it. For example, if you have composed a presentation for an alumni association meeting, you might include a clip showing the campus. You can set up PowerPoint to play back your video automatically; alternatively, you can choose to play it manually by clicking it.

Supported video file formats include AVI (Audio Video Interleave), MPEG (Moving Picture Experts Group), and WMV (Windows Media Video).

Video files are always linked to, rather than embedded in, PowerPoint presentations to reduce the size of the presentation file. For this reason, it is wise to first copy the video file into the same folder in which your PowerPoint presentation is stored; this ensures that your presentation can locate the file when necessary.

You can also insert sound clips into your presentation. When you do, PowerPoint adds a small speaker icon to the selected slide. When you position the mouse pointer over the speaker icon, a player control bar appears with buttons for playing the clip. (If the speaker icon clashes with your slide design, and if you have set up the sound to play automatically, you can hide the speaker icon by clicking it, clicking the Playback tab, and selecting the Hide During Show check box.)

Insert a Video Clip

1. Click the Insert tab.
2. Click the Video arrow.
3. Choose Video from File.

   The Insert Video dialog box appears.

4. Select the video file you want to insert.
5. Click Insert.

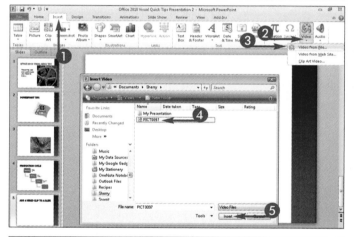

● The clip is added to the slide. You can move or resize the clip, as needed.

● Point to the clip and click to play the clip.

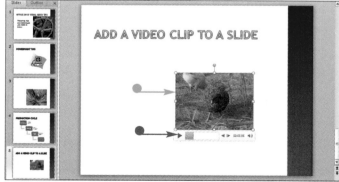

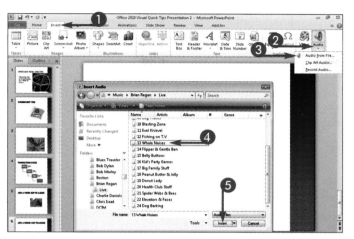

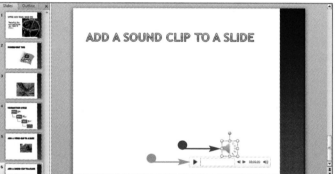

Insert a Sound Clip

1. Click the Insert tab.

2. Click the Audio arrow.

3. Choose Audio from File.

   The Insert Audio dialog box appears.

4. Select the audio file you want to insert.

5. Click Insert.

- The clip is added to the slide as a speaker icon. You can move or resize the speaker icon, as needed.

- Point to the icon and click to play the clip.

TIPS

More Options!

You can control how a video clip or sound clip plays in a movie using the settings found on the Playback tab (Audio Tools) or the Playback tab (Video Tools), one of the two special tabs that appear when you select the clip in the slide. You can use the Start setting to specify whether the clip plays when clicked or automatically. You can also loop the clip to play continuously or rewind when finished playing.

More Options!

If you want to look for media clips to insert, instead of inserting a clip of your own, click the Video arrow in the Insert tab and choose Clip Art Video. The Clip Art task pane opens; type a keyword describing the type of clip you want to find and click Go. To preview a clip, position your mouse pointer over it, click the down arrow that appears, and choose Preview/Properties.

New to PowerPoint 2010, you can use the built-in video editor to make simple edits to a video clip in your slide. You can easily remove unwanted portions of a clip so the presentation shows only the information you want to show. You can also assign styles to the clip to create fading edges, 3-D rotation, and more. You can even recolor your video clip to match the theme of your presentation.

Using the Trim Video dialog box, you can trim the front or end of a clip to suit your needs. For example, you may want to end a clip earlier to fit the timing needs of your presentation or cut off an awkward pause at

the beginning of a clip. The Trim Video dialog box includes playback controls to view and check your work, move forward and backward frame by frame, as well as details about the length of the clip.

You can use the Video Styles group of effects on the Video Tools Format tab to create an eye-catching border around the clip. You can also find tools on the tab for changing the shape, adding a color border, or assigning a special effect, such as a shadow or reflection. In addition to enhancements, Video Tools include a feature for correcting brightness and color issues with the clip.

Trim a Video Clip

① Select the video clip you want to edit.

Note: See the task "Add Video or Sound to Your Presentation" to learn how to insert a video.

② Click the Playback tab in the Video Tools tab group in the Ribbon.

③ Click Trim Video.

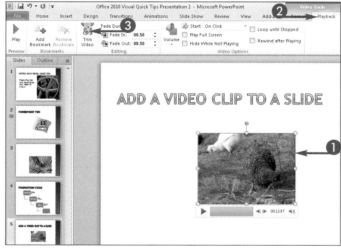

The Trim Video dialog box opens.

④ Click the Play button to view the clip and determine where you want to edit.

⑤ Click the start or end point bar you want to edit.

● Drag the start time bar to trim the beginning of a clip.

● Drag the end time bar to trim the end of a clip.

● You can also click the Previous Frame or Next Frame buttons to move the selected bar back or forward frame by frame.

⑥ Click OK to apply your edits.

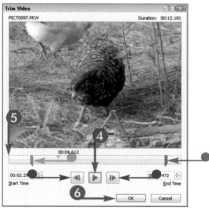

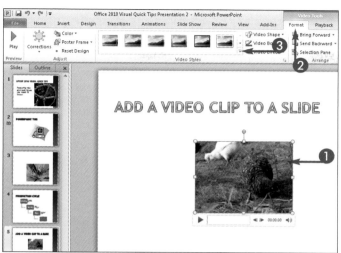

Assign a Video Style

1 Select the video clip you want to edit.

2 Click the Format tab on the Ribbon's Video Tools.

3 Click the Video Styles More button.

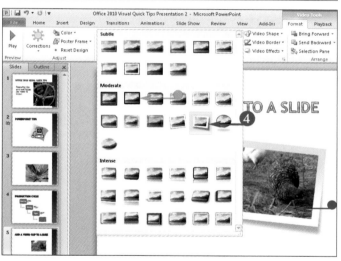

● As you peruse the effects and position the mouse pointer over an animation, PowerPoint's Live Preview feature demonstrates the effect on the selected video clip in the Slide pane.

4 Click the style you want to apply.

● PowerPoint applies the new style.

TIPS

Try This!

You can make the video clip's coloring match the assigned presentation theme. Click the Color button on the Format tab of the Video Tools and choose a color that matches your theme. PowerPoint then assigns a color tint to the clip.

More Options!

You can open the Format Video dialog box to find a variety of formatting options all in one spot. Click the Corrections button on the Video Tools Format tab, and then click Video Correction Options. This opens the dialog box to the Video settings. If you need to remove all of a clip's formatting changes, click the Reset Design button on the Format tab.

By default, items you add to your slides remain static. To add interest, you can animate the items on PowerPoint slides — that is, apply motion to the text or objects in your slide, such as images, bulleted lists, and the like. For example, you might animate a table on your slide to move in from the top of the screen.

The Ribbon's Animations tab contains options for setting up and working with animations in your presentation. You simply select the item in your presentation you want to animate, and

then choose the desired animation effect from the tab. PowerPoint previews the animation for you right after you apply it. Another option is to create a custom animation, as outlined here.

Be warned: You should avoid overusing animations. Otherwise, your presentation may seem too busy. Excessive use of animations can overshadow the message of your presentation. By using animations sparingly, you ensure they serve as effective attention grabbers rather than distractions.

① Click the object you want to animate to select it.

② Click the Animations tab.

③ Click the Animation gallery's More button.

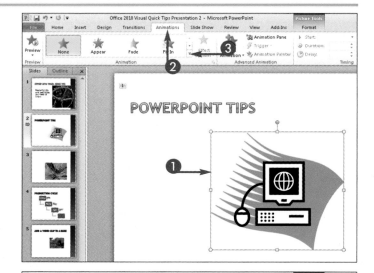

④ Click an effect.

● As you peruse the effects and position the mouse pointer over an animation, PowerPoint's Live Preview feature demonstrates the effect on the selected object in the Slide pane.

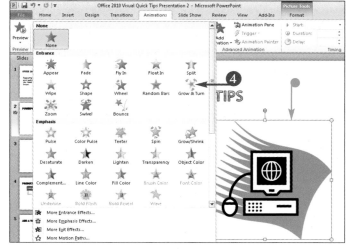

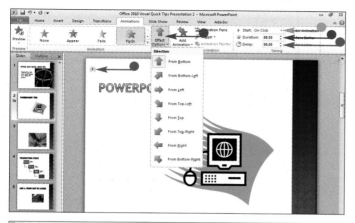

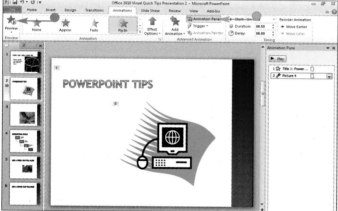

- PowerPoint displays a tiny number icon next to each animation you assign to a slide element.

- If the animation has a directional control, click Effect Options and set the desired direction or path.

- Click here and choose an option for starting the animation.

- Click here and choose a duration for the effect.

- Click here to set a delay time.

- If assigning more than one animation to a slide, click the Animation pane to view a list of effects. You can use the pane to reorder the effects or make changes to their status.

- To preview the effect again, click the Preview button.

Note: To remove an animation effect, select the object, click the More button in the Animation gallery, and click None. You can also click the effect's drop-down arrow in the Animation pane and click Remove.

TIPS

Try This!
You can apply multiple animations to an object. If you do, you can then specify the order in which the animations should occur. To change the order, click an animation you want to move in the Animation pane and then click the up and down arrow buttons along the bottom of the pane to move it up or down, respectively.

Did You Know?
If you select a complex object — for example, a SmartArt diagram — you can apply animation to each of its individual parts. Simply select the part you want to animate and apply the animation as normal.

Some presentations — for example, presentations that illustrate a process — should rely more on pictures than on text, tables, and graphs. If yours is one such presentation, consider using PowerPoint's Photo Album feature to set it up.

Using Photo Album, you can select the photos you want to include in your presentation and specify the order in which they should appear, as well as select a layout for the slides. Your choices include displaying one, two, or four pictures per slide. You can improve the appearance of your slide show by choosing a

frame shape for your photos and applying a theme.

If you think you need more than just photos to communicate your message, you can add picture captions. They can serve as descriptive or humorous labels. Alternatively, they might convey important information about the photos, such as the step or operation a photo depicts. For more extensive textual information, you can insert a text box; text boxes can also be used to insert a blank space in the slide — useful if you want to move the next photo in the album from one slide to the next.

---

① Click the Insert tab.

② Click Photo Album.

③ Click New Photo Album.

The Photo Album dialog box opens.

④ Click File/Disk.

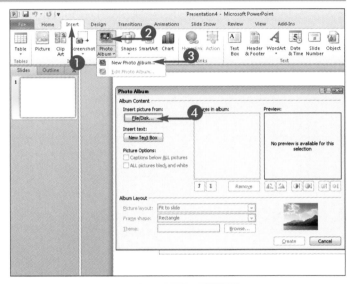

The Insert New Pictures dialog box opens.

⑤ Locate and select the photos you want to include in your presentation.

Note: *To select multiple photos that are not listed contiguously, press and hold Ctrl on your keyboard as you click the desired images.*

⑥ Click Insert.

Note: *If the images you want to insert are spread across multiple folders, repeat steps 3 to 5 for each folder containing the necessary images.*

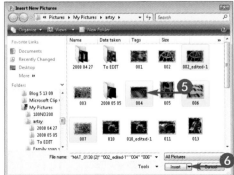

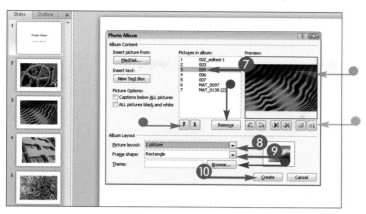

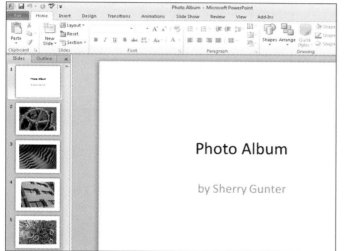

PowerPoint lists the images you selected.

⑦ Click an image in the list.

● A preview of the image appears.

● To change the order in which the selected image is listed, click here to move it up or down in the list, respectively.

● To remove the selected image, click Remove.

● Click these buttons to adjust the appearance of the image.

⑧ Click here and select how many images should appear on each slide.

⑨ Click here and select a frame shape.

● To apply a theme, click Browse and select a theme from the dialog box that appears.

⑩ Click Create.

PowerPoint creates the photo album presentation.

More Options!

You can edit a photo album presentation via the Edit Photo Album dialog box, which is identical to the Photo Album dialog box. To open it, click the Photo Album arrow and choose Edit Photo Album.

Try This!

To add captions to your photo album presentation, select the Captions Below ALL Pictures check box in the Photo Album dialog box (☐ changes to ☑). PowerPoint adds caption placeholders to the presentation slides; simply click a placeholder and type the desired text. To add a text box, click New Text Box in the Photo Album dialog box. PowerPoint inserts a text box placeholder after whatever image is currently selected in the Pictures in Album list.

Harnessing Access

Access 2010 is a program for creating databases to store business or personal information. You can use Access to create, retrieve, and manage large or small collections of information. To make it easier for you to create databases, Access provides several built-in templates, as well as additional templates online.

In Access, data is stored in tables. Each individual entry in a table is called a *record*. For example, in a Customers table, the information about each customer is a separate record. Each record is composed of one or more fields, which contain individual pieces of data. For example, a customer field might include a name, address, city, state, or ZIP code.

By default, tables appear as spreadsheet grids called *datasheets*, similar to the worksheets found in Excel. You can type directly into a datasheet. To make data entry more convenient, however, some people prefer to use *forms*, which are like dialog boxes that prompt for field entries. You can also import data from other programs such as Excel and Outlook.

You can filter the tables in a database to display only certain records, only certain fields, or both. You can run a one-time filter or you can create a query, which is like a saved filter. Tables and query results appear in plain datasheets, which are not very attractive when printed. In contrast, a report presents data from tables and queries in an attractive, customizable format.

Quick Tips

To expedite the database creation process, Access provides several built-in database templates. A *template* is a ready-to-use database that contains all the necessary components — tables, forms, reports, queries, macros, and relationships — to track a specific type of data. You can use a template database as is or customize it as needed.

In addition to the templates that install with Access, you can also use templates available on Office Online. To download an Office Online template, click a template category under the Office.com Templates area in Backstage view, click the desired template from the list that

appears, and click Download on the right side of the screen. Access downloads the template for you and opens it when the download is complete.

In addition to creating databases with templates, you can create forms within a database by using a template. Each Access form template contains a pre-created set of fields, so you do not have to create fields manually. Templates work well when you need a standard form with common fields. To create a form from a template, click the Create tab in the Ribbon, click Application Parts, and choose from the list of templates that appears.

---

1 With Access open, click the File tab.

2 Click New.

3 Click Sample Templates to open installed templates.

● To choose from online templates, click a category and view available templates from the Office.com Web site.

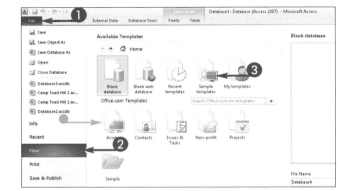

● A list of templates available from within Access appears.

4 Click the template you want to use.

5 Type a descriptive name for the new template.

● Click the folder button to navigate to a particular folder or drive in which to store the file.

6 Click Create.

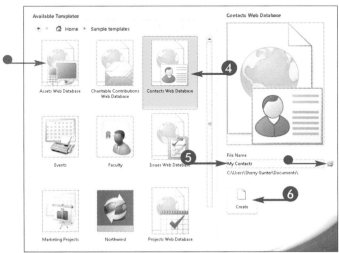

- Access creates a new database based on the template you chose. In this example, a helpful Getting Started screen appears, welcoming you to the new database.

More Options!

Looking for more templates? With an online connection, you can conduct a search for more templates on the Office Web site. Click in the search box in Backstage view and type a keyword or phrase, and then click the search arrow or press Enter. Access connects to the Web site and any resulting matches appear listed. You can also conduct a search on the Internet for other sources of Access template files. Some sources charge a fee for special template files; others may be free for downloading. Always use caution when sharing files from unsecure sites, making sure your virus protection and other safety measures are on and functioning.

Did You Know?

You can share your Access database files on the Web with assistance from Access Services in Microsoft's SharePoint Server 2010. You can also export your database files to PDF or XPS file formats, making it easy to share across platforms. In previous versions of Access, PDF and XPS formats were supported only through the help of add-ins you had to install. With PDF and XPS formats, you can capture all of your database information in a way that is easy to distribute via e-mail, Web storage, or portable storage media. Be sure to check out all the export options found on the External Data tab on the Access Ribbon.

Suppose you have an Excel worksheet that contains data you want to include in an Access database. You can import the worksheet right into Access, creating a new table. This table becomes part of the Access database; it does not retain any ties to Excel. (Note that in addition to importing the spreadsheet in its entirety, you can also import portions of it.)

For Excel data to import correctly into Access, it must be set up to mimic a datasheet in Access. Specifically, field names should appear in row 1; each record should be on its own row; and no formulas or functions should be included.

You use the Import Spreadsheet Wizard to import Excel data into Access. When you do, the wizard asks you various configuration-related questions, such as whether fields in the table you are creating should be indexed and whether duplicates are okay. It also gives you the option to name the table.

① Click the External Data tab.

② In the Import & Link group of tools, click Excel.

Note: *Be careful not to confuse the Excel button in the Import & Link group with the Excel button in the Export group.*

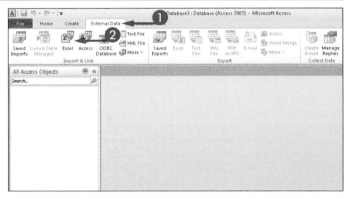

The Get External Data – Excel Spreadsheet dialog box opens.

③ Type the name and path (that is, the location) of the workbook that contains the worksheet you want to import in the File Name box.

● If you are not sure of the path, click Browse to browse for the file.

④ Click Import the Source Data into a New Table in the Current Database.

⑤ Click OK.

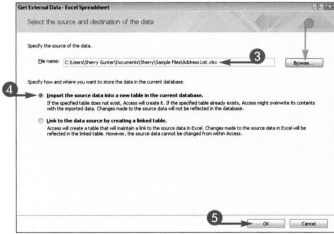

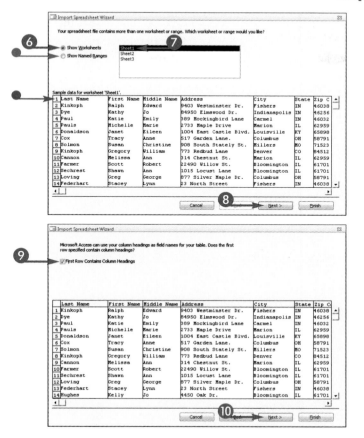

The Import Spreadsheet Wizard starts.

6 Click Show Worksheets.

● To select a range of data in the worksheet rather than an entire worksheet, click Show Named Ranges, and then select the named range in the list that appears.

7 Click the worksheet you want to import.

● A preview of the worksheet (or named range) appears.

8 Click Next.

9 If the first row of the imported worksheet contains column headings, select First Row Contains Column Headings; if not, leave the option unchecked.

10 Click Next.

More Options!

To link an Excel worksheet to your Access database rather than import it, use the Link Spreadsheet Wizard. To launch the wizard, choose the worksheet to which you want to link and then click to select the Link to the Data Source by Creating a Linked Table radio button in the Get External Data – Excel Spreadsheet dialog box and follow the on-screen prompts. After creating the link, any changes you make to the source data in Excel are immediately reflected in the linked table in Access. You cannot change the data in Access, however, to reflect back in the source data. The link works only in one direction.

Did You Know?

You can also export Access data into Excel in the structure of a table, form, query, or report. Although you cannot export multiple database objects in all at once, you can use the Excel tool on the External Data tab on the Access Ribbon to export objects into your workbook files. Click the Excel button in the Export group of tools on the tab to open the Export – Excel Spreadsheet Wizard to get started. The wizard walks you through the necessary steps to choose an object and a file format to export.

As you step through the Import Spreadsheet Wizard, you are given the option to set a primary key. A *primary key* is a field or set of fields in a table that contains a unique identifier for every record. For example, if your table contains customer information, the primary key would likely be the field that contains a unique ID number for each customer. If none of the fields in your imported data contain unique information, you can prompt the Import Spreadsheet Wizard to create a primary key for

you; when you do, a new field is added that contains a unique number for each record.

If the data you are importing will be regularly updated in Excel, it might be wise to link your Access database to the Excel worksheet instead of importing the spreadsheet into the database. That way, each time you open the linked worksheet in Access, it will contain the most recent data. To link a worksheet to an Access database, you use the Link Spreadsheet Wizard.

⑪ Click a field.

⑫ To change the name of the selected field, type a new name here.

⑬ To change a field's data type, click here and select a different data type from the list that appears.

⑭ To change the selected field's index settings, click here and choose the desired setting from the list that appears.

⑮ To omit a field, click here.

⑯ Click Next.

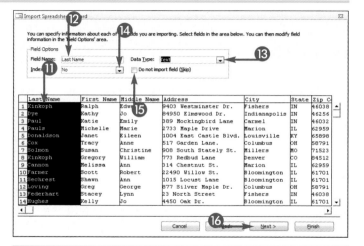

⑰ Choose how you want to determine a primary key.

● To let Access choose a key, leave this option selected.

● To choose a primary key from the fields in the imported worksheet, click here, and then select the desired field from the list that appears.

● Click here if the information you imported does not contain a field that would work well as a primary key.

⑱ Click Next.

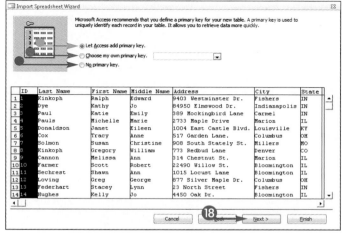

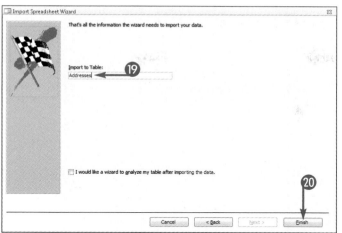

⑲ Type a name for the table.

Note: *The default name is the name of the tab from the worksheet.*

⑳ Click Finish.

Excel prompts you to complete the import process.

㉑ Click Close.

The Excel worksheet is imported as a new table.

TIPS

Did You Know?

You can prompt Access to analyze your imported data by selecting the I Would Like a Wizard to Analyze My Table after Importing the Data check box in the final screen of the Import Spreadsheet Wizard. When you click Finish, Access launches the necessary wizard to analyze your table. Not all of Excel's features import into Access. For example, graphical elements such as pictures and charts are not visible in Access. You can also open your data in Datasheet view any time you want to check the data over for possible errors later.

Did You Know?

You can also use the tried-and-true Cut, Copy, and Paste commands to move data from an Excel workbook file over to an Access database file. Anytime you cut or copy data using the Cut or Copy commands, the data is placed on the Windows Clipboard where you can paste it into other files, including an Access table.

Suppose you want to conduct an e-mail survey and track the results using an Access database. In that case, you can create a data-entry form that can be e-mailed to others via Microsoft Outlook. When a recipient of your survey completes the data-entry form and returns it to you via e-mail, you can assimilate the data he or she has shared into your Access database the instant the message lands in your inbox. You create and distribute the data-entry form using the Collect Data Through E-mail Messages Wizard. Note that the recipient of your e-mail need not use Outlook in order to complete the data-entry form the e-mail contains; any e-mail program will do.

You have two options with regard to what types of forms to include in your e-mail message: HTML or InfoPath. If you are not certain whether all the recipients of your message have the necessary software to view and interact with InfoPath forms, opt for HTML.

Using Outlook as a data-collection tool also works well for gathering and tracking status reports and organizing an event.

① Click the External Data tab.

② Click Create E-mail.

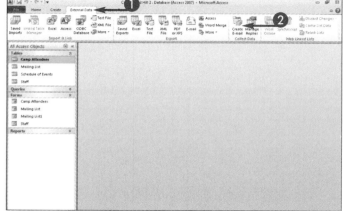

The Collect Data Through E-mail Messages Wizard starts.

③ Click Next.

④ Click HTML Form.

⑤ Click Next.

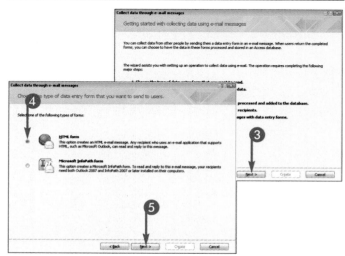

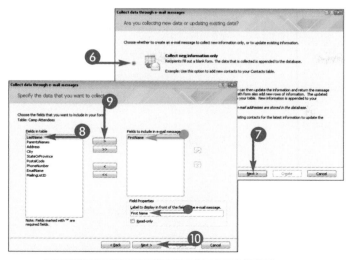

⑥ Specify whether you want the recipients of your data-collection e-mail to update existing information or enter new information. In this example, Collect New Information Only is selected.

⑦ Click Next.

⑧ Click a field in the Fields in Table list that you want to include in the e-mail data-collection form.

⑨ Click the Add button.

● The field is added to the Fields to Include in E-mail Message list.

● Type a descriptive label for the field to help the recipients of your e-mail form determine what data to enter.

⑩ Click Next.

⑪ If you want Access and Outlook to automatically process replies to your e-mail, adding the data those replies contain to your Access database, click here.

● To configure how Access and Outlook handle automatic processing of replies, click here.

⑫ Click Next.

More Options!
If you know that all the recipients of your e-mail form have the necessary software to handle InfoPath forms (for example, if you are polling users in your company only, and your IT department has assured you that their computers have been configured to handle InfoPath forms), then you might prefer to use that type of e-mail form over HTML. InfoPath forms are generally easier to use, and provide a better data-entry and editing environment. In addition, InfoPath forms can be configured to validate the data submitted by the user when he or she clicks Send. If any of the entered data is deemed invalid, InfoPath enables the user to correct his or her responses before submitting the form.

As you step through the Collect Data Through E-mail Messages Wizard, you are asked a series of questions. One is whether you want Access to automatically process replies to your e-mail when they arrive in your inbox and add the data those replies contain to your database. (Note that if you opt to process the data manually, you are not relegating yourself to tedious data entry; you simply launch the export operation that automatically transfers the collected data to your table by hand.)

You can also specify whether you want to enter the addresses of your recipients from within Outlook, or to use the addresses as they appear in your Access database. (Note that if you choose the latter, you are asked to indicate the table and field from which you want to draw the e-mail addresses.) When prompted, you can type a subject for the form e-mail, as well as any message text you want the e-mail to contain.

As you navigate the wizard steps, remember the options may vary based on the selections you make.

⑬ Indicate how you want to enter the recipients' e-mail addresses. You can choose to enter the e-mail addresses by using Outlook, or by using a field in the database.

⑭ Click Next.

⑮ Type a subject for your e-mail.

⑯ Type the text that you want your e-mail to contain.

⑰ Click Next.

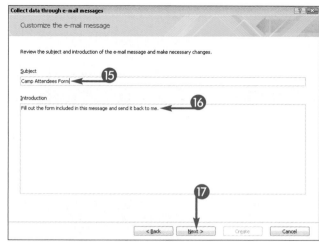

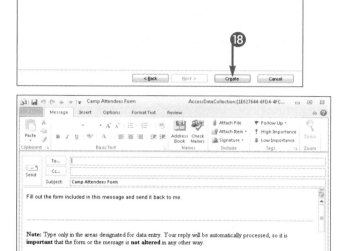

The wizard prompts you to create the e-mail message.

⑱ Click Create.

Access creates the e-mail form and launches an Outlook New Message window where you can address and send the message.

Important!

When someone receives your e-mail message containing a data-collection form, he or she can click Reply, respond to the prompts in the form, and then click Send. Depending on how you set up your form, either Outlook and Access will work together to automatically update your database with the submitted information, or you can manually launch an export operation from within Outlook to assimilate the data into your database. To do so, right-click the reply in your inbox that you want to process and click Export Data to Microsoft Office Access. Review the reply in the dialog box that opens and click OK.

Try This!

To resend a data-collection e-mail message, open the database containing the original message, click the Ribbon's External Data tab, and click Manage Replies in the Collect Data group of tools. The Manage Data Collection Messages dialog box opens; click the message you want to resend, click Resend This E-mail Message, and follow the on-screen prompts. You can use the Manage Data Collection Messages dialog box to view information about the messages, delete messages, and perform other management activities.

Suppose you are creating a form to record customers' contact information. If your business is limited to a certain state, you might make that state the default value in the State field. In this way, you can speed up data entry. You can set default values for fields that use the following data types: Text, Memo, Number, Date/Time, Currency, Yes/No, and Hyperlink. If you do not set a default value, the field remains blank until a value is entered.

Note that in order to set a default value, you must open the table containing the field for which you want to set the value in Design view. To do so, right-click the table in the Navigation pane and choose Design View from the menu that appears. Alternatively, if the table is already open in another view, right-click the table's tab and choose Design View.

① Open the table upon which the form is based in Design view and click the field name for which you want to set a default value.

● The Field Properties for that field appear.

② In the Default Value row, type the value you want to set.

Note: *When you move away from the text box, Access automatically adds quotation marks around what you typed.*

③ Click the Save button (🖫) to save the table.

● When you display the table's datasheet, the default value appears in new records.

Note: *The default value does not automatically populate existing records.*

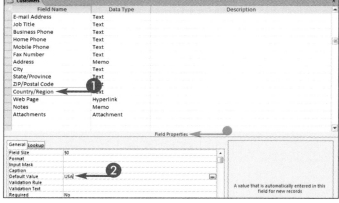

A primary key field is always required for each record. (As mentioned in the task "Import Data from Excel," a primary key is a field or set of fields in a table that contains a unique identifier for every record. For example, if your table contains customer information, the primary key would likely be a field that contains a unique ID number for each customer.)

You are not limited to making the primary key field required, however. You can make other fields required as well. (Note that doing so

does not change the primary key setting.) When a field is required, Access does not enable users to move past it during data entry until they have entered a value in the field.

In order to set a field as required, you must open the table containing the field in Design view. To do so, right-click the table in the Navigation pane and choose Design View from the menu that appears. Alternatively, if the table is already open in another view, right-click the table's tab and choose Design View.

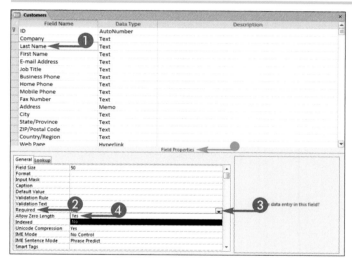

① In Design view, click the field name you want to make required.

● The properties for that field appear.

② Click in the Required row to display a drop-down arrow.

③ Click the Required drop-down arrow.

④ Click Yes.

⑤ Click the Save button (🖫) to save your changes.

If you or another user attempts to enter a new record in the table, a warning appears if you do not enter a value in a required field.

⑥ Click OK to clear the error and then type a value in the required field.

If a field in your table has an ambiguous or grammatically incorrect name, you can apply a caption to the field. For example, you might add the caption "Last Name" (note the space) to make a LastName field easier to identify. Captions appear in datasheet headings and on labels in forms and reports, so making them easy to understand can go a long way in speeding up the reading of your Access data.

To apply a caption to a field, you must open the table containing the field in Design view. To do so, right-click the table in the Navigation pane and choose Design View from the menu that appears. Alternatively, if the table is already open in another view, right-click the table's tab and choose Design View. You can also use the view tools on the Ribbon's Home tab to switch views, or the view icons in the lower right corner of the Access program window.

1 In Design view, click the field name.

● The properties for that field appear.

2 In the Caption row, type the desired caption.

3 Click the Save button (🖫) to save your changes.

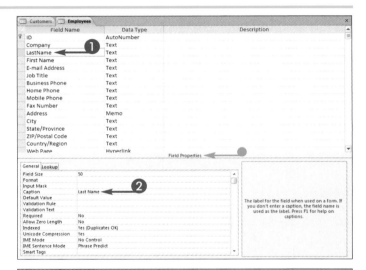

● When you display the table's datasheet, the field's caption appears as its column heading.

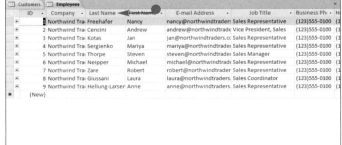

If you are entering the same value in the same field in a table or form over and over again, you can use a shortcut technique to copy the value of the previous record. Rather than retype it each time, you can summon the value with a keyboard shortcut. This can really reduce the amount of time you spend entering records into tables or forms.

To make the best use of this technique, type your record data in a table using Datasheet view. This allows you to easily see the previous record's values and determine if you need to re-enter the same information again.

This technique makes use of a little-known shortcut key. You can create all kinds of other custom shortcut keys to help you navigate through your database. For example, open a form in Design view and select the Caption property of a field name to which you want to navigate. Type an ampersand before the letter that you want to act as a shortcut key, such as P&hone. Save your changes and switch to Form view. Access adds an underscore to the letter you designate as your navigation shortcut. To navigate to the field in Form view, press Alt+H.

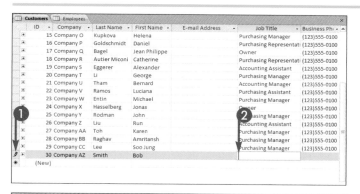

❶ Open or start a new record in Datasheet view.

❷ Click the field in which you want to copy a value.

❸ Press Ctrl+'.

❹ Press Tab to move to the next field.

● Access immediately copies the value from the previous record.

You can apply an input mask to a field to help minimize data-entry errors. Although it sounds rather like a beauty product you might smear onto your face, input masks help users enter the proper number and type of characters. They do so by providing a template for entering data in the field. For example, you might implement an input mask to include parentheses for the area code portion of a telephone number. Input masks act like quality control checks, helping users know what sort of data they are expected to enter into a table or form.

Access provides several predefined input masks from which you can choose. If none of these predefined input masks quite suits your needs, you can customize an input mask.

To apply an input mask to a field, you must open the table containing the field in Design view. To do so, right-click the table in the Navigation pane and choose Design View from the menu that appears. Alternatively, if the table is already open in another view, right-click the table's tab and choose Design View.

① **In Design view, click a field.**

● **The properties for that field appear.**

② **Click the Input Mask row.**

③ **Click the ellipsis button.**

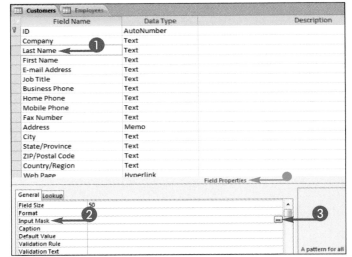

The Input Mask Wizard appears.

④ **Click the type of input mask you want to apply.**

● **To try the selected mask, click in the Try It field and type a sample entry.**

⑤ **Click Next to customize the mask.**

● **Click Finish if you decide not to customize the mask.**

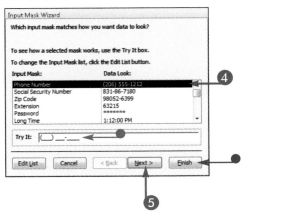

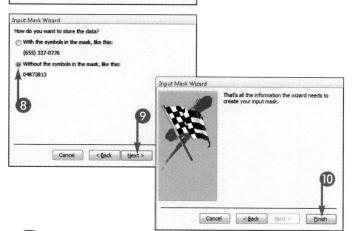

6 Modify the input mask as desired.

Note: See the tip for help.

● Optionally, click here and select a different placeholder character.

7 Click Next.

8 Click here to describe how you want the data stored.

Note: The option you select here determines how the data looks if you export it. If you do not export it, your selection here does not matter.

9 Click Next.

10 Click Finish.

Try This!

Input masks use special characters to represent the types of data they can accept. You use these special characters to customize an input mask. The following table contains the most commonly used characters; for more information, look up "Input Mask Character Reference" in Access Help.

Character	Use
0	Single digit, required
9	Single digit, optional
#	A digit, space, plus sign, or minus sign
L	Single letter, required
?	Single letter, optional
A	Single letter or number, required
a	Single letter or number, optional
&	Any character or a space, required
C	Any character or a space, optional

Input masks help users enter the proper number and type of characters, but they cannot restrict the field to certain entries based on logic. That is where data-validation rules come in. You can construct a validation rule that forces field entries to pass a logical test of their validity. For example, you could make sure that negative numbers are not entered into a numeric field. You can also create *validation text*, a custom message that appears when the rule is violated.

You create data-validation rules using Expression Builder. It can guide you in

determining the correct syntax for an expression. There are many types of expressions available in Expression Builder, including functions, constants, and operators. For example, you can create an expression to primarily test data including checking for one in a series of data, such as "New York" Or "Los Angeles" Or "Tokyo." You can also use expressions to perform mathematical operations, such as >5 which forces the user to enter values greater than 5. The possibilities are endless.

---

① **In Design view, click a field.**

● **The properties for that field appear.**

② **Click the Validation Rule row.**

③ **Click the ellipsis button.**

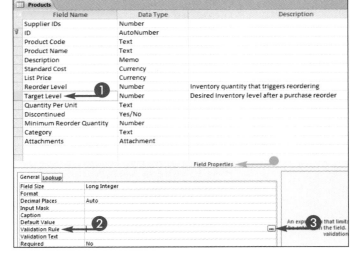

The Expression Builder dialog box opens.

④ **Enter the expression that represents the criteria to specify (here, that the value entered in the field should be greater than 0).**

⑤ **Click OK.**

Note: *You could have simply typed the validation rule into the row and skipped steps 3 to 5, but Expression Builder's tools can be useful for complex expressions.*

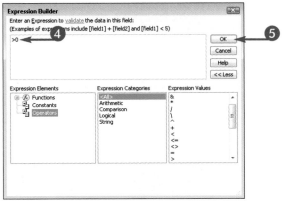

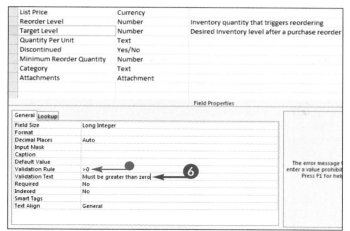

● The validation rule appears in the Validation Rule row.

⑥ Click in the Validation Text row and type the text you want Access to display in the error message.

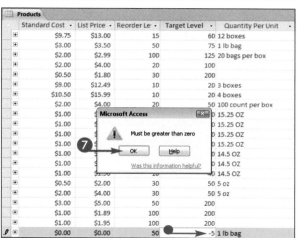

● When the rule is violated, a dialog box appears containing the text you specified in the Validation Text row.

⑦ Click OK and then re-enter the field text.

Did You Know?
You can create two types of data validation rules in Access: field validation rules and record (or table) validation rules. Field rules check the values entered into a field, whereas record rules control how you save a record in a table. As an example of a data validation rule, perhaps your table has a Date field, but you only want users to input dates on or after January 1, 2011. Your validation rule might look like this in the Expression Builder dialog box: >=#01/01/2011#. Such a rule prevents users from leaving the field until they enter the correct date. For a record validation rule, perhaps you are required to ship products within 30 days, so your record validation rule might ensure that no one ships anything with the wrong date. This type of rule might look like this: [RequiredDate]<=[OrderDate]+30.

Suppose you are maintaining a database of job candidates, and you want to attach each candidate's resume to his or her record. You can easily do so using Access. A single record can have multiple attached files of various types.

You can add an attachment to a record only if the table containing the record includes an Attachment field. To insert a field into a table, open the table in Design view, click the field above which the new field should appear, and click Insert Rows. Type a name for the new field in the Field Name column; then click in the Data Type column, click the drop-down arrow that appears, and choose Attachment.

To add an attachment to a record, the table containing the record must be open in Datasheet view. If it is not in Datasheet view, right-click the table's tab in the Access screen and choose Datasheet View in the menu that appears. Attachment fields are marked by a paperclip. The number in parentheses is the number of attachments the field currently contains.

① In Datasheet view, double-click the Attachment field in the record to which you want to add an attachment.

The Attachments dialog box opens.

② Click Add.

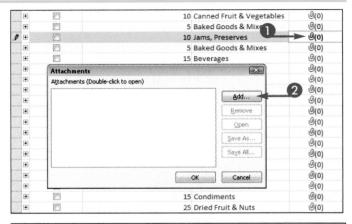

The Choose File dialog box opens.

③ Locate and select the file you want to attach.

④ Click Open.

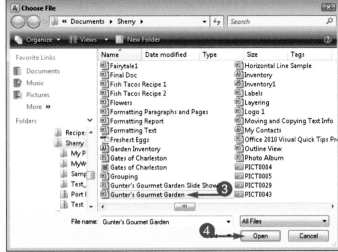

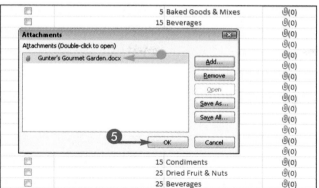

● The file is added to the list of files in the Attachments dialog box.

You can repeat steps 2 to 4 to attach more files if necessary.

⑤ Click OK.

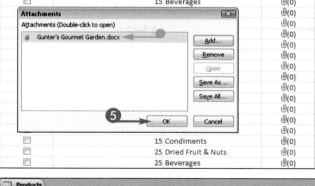

● The file is attached to the record.

More Options!
After you have attached files to a record, you can open those files, save them as separate files outside of Access, or remove them from Access at any time. You do so from within the Attachments dialog box. To open the dialog box, double-click the Attachment field that contains the attachment you want to work with. Then click the attachment in the list and click Open, Save As, or Remove. Click Save All to save all files attached to the record to a new location; when you do, a Save Attachments dialog box appears, enabling you to either choose or create a folder in which to save the attached files.

Attaching a file to a database record works well if the file is static. If, however, it is dynamic — that is, it will be changed over time — you should insert the file as an OLE object rather than as an attachment. That way, the version of the file in the Access database will match the original, even if the original is changed in some way.

You can insert an OLE object into a record only if the table containing the record includes an OLE Object field. To insert a field into a table, open the table in Design view, click the field above which the new field should appear, and click Insert Rows on the Ribbon's Design tab. Type a name for the field in the Field Name column; then click in the Data Type column, click the drop-down arrow that appears, and choose OLE Object.

To insert an OLE object into a record, the table containing the record must be open in Datasheet view. If it is not in Datasheet view, right-click the table's tab in the Access screen and choose Datasheet View in the menu that appears.

① In Datasheet view, right-click the OLE Object field in the record into which you want to insert an OLE object.

② Click Insert Object.

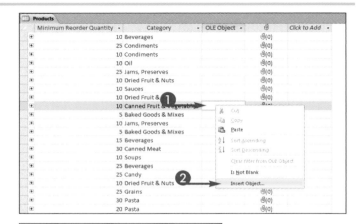

The Microsoft Access dialog box opens.

③ Click Create from File.

④ Click Browse.

The Browse dialog box opens.

⑤ Locate and select the file you want to insert as an OLE object.

⑥ Click OK.

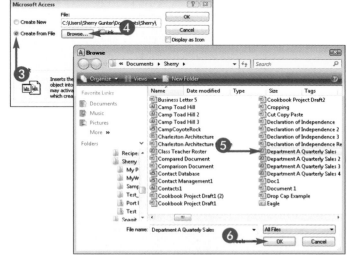

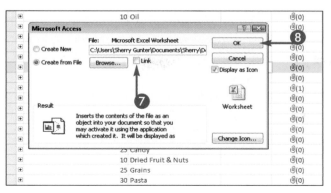

7 Click the Link check box to select it.

8 Click OK.

● Access inserts the file into the record as an OLE object.

More Options!

In addition to inserting an existing file into a record as an OLE object, you can also create a new object to insert. To do so, click Create New instead of Create from File, select the type of object you want to create, and click OK. OLE objects can include charts, bitmap images, video clips, Word documents, sound clips, Excel worksheets, and more. Scroll through the Object Type list that appears in the Microsoft Access dialog box to see what you can create. When you choose to create a new OLE object, the necessary tools open to make the object. For example, if you choose a Microsoft Excel Chart, a window of Excel tools opens for you to create the chart.

Try This!

After inserting a file as an OLE object, you can open the file and edit it from within Access. To do so, double-click the field containing the object; the file opens in its native application. Make any necessary edits and simply close the native application's window to save your changes. To remove an OLE object from a record, click the field containing the object, click the Home tab in the Ribbon, and click Delete. Access immediately removes the OLE object, no questions asked.

You can use a filter to show only records that match criteria that you specify. For example, you can filter for blank or nonblank records, records containing a specific value in a particular field, multiple values, a particular text string, by form, and so on.

If you filter by form, you can save your filter parameters. That way, you can rerun the Filter By Form filter at a later time. When you save a filter, a new query is created in the database. A *query* is something you use to display data from a table in some modified way. Queries created from filters work just like any other query.

To create a Filter By Form filter, display the table you want to filter, click the Home tab, click Advanced, and click Filter By Form. Then click in the field by which you want to filter, click the drop-down arrow that appears, and choose the desired value. The results display only those records that have the value you chose in the corresponding field.

Save the Filter

① After you create a Filter By Form filter (but before you apply it), click the Home tab.

② Click Advanced.

③ Click Save As Query.

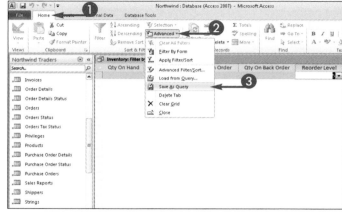

The Save As Query dialog box opens.

④ Type a name for the query.

⑤ Click OK.

The query is added to the Navigation pane.

Run the Filter Query

① With the table you want to filter open in Access, double-click the filter query in the Navigation pane.

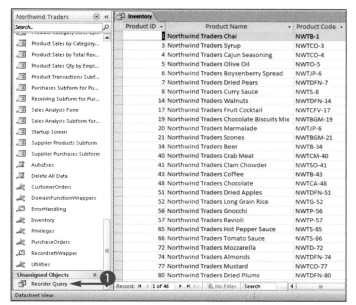

● The filtered results open in a new datasheet.

Did You Know?

In Access, it is not uncommon to find yourself working with the same type of filters on a regular basis. It makes sense to save these filters to reuse them again rather than rebuild them each time. Although you are not allowed to save more than one filter for each form or table, you can save them as queries instead and apply them when you need them. For example, with filters, only the most recent filter is saved in Datasheet or Form view, but with queries, you can apply one whenever you need it regardless of when it was created. What a handy little technique, yes?

One reason people create reports and queries is to extract summary statistics about data, such as the sum or average of the values in certain fields. A new feature introduced back in Access 2007 is the ability to display such information directly on the datasheet, without having to create a query or report.

Available statistic types include Sum (this results in a total of the values in the selected column), Average (this averages the values in the selected column), Count (this totals up the number of rows in the selected column that contain a value), Maximum (this reveals the maximum value in the selected column), Minimum (this reveals the minimum value in the selected column), Standard Deviation (this measures how widely values in the selected column are dispersed from an average value), and Variance (this measures the statistical variance of all values in the selected column).

① With the table for which you want to display summary statistics open in Access, click the Home tab.

② Click Totals.

● A Total row appears below the records in the table.

③ Click in the Total row for the field you want to total.

④ Click here and choose the desired statistic type.

   In this example, the SUM statistic is applied.

● The information appears in the Total row.

⑤ To hide the Total row, click Totals again.

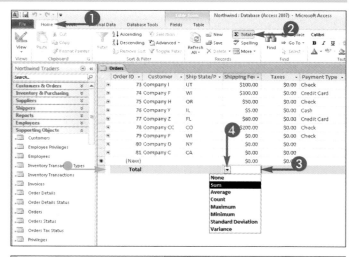

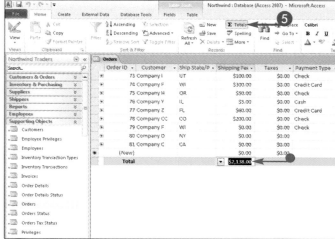

Access is a relational database. Relational databases are powerful because they can contain multiple related tables — for example, tables that share one or more fields.

In a complex database, relationships are often created among the various objects in the database. Indeed, very rarely would a table or similar object stand alone. Therefore, you should not delete an object until you understand what other objects are affected by that deletion. For example, if you delete a table

on which a form is based, the form based on the table is orphaned.

One way to view an object's dependencies is to use the Relationships window. To open this window, click the Database Tools tab and click Relationships. Another way is to use Access's Object Dependencies feature, which enables you to see all the dependencies of a particular object. (Note that to see all dependencies for all objects at once, you can use the Database Documenter feature, covered in the next task.)

① With the table whose dependencies you want to examine displayed, click the Database Tools tab.

② Click Object Dependencies.

Note: *Access may notify you that generating object-dependency information may take a few moments. If so, click OK.*

● The Object Dependencies task pane opens.

③ Click a type of dependency to view.

● Any queries, forms, or reports based on the table appear here.

④ Click to view an object's dependencies.

● If any dependencies have a plus sign next to them, you can click it to expand it, too.

⑤ To close the Object Dependencies task pane, click here.

Whereas Access's Object Dependencies feature enables you to view all the dependencies of a particular object, the program's Database Documenter feature allows you to see all dependencies for all objects in a database. Using this feature results in a full report of the database, including details about each object in the database and how it relates to other objects the database contains. Generating such a report might help another database designer understand the structure of your database.

When you run the Database Documenter feature, the feature launches the report it generates in Print Preview mode, enabling you to print out the report with the click of a mouse. Alternatively, you can export the report to an Extensible Markup Language (XML) file or Hypertext Markup Language (HTML) document, or even merge it with Microsoft Word. To export, rather than print, the report, simply click More in the Print Preview tab's Data group and select the desired output from the menu that appears.

① With the database you want to document open in Access, click the Database Tools tab.

② Click Database Documenter.

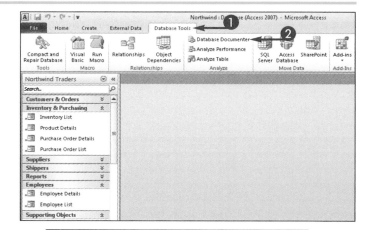

The Documenter dialog box opens.

③ Click a tab.

④ Mark the check box for each object or item you want to include.

⑤ Click Options.

The Print Table Definition dialog box opens.

● Click the check box to include the database's properties in the generated report.

● Click the check box to include a Relationships diagram in the report.

⑥ Click OK.

⑦ Click OK.

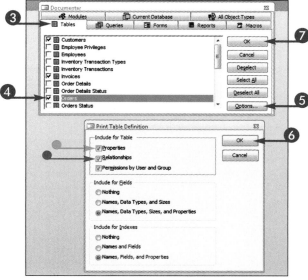

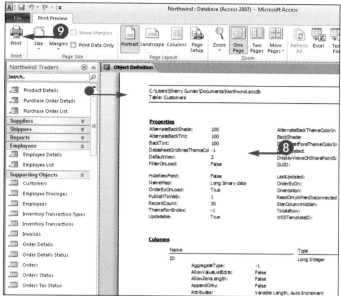

● The information appears in a report in Print Preview mode.

⑧ To zoom in on the report, click it. Click again to zoom out.

⑨ Click Print.

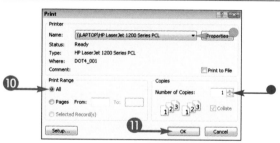

The Print dialog box opens.

⑩ Change printing options as needed.

● Click here to choose a different printer.

● Click here to increase the number of copies.

⑪ Click OK to print the report.

Try It!

You can use the Database Documenter tool as a way to help you learn more about a particular database. This is especially helpful if you are new to the database you are working with or new to Access in general. By generating a report based on a particular object in a database, such as a query or form, you can view details about how the object works with various types of data and other objects, viewing properties for the various elements that comprise the object, such as buttons, labels, text boxes, and other controls.

Reports are simply special views of your data, which are designed to be printed. Reports can be created with very basic formatting settings or can involve complex, custom layouts.

Access enables you to generate reports very easily, especially if you use the default settings. To create a report, click the table or query for which you want to generate a report in the Navigation pane, click the Create tab, and click Report.

After you have created the report, you can export it to Word. Doing so enables you to

apply Word's full-featured formatting functionality to the report. To export the report to Word, you launch the Export Wizard, which steps you through the process of converting the report to a Word document.

In addition to exporting reports to Word, you can also export other types of Access objects, such as tables and queries. As with reports, you launch the export operation from within Print Preview mode.

① With the report you want to export open in Access, click the External Data tab.

② Click the More button.

③ Click Word.

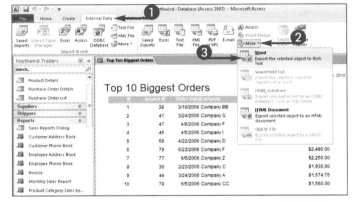

The Export – RTF File Wizard opens.

④ Type the path (that is, the location) of the folder in which you want to save the resulting Word file as well as a name for the file.

● If you are not sure of the path, click Browse to browse for the folder in which you want to save the file.

● If you want to launch the Word document containing the report after the export is complete, click here.

⑤ Click OK.

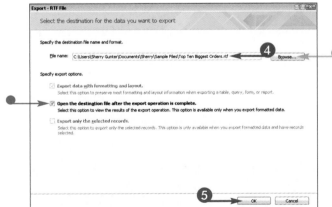

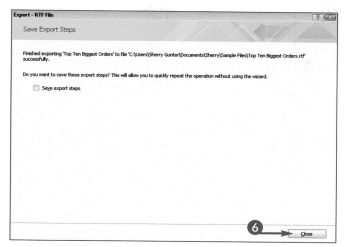

Access notifies you when the export is complete.

⑥ Click Close.

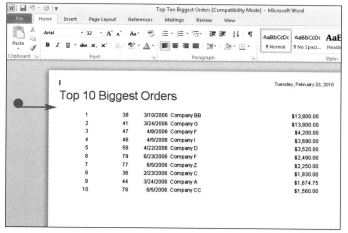

● Access exports the report to Word.

Did You Know?

If you will need to export this report to Word at some later date, you can save your export settings. Select the Save Export Steps check box in the Export Wizard's final screen. A series of additional fields appears; type a name for the export settings in the Save As field, type a description in the Description field, and click Save Export. (To automatically run the export operation at fixed intervals, such as once a week or once a month, select the Create Outlook Task check box before clicking Save Export; Access launches an Export Task dialog box, where you can set the necessary parameters.)

In addition to standard reports, Access can create mailing labels. This enables you to print labels without exporting the data first into a word-processing program and to set up reusable label definitions for recurring mailings.

Labels are a special type of report. They print multiple records per page, in a layout designed to correspond to self-stick labels that feed into your printer.

After choosing the size and formatting for the label, you set up the fields that should appear

on it. These come from the table or query that you selected before you started the Label Wizard.

You can format the labels you create, changing the background color, adjusting the font and font color, and more. For additional formatting options, you can export the labels to Word. To do so, click the External Data tab, click More, click Word, and follow the on-screen instructions.

① Click the Create tab.

② Click Labels.

The Label Wizard appears.

③ Click here and select the manufacturer of the labels you plan to use.

④ Click the product number.

⑤ Specify the unit of measure.

⑥ Indicate whether the label type is Sheet feed or Continuous.

⑦ Click Next.

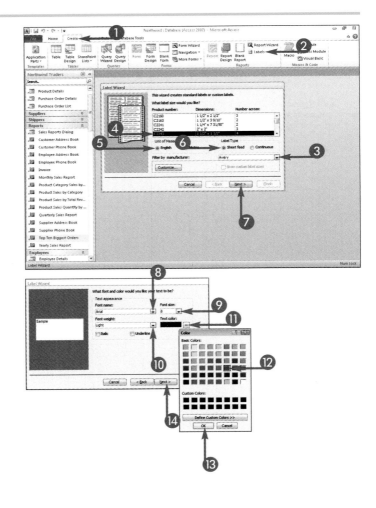

⑧ Click here and choose a font for your labels.

⑨ Click here and choose a font size.

⑩ Click here and choose a font weight.

⑪ Click here to choose a text color.

A Color dialog box opens.

⑫ Click the desired text color.

⑬ Click OK.

⑭ Click Next.

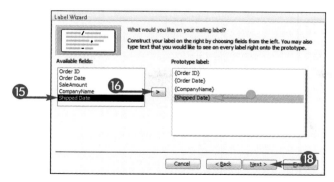

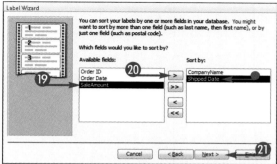

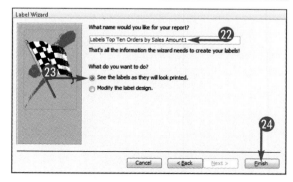

⑮ In the Available Fields list, click the field that contains the information you want to appear first on the label's top line.

⑯ Click the Add button.

● The field is added to the Prototype Label list.

⑰ Repeat steps 15 and 16 to add more fields to the label, inserting any necessary punctuation, spaces, and paragraphs as needed.

⑱ Click Next.

⑲ In the Available Fields list, click the field by which you want the labels to be sorted.

⑳ Click the Add button.

● The field is added to the Sort By list.

㉑ Click Next.

㉒ Type a name for the labels.

㉓ Specify whether you want to see the labels as they look printed or modify their design.

㉔ Click Finish.

Access creates the label sheet.

TIP

Did You Know?
You can change the labels' formatting attributes, such as their font, color, and so on. To do so, double-click the label object in the Navigation pane to display the labels. Next, right-click the labels' tab and choose Design View. Then, click the portion of the label you want to change. For example, to change the font used in the top line of text, click the box containing that line; alternatively, click outside the text fields to select the entire label. Finally, use the tools in the Ribbon's Design tab to make the desired changes or use the text formatting tools on the Home tab.

If you frequently use Access to complete the same task — for example, to format the entries in a table a certain way — you can expedite the process by creating a macro. When you create a macro, you essentially record a series of actions. Then, you can run the macro you created to automatically perform the actions.

Unlike other Office programs, which enable you to "record" macros by essentially tracking the steps you take to complete a task, Access

requires you to select the actions, arguments, and other elements of a macro from a list. You create a macro in Access by using Macro Builder, listing the actions you want Access to carry out when the macro is run, and in what order.

Once a macro has been created, you can easily run it with the click of a button. Using macros can save you loads of time and effort, automating tasks that might normally require dozens of keystrokes or clicks.

① **Click the Create tab.**

② **Click Macro.**

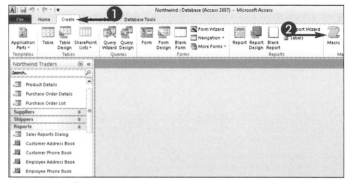

● **The Macro Builder appears.**

③ **Click the first empty cell's drop-down arrow in the Action column.**

④ **Choose the action you want the macro to take from the drop-down list (here, OpenQuery).**

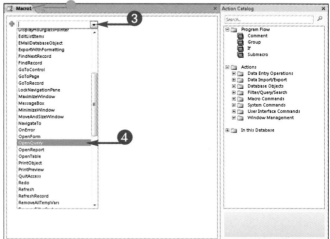

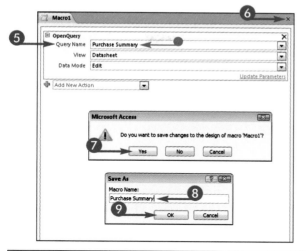

⑤ Set arguments for the macro.

● In this case, because the selected action was OpenQuery, the query name to be run must be selected.

⑥ Click here to close Macro Builder.

Access asks whether you want to save the macro.

⑦ Click Yes.

A Save As dialog box opens.

⑧ Type a name for the macro.

⑨ Click OK.

● Access saves the macro and adds it to the Navigation pane.

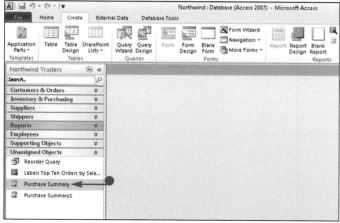

Apply It!

To run a macro you have created, right-click it in the Navigation pane and choose Run from the menu that appears. (Macros are easily identified in the Navigation pane by their unique yellow, scroll-like paper icon, the same icon found on the Macro button on the Ribbon's Create tab as well as the Run Macro tool on the Database Tools tab.) Alternatively, you can also click the Database Tools tab on the Ribbon, click Run Macro, and, in the dialog box that appears, click the Macro Name drop-down arrow, choose the macro you want to run, and click OK.

Customizing Your Database and Forms

To be sure, Access databases can hold volumes of data — so much so that it can sometimes be difficult to comprehend. Fortunately, you can mitigate this difficulty by using Access's formatting tools. For example, you can apply themes to your forms and reports to create a more polished and professional look, as well as add pictures to them to give them some visual interest. To expedite data entry, you can change the tab order of your forms — that is, the order in which the insertion point is moved from one field to another when Tab is pressed.

To draw attention to data that meets criteria you set, you can apply conditional formatting. For example, you might set a rule to highlight fields that contain values greater than, less than, equal to, or between a range of specified values. This enables you to detect problems, patterns, and trends at a glance.

Another way to display your data is in PivotTable or PivotChart form. A PivotTable is an interactive table that summarizes your data by using format and calculation methods you specify. PivotTables are useful in that they enable you to create many different views of your data rather than a fixed report. This way you can decide which one is most useful. A PivotChart is like a PivotTable, except it expresses the data graphically rather than as text and numbers.

Quick Tips

If you choose to create a form, you might reasonably want to format that form for added eye appeal. This is particularly true if other users will be entering data using your forms. One way to add eye appeal is to simply apply formatting changes to the form manually — for example, choosing a background color, border style, font, and so on from the Format tab on the Ribbon. An easier way, however, is to use Access's themes. Themes enable you to apply a background color, fonts, borders, and so on to the form in a single operation.

Of course, before you can apply a theme to a form, you must create your form. To create a form in Access, first display the table or query on which you want the form to be based in Access. In this task, Layout view is used; you can also apply a theme to a form in Design view. Then click the Create tab in the Ribbon and click the Form button. Access creates the form. Be sure to save the form.

You can also customize the themes you use in Access and save them to reuse in other Access databases and other Office programs. To learn more about customizing a theme, see Chapter 8. Although geared towards PowerPoint, the principles applied in the tasks "Customize a Theme" and "Save a Custom Theme" can also be used in Access to tailor a theme to suit your needs.

① With the form you want to format open in Access, click the Design tab, one of the three Form Layout Tools tabs on the Ribbon.

② Click Themes.

● A gallery of theme choices appears. To preview a theme, position the mouse pointer over the theme.

③ Click the desired theme.

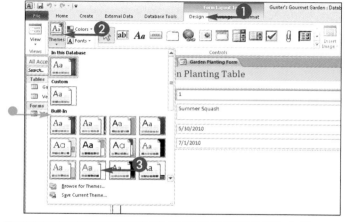

● Access applies the theme to the form.

If you have ever purchased anything on the Internet, chances are you have entered your billing and shipping information in an online form. You probably already realize, then, that you can move from one field of a form to the next by pressing Tab on your keyboard.

The order in which the insertion point is moved from one field to another when Tab is pressed is the form's *tab order*. By default, the tab order is the order in which fields are added to a form. You can change this tab order, however, to any order you want. You might change a form's tab order if, for example, you

added a field to the middle of your form at the last minute.

To change the tab order, you must display the form in Design view. To do so, right-click the form in the Navigation pane and choose Design View from the menu that appears, or click the View button and choose Design View.

You can also remove a control from the tab order. Switch to Design view and select the control you want to remove from the tab order in your form. Press F4 to display the Property Sheet task pane, click the Other tab, and change the Tab Stop property's Yes field to No.

① With the form you want to change open in Design view, click the Design tab.

② Click Tab Order.

The Tab Order dialog box opens.

③ Click a section containing the fields you want to reorder.

④ Click the box to the left of a field's name to select that field.

⑤ Drag the selected field name up or down in the list, releasing when it is in the desired location.

● Alternatively, click Auto Order to base the tab order on the field order.

Note: *Auto Order orders fields from top to bottom. If two fields have the same vertical position, it orders them from left to right.*

⑥ Click OK.

The dialog box closes, and the new tab order is placed in effect.

Another way to make your forms more visually appealing is to insert an image into the form. For example, you might insert your company logo, or an image that relates to the type of data the form requests, such as a picture ID or product image.

Depending on how large you want the image, you may need to move a few of your form elements to make room for the image. You can easily resize fields in Design view by dragging a border or corner of the field box.

After you insert an image, you can resize it as needed, either by dragging the image's corner

handle or by opening its Property Sheet. (To open a picture's Property Sheet, right-click the picture, and choose Properties. Change the sizing settings by clicking the Format tab and adjusting the Width and Height properties.) You can insert an image into the form body, or you can add a thumbnail size to the form's header.

In addition to enabling you to insert pictures into forms, Access allows you to add images to reports. You add images to both forms and reports using Design view.

---

① **Open the form you want to edit in Design view.**

② **Click the Design tab.**

③ **Click Insert Image.**

● Any previous images you inserted appear listed in the gallery.

④ **Click Browse.**

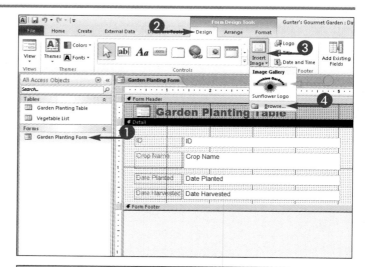

The Insert Picture dialog box opens.

⑤ **Locate and click the image you want to insert.**

⑥ **Click OK.**

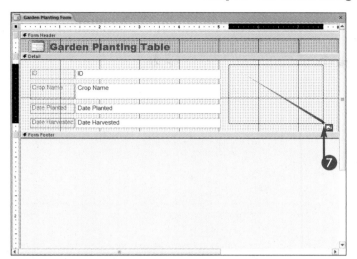

7 Click and drag a placeholder to insert the image.

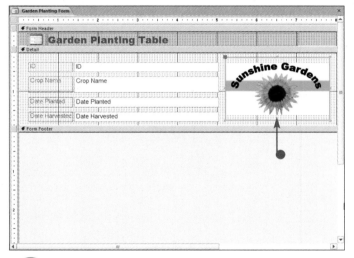

● The image is inserted into the box.

More Options!
To insert a logo into the form's header, click the Logo button on the Design tab. Like the Insert Image command, the Logo button summons the Insert Picture dialog box where you can select the image you want to use. Click Open; Access inserts a thumbnail size image into the header area of the form. You can move and resize the image as needed.

More Options!
As mentioned, you can also insert images in reports. Simply open the report in Design view and follow the same basic steps you used to insert an image into a form: switch to Design view, click the Design tab, click Insert Image, locate and click the image you want to insert. You can resize or move the image to fit anywhere on the report.

Add a Background to a Report

If you choose to create a report about your data, you might want to format that report for added eye appeal. One way to do so would be to simply apply formatting changes to the report manually — for example, choosing a border style, font, and so on from the Format tab on the Ribbon. Another easy way to add visual impact is to include a background picture in your report.

Of course, before you can apply any formatting to a report, you must first create the report. To create a report in Access, first display the table or query on which you want the report to be based in Access, click the Create tab in the Ribbon, and click the Report button. Access creates the report.

You can apply a background image to a report in Layout or Design view. When choosing a background, try to pick something that complements your report and does not distract from the information the report conveys. Digital photographs make good backgrounds. Logos tend to get lost behind the data, but photographs fill the entire page.

---

① Open the report you want to edit in Layout or Design view.

● To switch views, click the View button and choose Design view, or right-click the report name in the Navigation pane and choose Design view.

② Click the Format tab.

③ Click Background Image.

● Any previous images appear listed in the gallery.

④ Click Browse.

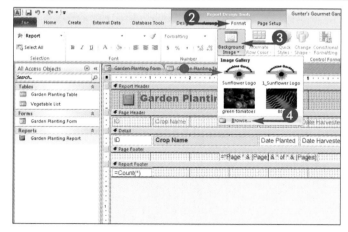

The Insert Picture dialog box opens.

⑤ Locate and click the image you want to insert.

⑥ Click OK.

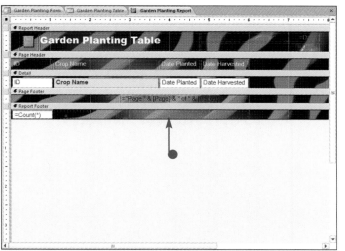

● The image is added as the report background.

Note: If you are unhappy with the background image, click the Undo button ( ) in the Quick Access toolbar to remove it.

More Options!

You can apply simple formatting techniques to your report text using the commands found on the Format tab on the Ribbon. For example, you can click a field in the report and click the Bold button (B) to make the text bold, or click the Font Color (A) button and choose a color from the palette to add color to your text. To change all the data at once, click the Select All button and then apply the formatting commands.

More Options!

You can also apply one of Access's many themes to a report. A theme is a pre-set collection of formatting, including color and font. To apply a theme, click the Design tab on the Ribbon, click the Themes button and choose from the gallery of available themes. You can use the Colors and Fonts buttons located next to the Themes button to customize your theme.

Color-Code Your Data with Conditional Formatting

You can use Access's conditional formatting functionality to assign certain formatting to fields in forms and reports when the value in a field meets a specified condition. For example, if you have a report with a Balance field, you might opt to present all negative values in that field in red text. This enables you to detect problems, patterns, and trends at a glance.

Access offers several predefined rules for conditional formatting. For example, you can set a rule to highlight data that is greater than, less than, equal to, or between a range of specified values; contains specific text; is a duplicate value; is among the top ten or bottom ten values; is above average or below average; and more. You can format data that meets conditions you set by changing the font or background.

You can apply conditional formatting from Design view or Layout view (as covered here).

① With your form or report open in Layout or Design view, click the field to which you want to apply conditional formatting.

② Click the Format tab.

③ Click Conditional Formatting.

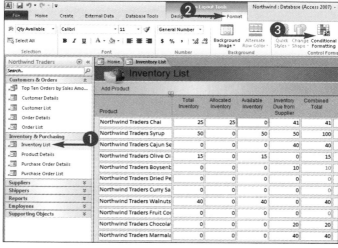

The Conditional Formatting Rules Manager dialog box opens.

④ Click New Rule.

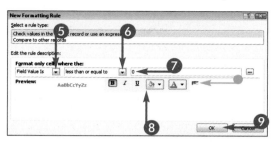

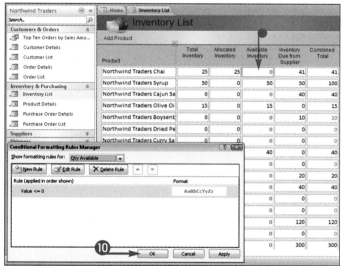

The New Formatting Rule dialog box opens.

⑤ Click here and specify whether the condition should pertain to the field value, expression, or field focus.

Note: Depending on what option you select, different settings are available.

⑥ Click here and choose a comparison operator.

⑦ Type the condition's value.

⑧ Choose from various formatting options to indicate how values that meet the condition should be formatted.

● Click the Enable/Disable button to enable or disable the conditional formatting. (This lets you preserve the conditional settings, but opt out of applying the conditions when you do not want them used.)

⑨ Click OK.

⑩ Click OK.

● The conditional formatting is applied to any records whose field value meets the condition you set.

TIPS

Did You Know?

You are not limited to applying a single rule. You can apply multiple rules to a field using the Conditional Formatting Rules Manager and following the same steps outlined in this task. The order in which the rules have conditional formatting applied depend on the order in which they are listed in the dialog box. You can move a rule up or down in the list.

Remove It!

To remove the conditional formatting, open the Conditional Formatting Rules Manager dialog box, select the rule you want to delete, and then click the Delete Rule button. To edit a rule rather than remove it entirely, click the Edit Rule button.

Summarize a Datasheet with a PivotTable

You can easily filter and analyze your database data using a PivotTable. A PivotTable is an interactive table that summarizes your data using format and calculation methods you specify. PivotTables are useful in that they enable you to create many different views of your data rather than a fixed report. This way you can decide which one is most useful.

You create a PivotTable by displaying the table or query containing the data you want to summarize in PivotTable view and then dragging the desired fields in the table or

query to the blank PivotTable grid that appears.

After you have the PivotTable in place, you can enhance it by filtering by certain fields, or by certain values in a particular field. You can add fields to it specifically for the purpose of filtering, or you can exclude certain values from individual rows or columns.

If, after creating a PivotTable, you realize that it contains too many individual entries to be meaningful, you can group the entries into summary items.

---

① Display the table or query from which you want to create a PivotTable in Datasheet view.

② Click View.

③ Click PivotTable View.

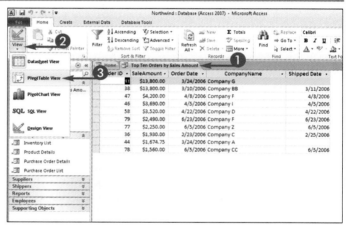

● A blank PivotTable grid appears with placeholders.

● The PivotTable Field List opens, listing the fields in the query or datasheet.

Note: *If the Field List does not appear, click Field List in the Design tab's Show/Hide group to display it.*

④ Click and drag a field in the PivotTable Field List to the Drop Row Fields Here placeholder.

● Data from the selected field appears in a column at the left.

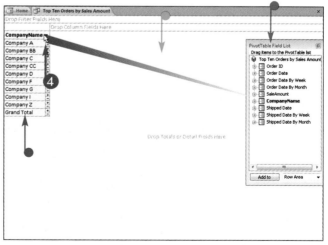

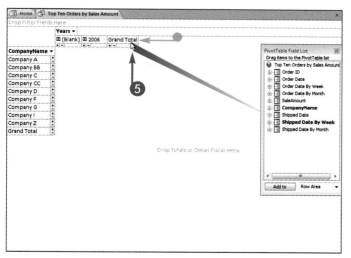

⑤ Click and drag a field in the PivotTable Field List to the Drop Column Fields Here placeholder.

● Data from the selected field appears in a row along the top.

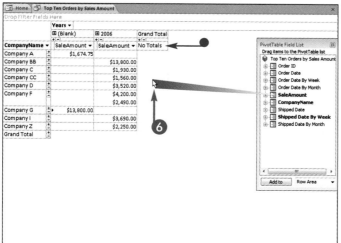

⑥ Click and drag a field in the PivotTable Field List to the Drop Totals or Detail Fields Here placeholder.

● The data appears in the center of the grid in the appropriate row and column.

Note: *You can have multiple fields in the same placeholder area. If a field is already in the area, simply drag another one on top of it.*

More Options!

To filter your PivotTable, drag the field by which you want to filter to the Drop Filter Fields Here area, click the drop-down arrow to the right of the filter field, and clear the check boxes for any values you do not want. To filter for certain values in individual fields, click the drop-down arrow next to a field name, clear the check box for each value you do not want to include, and click OK.

More Options!

To remove a PivotTable field, right-click it and choose Remove from the menu that appears. To group entries in a PivotTable, select the entries you want to group and click Group in the Design tab. To ungroup a grouped entry, select the group and click Ungroup.

Summarize a Datasheet with a PivotChart

You can view your data using a PivotChart. A PivotChart is an interactive chart that summarizes your data using format and calculation methods you specify. PivotCharts are useful in that they enable you to create many different views of your data rather than a fixed report. This way you can decide which one is most useful.

A PivotChart is like a PivotTable, except it expresses the data graphically rather than as text and numbers. Indeed, PivotTables and PivotCharts are two different views of the same data, so you can switch freely between them. (To do so, right-click the PivotTable or PivotChart's tab and choose PivotChart View or PivotTable View, respectively.) If you switch to PivotChart view while there are fields in PivotTable view, the fields carry over unless they are cleared first.

You create a PivotChart by displaying the table or query containing the data you want to summarize in PivotChart view and then dragging the desired fields in the table or query to the blank PivotChart that appears.

① Display the table or query from which you want to create a PivotChart in Datasheet view.

② Click View.

③ Click PivotChart View.

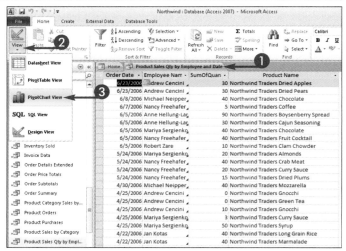

● A blank PivotChart appears with placeholders.

● The Chart Field List opens, listing the fields in the query or datasheet.

Note: *If the Field List does not appear, click Field List in the Design tab's Show/Hide group to display it.*

④ Click and drag a field in the Chart Field List to the Drop Category Fields Here placeholder.

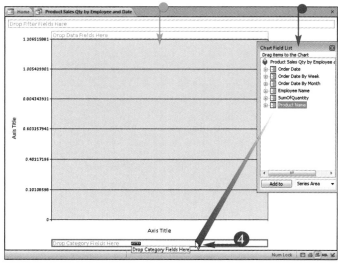

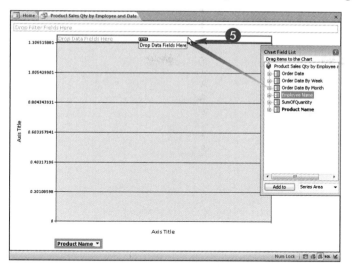

⑤ Click and drag a field in the Chart Field List to the Drop Data Fields Here placeholder.

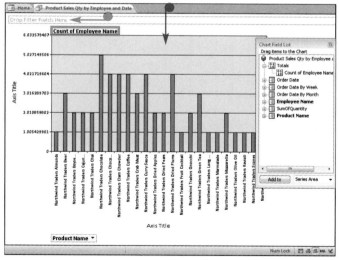

● The data is displayed as a PivotChart.

● You can also drag a field to the Drop Filter Fields Here placeholder.

Note: *The Chart Field List covers the Drop Series Fields Here placeholder by default. To move the box, click its title bar and drag to the desired location.*

More Options!
To change the chart type, right-click the PivotChart and select Change Chart Type. The chart's Properties dialog box appears with the Type tab displayed; choose a chart category from the list on the left, and then choose a specific chart type from the pane on the right.

Streamlining Outlook Tasks

E-mail is a primary method of communicating these days — so much so that many people are deluged with messages every day. Microsoft Outlook's Mail component enables you to view, respond to, forward, and compose new e-mails, as well as create folders for organizing the e-mails you send and receive.

With these basics mastered, you can graduate to using Outlook's more advanced e-mail functions. You can use Outlook to create distribution lists, which are useful if you frequently send e-mails to the same group of contacts — for example, to your team members at work — because they enable you to simply enter the name of the distribution list in the message's To field

instead of adding each contact individually. You can also append a signature to the end of your messages, encrypt messages that contain sensitive data, recall messages sent in error, establish an automated message to be sent when you are out of the office, establish rules for managing messages, filter junk e-mail, archive e-mails to save space, and subscribe to RSS feeds.

Note that to use Outlook's Mail function, you must first set up an account with and obtain an e-mail address from an Internet service provider (ISP). Then, you can use Mail's Add New E-mail Account Wizard to automatically configure Mail to send and receive messages using that address.

Quick Tips

You can use Outlook to manage multiple e-mail boxes. You can easily add additional accounts to your existing Outlook setup. For example, you can synchronize services from Hotmail, Gmail, or other e-mail providers. When you add other e-mail accounts, Outlook lists them in the Navigation pane on the far left side of the Inbox view. You can select which e-mail account to view and work with in the Outlook window, expanding and collapsing accounts like folders.

When adding other accounts, Outlook attempts to connect to the server and retrieve the e-mail information required for you. If all goes well,

the procedure works quietly in the background. However, depending on your e-mail provider, you may need to enter the information manually. Most e-mail accounts use a designated IMAP account type, an incoming mail server (POP3), and an outgoing mail server (SMTP). You need to know the server names, along with your logon information, typically your user name and password. Check with your service provider to find out specific details, or if you are using a different e-mail program, you can check its settings before migrating your e-mail to Outlook.

---

① To add an account from Mail view, click File.

Note: *You can press Ctrl+1 to quickly switch over to Mail view in Outlook.*

② Click Info.

③ Click Account Settings.

④ Click Account Settings.

The Account Settings dialog box appears.

⑤ Click the E-mail tab if it is not already selected.

⑥ Click New.

The Add New Account dialog box opens.

⑦ Click Microsoft Exchange, POP3, or IMAP (○ changes to ◉).

⑧ Click Next.

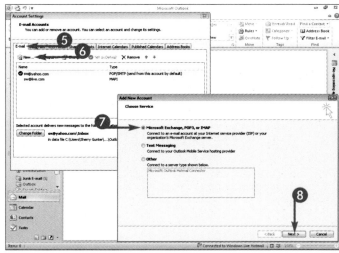

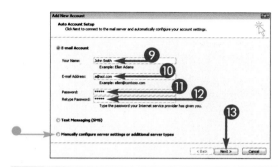

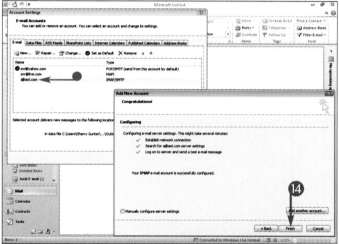

⑨ Type your name.

⑩ Type your e-mail address for the new account.

⑪ Type your account password.

⑫ Retype the password here.

● To configure the account manually, skip steps 9 to 12 and click this option instead (◎ changes to ◉).

⑬ Click Next to continue.

Outlook attempts to configure your e-mail server settings, establish a connection, and log onto the server.

⑭ Click Finish.

Note: *If the automatic configuration did not work, you can click the Back button and configure the account manually.*

● The account is added to the Account Settings dialog box.

TIPS

Important!

If you are a Hotmail or Windows Live user, Outlook may prompt you to download and install Outlook Connector, a program to help you use Outlook with your Hotmail or Windows Live account. Just follow the prompts to download the add-on, and then follow the prompts to install the software. You must restart Outlook to continue adding the Hotmail or Windows Live account.

More Options!

You can revisit the Account Settings dialog box to edit accounts, add new accounts, or remove old accounts. To remove an account, click its name in the list box and click the Remove button. To edit an account, click the Change button and change the settings. The top account listed is considered the default account. You can use the arrow buttons to move another account to the default position (⬆ and ⬇).

Create Your Own Quick Steps

You can use the Outlook Quick Steps feature to turn routine tasks into a single action. New to Outlook 2010, you can use Quick Steps to send an e-mail to an archive folder, reply and delete e-mails, send meeting replies, and more. Quick Steps are a great way to increase your productivity and conquer several actions at once. You can even assign shortcuts to a Quick Step that let you activate the task with a keyboard shortcut key combination.

Outlook installs with several Quick Steps already in place and ready to activate with a click. For example, you can quickly move an e-mail, create a team e-mail, reply and delete

e-mail, forward an e-mail to your manager, mark an e-mail as done, or create a new e-mail — all with a single click. You can find the Quick Steps listed in the Quick Steps group of the Home tab when you view your Inbox.

Just about any Quick Step you create requires some fine-tuning, such as specifying where to move an e-mail, or the name of a manager to forward a message to, but once you have set up the step, it is ready to go in the Quick Steps gallery on the Ribbon.

In this task, you learn how to move an e-mail. If you choose another type of Quick Step to create, similar steps are followed.

① Click the Home tab in Inbox view.

② In the Quick Step group of tools, click the More button.

③ Click New Quick Step.

④ Click Move to Folder.

Note: *If you choose another type of Quick Step, different steps are required.*

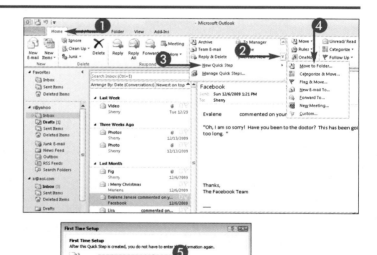

The First Time Setup dialog box appears.

⑤ Type a name for the Quick Step.

⑥ Choose a folder in which to move the e-mail.

● To create a new folder, click Other Folder and click New.

⑦ Click Options.

268

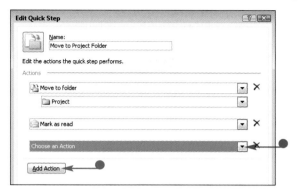

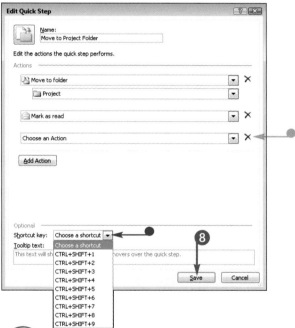

The Edit Quick Step dialog box opens.

● To add additional actions for more complex Quick Steps, such as flagging a message or marking it completed, click Add Action.

● To specify what type of additional action to add, click here and choose a type.

● To remove an action, click the delete icon.

● To assign a shortcut key, click here and choose a shortcut.

⑧ Click Save.

TIPS

More Options!
You can manage your Quick Steps using the Manage Quick Steps dialog box. You can edit existing Quick Steps, create a duplicate Quick Step, or remove Quick Steps you no longer need. You can also reorder the way in which Quick Steps are listed in the Quick Steps gallery on the Ribbon. To open the dialog box, click the More button on the Quick Steps group and click Manage Quick Steps.

More Options!
You can create a tooltip that appears when you position the mouse pointer over the Quick Step name in the gallery. In the Edit Quick Step dialog box, click inside the Tooltip text box, type a short description of the Quick Step, and save it. The next time you position the mouse pointer over the Quick Step name, a tooltip pop-up displays the description.

Create a Distribution List

Normally, to send an e-mail to multiple people, you must enter each name in the To or Cc field individually, either by typing it or by clicking the corresponding To or Cc button and selecting the recipients from the contacts listed in the Select Names dialog box that appears. The task is tedious, especially if you frequently send e-mails to the same group of contacts — for example, to your team members at work. To speed up your work, you can place those people in a *distribution list.*

A distribution list in Outlook is stored as a Contacts group in your Address book. You can create a stored list of everyone in the group; then, any time you need to send a message to the group, you can simply type the name of the distribution list in the message's To or Cc field instead of adding each contact individually. Alternatively, you click the To or Cc button in the message window and, in the Select Names dialog box that appears, click the list's name.

Distribution lists are perfect for group e-mailing tasks, and you can easily edit the list to include new people or remove others from the group.

① Click Contacts.

② Click New Contact Group.

Note: *You can press Ctrl+3 to quickly switch over to Contacts view in Outlook.*

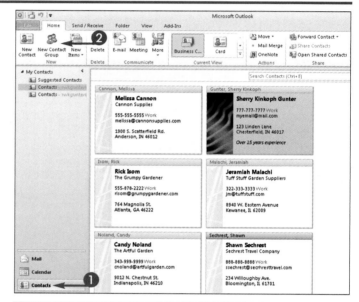

An empty Contact Group window opens.

③ Type a name for the group.

④ Click Add Members.

⑤ Click From Outlook Contacts.

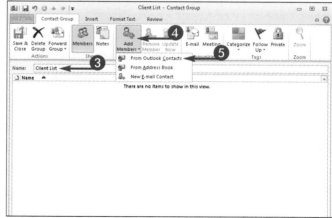

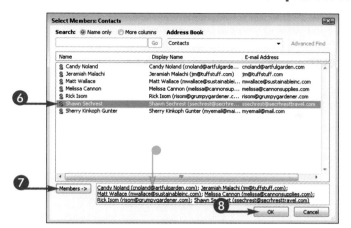

The Select Members: Contacts dialog box appears.

6 While pressing and holding Ctrl, click each contact you want to include in the distribution list.

7 Click Members.

Note: You can also click a name, and then click Members to add a contact one by one.

● The contacts you selected appear in the Members field.

8 Click OK.

● The contacts you selected now appear in the distribution list window.

9 Click Save & Close.

● The distribution list is saved and added to the Contacts.

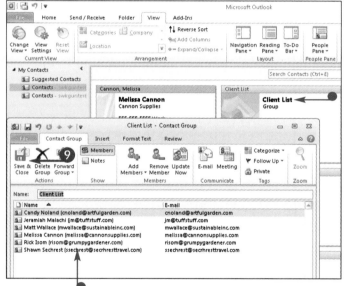

TIPS

Apply It!

Now that you have created a distribution list, Outlook makes it easy to apply it to an e-mail message. Using Outlook Mail, open a new message window as you normally would and click the To button, double-click the name of the distribution list, and click OK. Outlook adds the list to the To box, and you can finish creating and sending the e-mail.

More Options!

To edit a distribution list, locate the list's entry in your Outlook Contacts and double-click it to open it. To add more recipients to your list, follow steps 4 to 8 in this task. To remove a member, click his or her entry in the list and then click Remove Member. Clicking Update Now updates the list to reflect changes to contacts included in the list. Click Save & Close to exit the window.

You can use Outlook to create a signature — that is, a string of text that appears at the bottom of messages you send. Also called a signature block, an e-mail signature acts as a sign-off at the end of your e-mail message. You may have noticed signatures used in other e-mails you receive. Signatures are a great way to promote yourself or your company, or add a bit of personality to your correspondence. Signature text might include your name, e-mail address, and other contact information;

alternatively, it could spell out the name of your business, display a link to your Web site, or even include a picture. Some users even include a special quote or saying.

For best results, try to keep your e-mail signature to six lines or less. Although you can use a graphic in a signature, not all e-mail programs will display it based on security settings. The point of a signature is to make it easy for people to identify and contact you.

① Click the File tab.

② Click Options.

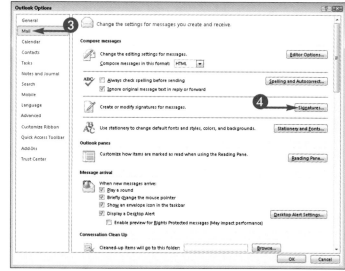

The Outlook Options dialog box opens.

③ Click the Mail tab.

④ Click Signatures located in the Compose Messages section.

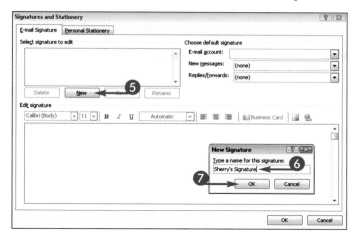

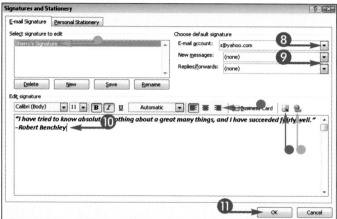

The Signatures and Stationery dialog box opens with the E-mail Signature tab open.

⑤ Click New.

The New Signature dialog box opens.

⑥ Type a name for the signature you want to create.

⑦ Click OK.

● The new signature's name appears selected in the list.

⑧ Click here and select the e-mail account to which the signature should apply.

⑨ Specify which messages should contain the signature.

⑩ Type the signature text.

● These controls enable you to customize the font and the text alignment.

● Click here if you want to add a picture to the signature.

● Click here to insert a hyperlink into the signature.

⑪ Click OK.

⑫ Click OK to close the Outlook Options dialog box.

Important!

To change your signature, simply open the Signatures and Stationery dialog box again, click the signature you want to edit in the list, and make the necessary changes. When you finish, click OK.

Try This!

To add your electronic business card to your signature, click the Business Card button in the Signatures and Stationery dialog box. In the Insert Business Card dialog box, click your contact entry to preview it, and click OK to add it to your signature. (You learn how to create an electronic business card in Chapter 12.)

If your message contains highly sensitive information meant for the recipient's eyes only, you can encrypt it. When you encrypt a message, Outlook scrambles the text it contains. Only recipients with the necessary "keys" can decipher the message.

To share the necessary keys with the recipient, you must exchange certificates. (A *certificate* is a digital ID.) Once you have obtained a digital certificate, you can use it to digitally "sign"

your encrypted message. The recipient can then save your information, including the digital ID, to his or her contacts. For information about obtaining certificates and digitally signing your e-mail messages, see the tips at the end of this task.

You can encrypt your messages on an as-needed basis. You encrypt single messages from the Security Properties dialog box.

---

① Compose your message.

② Click the Options tab in the message window's Ribbon.

③ Click the dialog box launcher in the Tracking group.

The Properties dialog box appears.

④ Click Security Settings.

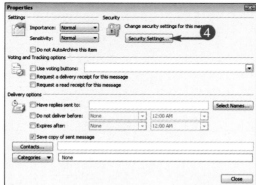

The Security Properties dialog box appears.

⑤ Click the Encrypt Message Contents and Attachments check box (☐ changes to ☑).

● To make changes to the encryption, such as choosing a specific digital certificate, click Change Settings and make your changes.

⑥ Click OK to close the Security Properties dialog box.

⑦ Click Close to close the Properties dialog box.

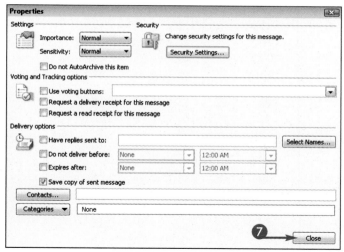

TIPS

Important!

To obtain a certificate, or digital ID, click Get a Digital ID in the Outlook Trust Center's E-mail Security tab. To access this screen, click the File tab, click Options, click the Trust Center tab, and click the Trust Center Settings button. Click the E-mail Security tab. Under the Digital IDs (Certificates) section, click the Get a Digital ID button. Doing so launches a special Web page with links to several organizations that issue certificates.

More Options!

To encrypt all outgoing messages in Outlook, click the File tab and click Options. Click the Trust Center tab and click Trust Center Settings. From the Trust Center dialog box, click the E-mail Security tab and then click the Encrypt Contents and Attachments for Outgoing Messages check box (☐ changes to ☑). Click OK to close the Trust Center, and then click OK again to close the Outlook Options dialog box and apply your changes.

Recall a Message

Suppose after sending your message you realize it contains an error. Assuming the recipient has not yet received the message, you may be able to recall it. When you recall a message, Outlook gives you the option of replacing it with an updated version.

Note that to recall or replace a sent message, you and the message's recipient must be using a Microsoft Exchange 2000, 2003, 2007, or 2010 account. If your account is a home or

personal account, chances are it is probably not an Exchange account.

To determine whether your Outlook account is a Microsoft Exchange account, press and hold Ctrl on your keyboard as you right-click the Outlook icon in the notification area in the Windows taskbar; then click Connection Status. The Microsoft Exchange Connection Status window opens, indicating whether you are indeed using an Exchange account.

---

① **Open the message you want to recall.**

Note: *To open the message, double-click it in the Sent Items folder.*

② **Click the File tab.**

③ **Click Info.**

④ **Click Resend or Recall.**

⑤ **Click Recall This Message.**

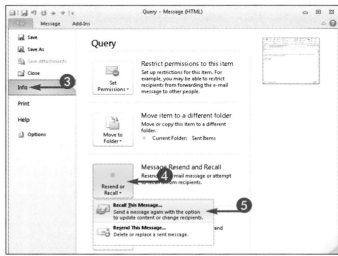

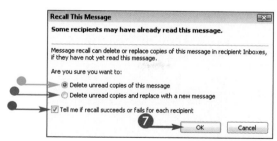

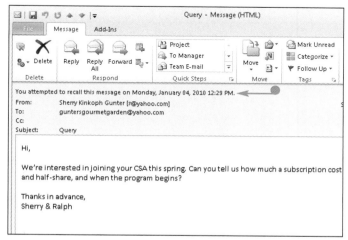

The Recall This Message dialog box appears.

⑥ Select the desired recall option:

● Click here to delete the message from the recipient's Inbox (provided it has not yet been read), or replace it with a new one.

● If you want Outlook to replace the deleted message with a new one, make the necessary changes to the message and send it.

● If you want Outlook to inform you whether the recall is successful (or not), click here.

⑦ Click OK.

● Outlook marks the message with a notation.

More Options!
By default, Outlook checks your messages for spelling errors as you type. You may want to check for grammar problems, too. The grammar checker is not turned on by default. To turn it on, click the File tab and click Options to open the Outlook Options dialog box. Click Mail, and then, under the Compose Messages section, click the Spelling and AutoCorrect button to open the Editor Options dialog box to the Proofing settings. Click the Mark Grammar Errors as You Type check box (☐ changes to ☑). Click OK, and then click OK again in the Outlook Options dialog box to exit and apply the new setting. Any grammar problems appear underlined in green wavy lines as you type your messages.

Set Up an Out-of-Office Reply

Suppose you will not have access to e-mail for a time — for example, if you are on vacation. You can configure Outlook to automatically send an out-of-office reply anytime you receive an e-mail during your absence, indicating that you do not have access to your account but will respond to the sender as soon as possible.

The first step when creating an out-of-office reply is to compose the message you want Outlook to send on your behalf and save it as a template. To compose the message, create a new message as normal (click the New E-mail button in Outlook Mail). Type the message

you want to include in your out-of-office reply, including a subject such as "Out of Office" or something that signifies the automatic response. Finally, click the File tab in the message window, click Save As, type a name for the message (such as "Out of Office Reply"), click Save as Type, choose Outlook Template (*.oft) from the list that appears, and then click Save. (Note: If the message window does not close automatically, click its Close button to close it.) After you have created a reply message, you are ready to create a rule to use it.

① **In Outlook Mail, click the Home tab.**

② **Click Rules.**

③ **Click Manage Rules & Alerts.**

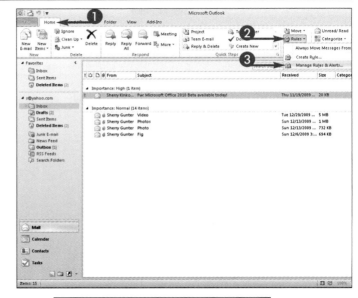

The Rules and Alerts dialog box appears.

④ **Click New Rule.**

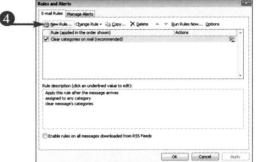

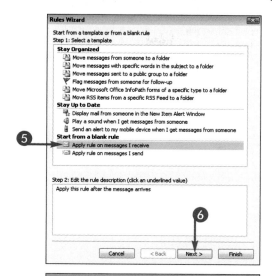

The Rules Wizard dialog box appears. This is the first of several to walk you through the procedure.

⑤ Under the Start from a Blank Rule category, click Apply Rule on Messages I Receive.

⑥ Click Next.

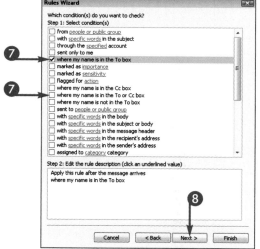

⑦ Click Where My Name Is in the To Box or Where My Name Is in the To or CC Box (☐ changes to ✔).

⑧ Click Next.

Did You Know?

Outlook rules are simply a set of instructions that tell the program what to do with the messages you receive in your Inbox. You can create rules to automatically delete e-mails, move them to other folders, or forward them to other people. By establishing conditions, exceptions, and actions, you can tell Outlook how to handle all of your e-mail messages. Learn more about creating rules in the next task, "Manage Messages Using Rules."

The precise steps for setting up an out-of-office reply differ depending on what type of Outlook account you have. This task outlines how to set up an automatic reply for a Post Office Protocol (POP) or Internet Message Access Protocol (IMAP) account, a process that involves setting up a message template and then creating a rule that employs that template.

If you use an Exchange account rather than a POP or IMAP account, you follow a different — and, frankly, simpler — series of steps to set up an out-of-office reply. Check out the Microsoft Exchange Help files to learn more about the process.

Note that in order for Outlook to send your out-of-office reply, your computer must be on with Outlook running. In addition, Outlook must be set up to periodically check for incoming messages.

Even if you receive more than one message from a sender while you are away, Outlook sends your out-of-office reply only once — provided the program is not restarted during your absence, in which case it resets the list it keeps of senders to which it has responded.

⑨ Click Reply Using a Specific Template (☐ changes to ✔).

⑩ Click the Reply Using a Specific Template link.

The Select a Reply Template dialog box appears.

⑪ Click here and select User Templates in File System.

⑫ Click the template you created to select it.

⑬ Click Open.

⑭ Click Next in the Rules Wizard dialog box.

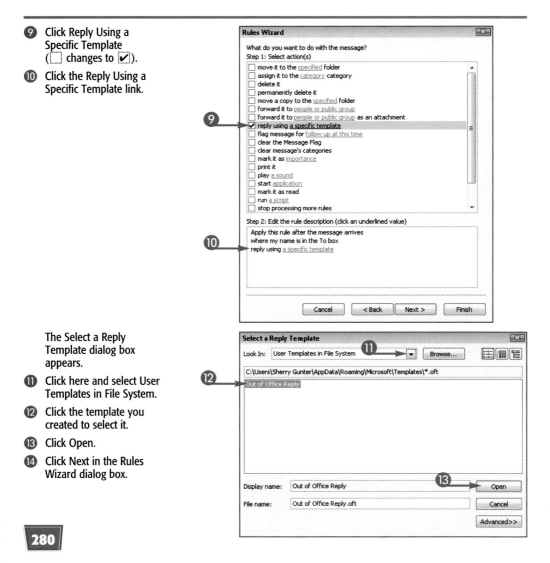

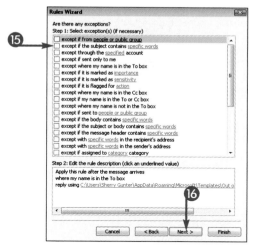

⑮ Optionally, click any exceptions you want to apply to the out-of-office reply rule.

⑯ Click Next.

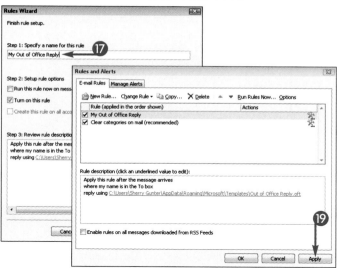

⑰ In the final wizard dialog box, type a name for the rule.

⑱ Click Finish at the bottom of the wizard dialog box.

Outlook adds the rule to the Rules and Alerts dialog box.

⑲ Click Apply to apply the selected rule.

Remove It!
To disable the out-of-office reply, revisit the Rules and Alerts dialog box (click the Rules button on the Inbox Home tab and click Manage Rules & Alerts). In the dialog box, deselect the rule you want to turn off (☑ changes to ☐). Click OK to apply the change. To remove a rule entirely, select it and click the Delete button or press Delete.

Manage Messages Using Rules

Suppose you want all messages you receive from a specific sender to be filed in a particular folder automatically. To accomplish that, as well as many other automated Mail tasks, you can set up a rule. Any messages that meet the criteria defined in the rule are handled in the manner you specify.

Quite simply, rules are just sets of instructions that tell Outlook what to do with your messages. To create rules in Outlook, you use the program's Rules Wizard. The Rules Wizard walks you through the process of setting up

automatic responses to messages in your Inbox, letting you customize how you want a message task handled through conditions, actions, and exceptions.

In this task, you learn how to create a rule to move messages from your Inbox to a designated folder. In addition to creating rules based on predefined templates provided by Outlook, you can create new rules from scratch. Alternatively, if you established rules in an earlier version of Outlook, you can import those rules into this version.

---

① In Outlook Mail, click the Home tab.

② Click Rules.

③ Click Manage Rules & Alerts.

The Rules and Alerts dialog box appears.

④ Click New Rule.

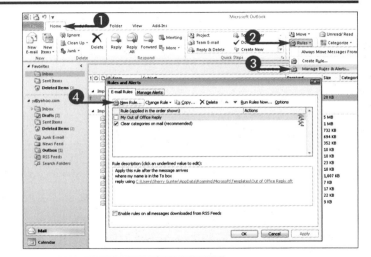

The Rules Wizard dialog box appears.

⑤ To move messages from a certain sender to a folder, click Move Messages from Someone to a Folder.

⑥ Click Next.

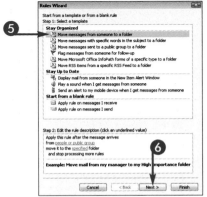

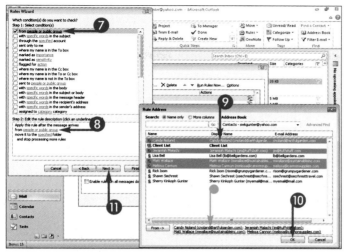

⑦ Click the condition that meets your needs to select it — here, From People or Public Group.

⑧ To specify the sender to whom the rule will apply, click the People or Public Group link.

The Rule Address dialog box opens.

⑨ Double-click the names of any people or distribution lists you want to adhere to the rule.

● The name(s) you double-clicked appear in the From field.

⑩ Click OK.

⑪ Click Next.

⑫ To choose the folder to which messages from the specified sender should be moved, click the specified link.

TIPS

More Options!
In addition to creating rules based on predefined templates that Outlook provides, you can create them from scratch. To do so, launch the Rules Wizard dialog box, choose the desired option under Start from a Blank Rule, click Next, and follow the on-screen prompts. For example, see the previous task, "Set Up an Out-of-Office Reply," to learn how to generate an automated e-mail response for when you are out of the office. You might also create rules to pre-filter messages before they arrive in your Inbox, redirect them to other folders, or notify you when you receive an important message.

More Options!
If you established rules in an earlier version of Outlook, you can import those rules into this version. (Note that to import your rules from a previous version of Outlook, you must first export them from that earlier version.) To access the tools for importing and exporting rules, as well as for upgrading any rules you import for better performance in Outlook 2010, click the Options button in the Rules and Alerts dialog box.

continued

You are not limited to creating rules that place messages from a certain sender in a specific folder. For example, you might create a rule that dictates that all messages from a particular sender (for example, your boss) be flagged for immediate attention. You can also set exceptions — that is, situations in which the rule you create is ignored. For example, you might specify that the rule be ignored when messages contain a certain word in the body text or subject line.

The advantage of using Outlook rules is that you control when a rule applies and any

exceptions to the rule. You can keep a list of rules in the Rules and Alerts dialog box and turn them on or off as needed. You can also edit rules to change their settings and conditions.

The order in which rules are listed in the Rules and Alerts dialog box are the order in which Outlook carries them out. If you want a particular rule to take place first in the list, make sure the rule is listed first in the dialog box.

The Rules and Alerts dialog box opens.

⑬ Navigate to and select the folder in which you want to save messages from the selected senders.

● To create a new folder to hold the messages, click New and create a new folder.

⑭ Click OK.

⑮ Click Next in the Rules Wizard dialog box.

⑯ If there are circumstances in which you want your new rule to be ignored, click them among the exceptions list and define them using the available links.

⑰ Click Next to continue.

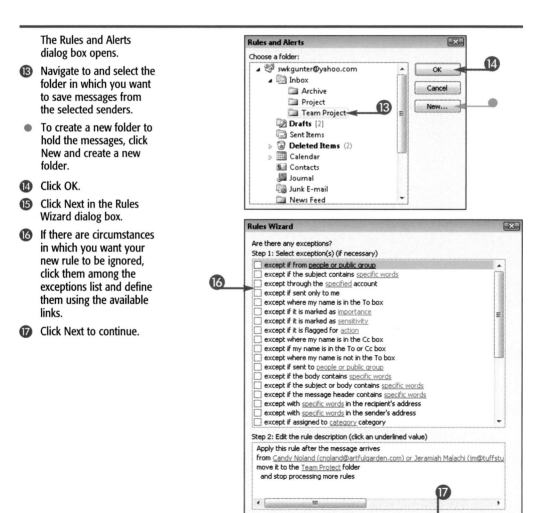

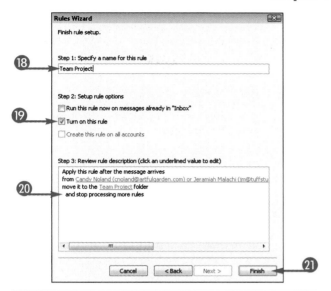

⑱ Type a name for the rule here.

Note: *To apply the rule to messages already in your Inbox, click Run This Rule Now on Messages Already in "Inbox."*

⑲ Verify that Turn On This Rule is checked.

⑳ Review the rule description.

㉑ Click Finish.

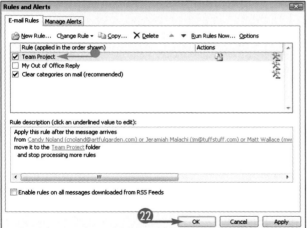

● The new rule is added to the list and enabled by default.

㉒ Click OK to close the Rules and Alerts dialog box.

Outlook applies the rule to messages meeting the criteria you specified.

Try This!

If you want to create a rule that applies to a certain sender, and you have a message from that sender in your message list, you can expedite the rule-creation process. First, right-click a message from the sender and click Rules and then Create Rule in the shortcut menu. In the Create Rule dialog box, under When I Get E-mail with All of the Selected Conditions, select the check box next to the necessary conditions, such as the From check box. Next, under Do the Following, select the check box next to the actions you want Outlook to take when the conditions are met. Outlook may prompt you for additional information; respond as necessary. Finally, click OK, and Outlook creates the rule.

Clean Up Folders and Conversations

You can use Outlook 2010's new Clean Up tool to clean up your Inbox folders and messages. The Clean Up tool keeps your most recent messages in view, but moves older, redundant messages out of the way or allows you to delete them entirely. This can free up some much-needed space on your computer.

You can apply the Clean Up tool to a specific folder or to an ongoing e-mail conversation. For example, perhaps you are on a distribution list for your sales department. Usually a good

thing, the list is also used to coordinate an office pizza party that you do not plan on attending. Instead of being inundated with a bunch of messages and replies, you can use the Clean Up tool to ignore the entire thread and all of its messages, or choose to delete the messages pertaining to the pizza party.

You can use the Clean Up feature's settings to control where message items go and what items are moved.

---

① **In Mail view, click the Home tab.**

② **Click Clean Up.**

③ **Click Clean Up Folder.**

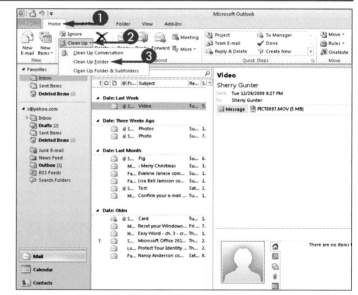

The Clean Up Folder dialog box opens.

④ **Click Settings.**

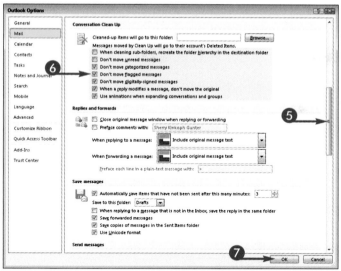

The Outlook Options dialog box opens to the Mail options.

⑤ Scroll to the Conversation Clean Up options.

⑥ Click any clean up settings you want to apply (☐ changes to ☑).

⑦ Click OK.

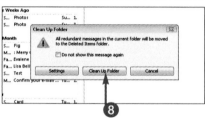

⑧ Click Clean Up Folder.

Outlook cleans up the Inbox folder as specified.

Try This!

If you ever have a distracting e-mail conversation in your Inbox that you prefer not to pay any attention to, apply the Ignore button to move it and any future iterations to the Deleted Items folder. To activate the feature, click the Home tab while in Mail view and click the Ignore button found in the Delete group of commands. To stop ignoring a conversation, open the Deleted Items folder, click the conversation, click the Ignore button again, and click Stop Ignoring Conversation. You can recover a conversation only if it has not been permanently deleted from the folder.

More Options!

Instead of removing conversations, you can also change how you view them. Click the View tab, click the Conversations button, and choose how you want to view the messages and threads.

Using e-mail opens you up to a deluge of junk e-mail messages, called *spam*. Indeed, you probably sift through dozens of spam e-mails to locate "real" messages every day. You can use Outlook Mail's Junk E-mail Filter to automatically divert spam from your Inbox into a Junk E-mail folder.

By default, Outlook Mail applies a low level of protection from junk e-mail. To change the level of protection, click the Home tab, click Junk, and click Junk E-mail Options. The Junk E-mail Options dialog box opens; in it, you

can specify the level of protection from junk e-mail that you want.

You should periodically check Outlook's Junk E-mail folder to ensure that no "authentic" messages have been diverted. If one is, you can mark it as "not junk"; this moves the message to the message list and, optionally, adds the sender to your Safe Senders list. On the flip side, if the Outlook filter fails to detect a junk e-mail message and allows it into your Inbox, you can set up Outlook to block all e-mail from the message's sender.

Block Messages from a Sender

① Right-click the message.

② Click Junk.

③ Click Block Sender.

● Outlook notifies you that the sender has been added to your Blocked Senders list, and that the message has been moved to the Junk E-mail folder.

④ Click OK.

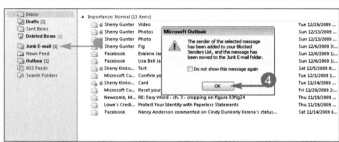

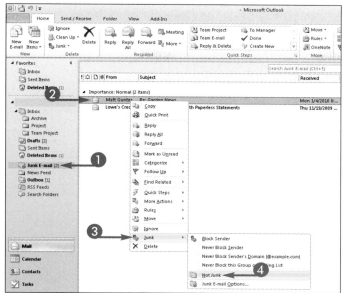

Mark a Message as Not Junk

1. Click the Junk E-mail folder in the folder list.

   Outlook displays the contents of the Junk E-mail folder in the message list.

2. Right-click the message you want to mark as not junk.

3. Click Junk.

4. Click Not Junk.

The Mark as Not Junk dialog box appears.

5. To always trust e-mail from the sender, verify that this option is checked.

6. Click OK.

   Outlook moves the message to your Inbox.

Try This!

To ensure that any sender who is listed in Contacts is considered "safe" by the Junk E-mail Filter, open the Junk E-mail Options dialog box. Click the Junk button on the Home tab, and then click Junk E-mail Options to open the dialog box. In the Safe Senders tab, verify that the Also Trust E-mail from My Contacts check box is checked. Optionally, click the Automatically Add People I E-mail to the Safe Senders List check box to select it. When you finish, click OK.

Did You Know?

Phishing typically involves an e-mail message that appears to be from a legitimate source, such as a bank, informing the user that his or her account information must be updated. When the user clicks the link provided, however, he or she is directed to a bogus site designed to mimic a trusted site in order to steal personal information. Outlook's anti-phishing features help detect these fraudulent messages automatically, disabling any links in messages it deems suspicious and alerting you to the problem in the message window's InfoBar.

Archive E-mails to Create Space

If you use Outlook with any regularity, you quickly discover that the sheer volume of e-mail messages, not to mention calendar entries and other Outlook items, can prove overwhelming. To mitigate this, Outlook automatically archives old files. If the default settings for this automatic operation do not suit you, you can change them.

You can use Outlook's Options dialog box to access the AutoArchive settings. You can control the frequency in which messages are archived, how old they must be for archiving,

and even where you want the archived messages stored. You can also choose to permanently delete the messages instead of storing them. By default, Outlook is set up to run the AutoArchive feature every 14 days.

In addition to changing Outlook's AutoArchive settings, as outlined here, you can also launch an archive operation manually. To do so, open Outlook's Folder tab, click AutoArchive Settings, and select the desired option in the Junk E-Mail Properties dialog box that appears.

---

① Click the File tab.

② Click Options.

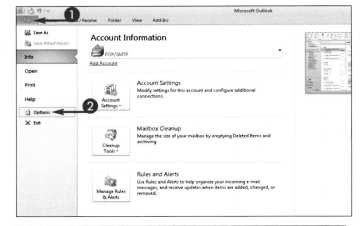

The Outlook Options dialog box opens.

③ Click Advanced.

④ Click the AutoArchive Settings button under the AutoArchive section.

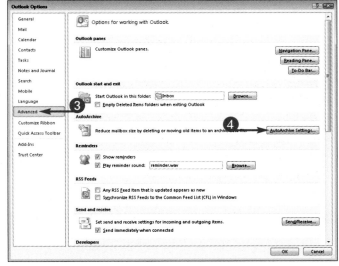

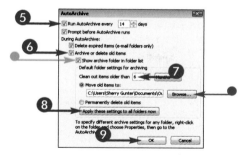

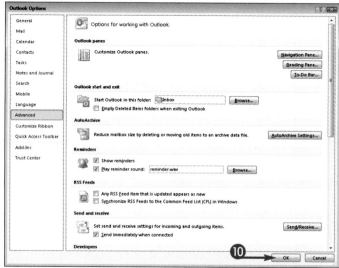

The AutoArchive dialog box opens.

⑤ Click Run AutoArchive Every *x* Days (▢ changes to ☑) and type the desired interval.

⑥ Click Archive or Delete Old Items (▢ changes to ☑).

● Click to display the Archive folder in the folder list (▢ changes to ☑).

⑦ Indicate how old an Outlook item must be to be archived.

● Click Browse and select where old items should be stored if using another storage location.

⑧ Click Apply These Settings to All Folders Now.

⑨ Click OK to close the AutoArchive dialog box.

⑩ Click OK to close the Outlook Options dialog box.

Remove It!

Alternatively, you may decide you want to disable Outlook's AutoArchive functionality altogether. To do so, click the File tab and then click Options. In the Outlook Options dialog box, click the Advanced tab and click AutoArchive Settings. Finally, in the AutoArchive dialog box, deselect the Run AutoArchive Every *x* Days check box (☑ changes to ▢). To prevent AutoArchive from running on a particular folder, right-click the folder in the folder list, click Properties, click the AutoArchive tab, and click Do Not Archive Items in This Folder.

Just because an item has been archived does not mean you cannot view it if need be. For example, you may need to check on an e-mail message from your boss you archived three months ago, or locate an e-mail with a software code from an online store. You can view archived items from the Archive folder in Outlook's Navigation pane.

In addition to viewing archived items, you can restore archived items back to their original folder or to a different folder, either individually or as a group. The easiest method of retrieving a message is to simply drag it out of the archived folder and into the folder in which you want to keep the message. To move a group of messages, press and hold Ctrl while clicking each message in the group. You can also press and hold Shift and click the first and last message in the group to move.

View an Archived Message

1 Click the Folder List icon to display all the folders in the Navigation pane.

2 Click the archive folder you want to open.

3 Double-click the message you want to open.

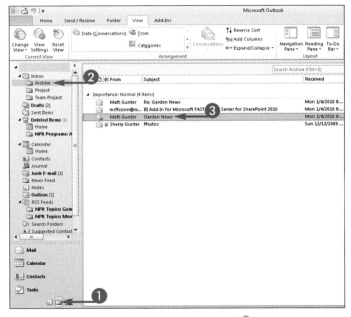

● Outlook displays the message in its own message window.

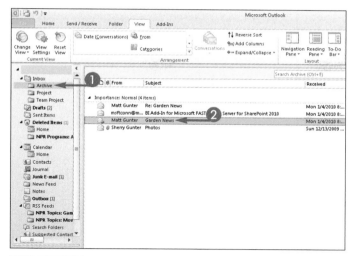

Retrieve an Archived Message

1. Using the Navigation pane, display the Archive folder containing the message you want to retrieve.

2. Locate and select the message you want to recover.

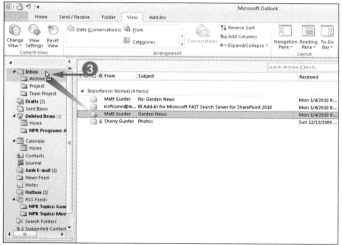

3. Click and drag the message you want to recover and drop it into another folder.

The message is moved to the designated folder.

Did You Know?

Where do your archived items go exactly? The first time AutoArchive runs, the archive file created depends on your operating system. If you are using Windows 7, archived e-mails are stored in the following path: C:\Users*YourUserName*\Documents\Outlook Files\archive.pst.

Really Simple Syndication, or *RSS* for short, is a technology that enables Web content to be syndicated — that is, converted to a Web feed. This content might include blogs, podcasts, news, and so on. When you use Outlook to subscribe to an RSS feed, Outlook automatically downloads new posts from those feeds. That means that instead of visiting several Web sites to stay informed, you can simply view these various feed posts in Outlook.

You can subscribe to a feed from the Web site that hosts the feed. (Note that if you use Internet Explorer 8 to subscribe to a feed, you can then access and manage the feed from within Outlook 2010. Internet Explorer 8 indicates when it has detected an RSS feed by changing its RSS Feed button from gray to orange.)

Alternatively, if you know the Web address, or URL, of the feed that interests you, you can subscribe to that feed from within Outlook. When you do, Outlook automatically checks for and downloads feed updates. Subscribing to a feed is typically free.

---

① Click the File tab.

② Click Info.

③ Click Account Settings.

④ Click Account Settings.

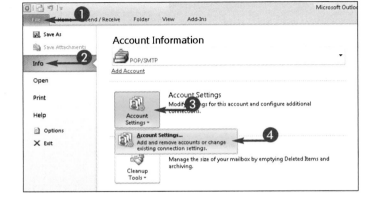

The Account Settings dialog box opens.

⑤ Click the RSS Feeds tab.

⑥ Click New.

The New RSS Feed dialog box opens.

⑦ Type the URL for the feed to which you want to subscribe.

⑧ Click Add.

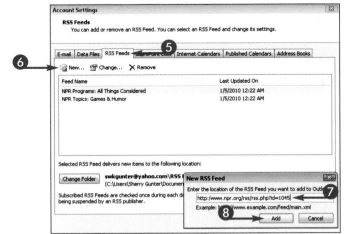

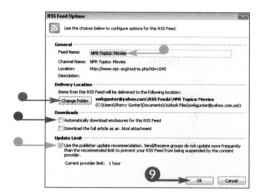

The RSS Feed Options dialog box appears.

● The name of the feed appears here.

● To change the folder in which feed updates are saved, click Change Folder.

● Click here to automatically download feed enclosures (☐ changes to ☑).

● The publisher of the feed to which you are subscribing likely limits how frequently you can check for new postings. Click here to ensure Outlook does not check more frequently than is permitted (☐ changes to ☑).

⑨ Click OK.

⑩ Click Close in the Account Settings dialog box.

⑪ In Outlook Mail, double-click the RSS Feeds folder in the folder list.

● The feed to which you subscribed is listed.

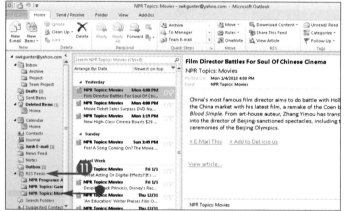

Did You Know?

You can share a favorite RSS feed with others. With the RSS folder open, click the Share This Feed button on the Home tab. This opens a new message window with the RSS feed link attached. Simply fill in the rest of the message window components and send the e-mail.

Remove It!

If you find that a particular feed is not as interesting or useful as you would like, you can unsubscribe from it. To do so, right-click the RSS folder for the feed you want to remove, and click Delete Folder in the menu that appears. When prompted, click Yes to confirm the deletion.

Managing Multiple Priorities with Outlook

Whether you are a seasoned user of earlier versions of Outlook or completely new to the program, you will appreciate Microsoft's efforts to streamline the program's interface. By default, the program displays the Mail component, consolidating it with your calendar, upcoming appointments, and tasks on a single screen.

In addition to enabling you to send and receive e-mails, Outlook is designed to help you keep track of appointments, manage your contacts, maintain a to-do list, keep a journal to track your time, and more.

Of course, Outlook contains many basic-level tools designed to make you more efficient. More advanced tools, however, can really help you stay organized. For

example, you can categorize your Outlook items so you can color-code them. Outlook's automatic journal tools enable you to track the time you spend on a project. If you find yourself overloaded, you can delegate a task you create in Outlook to someone else. You can also use Outlook's Contacts map feature to pinpoint an address contained in a contact record and map out how to find the location.

With Outlook 2010, sharing your information with others has never been easier. For example, you can easily create an electronic business card, which you can exchange with others in much the same way paper-based cards are shared. In addition, you can send a snapshot of your calendar to another Outlook 2010 user.

Quick Tips

Create an Electronic Business Card

Just as you likely exchange paper-based business cards with others, you can also exchange business cards created with Contacts. You can send your business card to others via e-mail, either as an attachment or as part of your e-mail message's signature.

The first step in creating an electronic business card is to create a contact entry in Outlook for yourself. To do so, click the Contacts button in Outlook's Navigation pane, click New Contact on the Ribbon's Home tab, and enter your contact information in the window that

appears. Once you have created your own contact, you can proceed to turning the information into an e-card.

In addition to including vital information such as your name, phone number, e-mail address, and so on, your electronic business card can include a photo and/or a logo. You can also customize the design of your electronic business card. For example, you can change the font size and text alignment of elements on the card. You can also add extra fields of text to the card for quotes or taglines.

---

① **Open your contact record window.**

Note: *You can quickly double-click a contact in the Contacts list to quickly open the contact window.*

② **Click the Contact tab.**

③ **Click Business Card.**

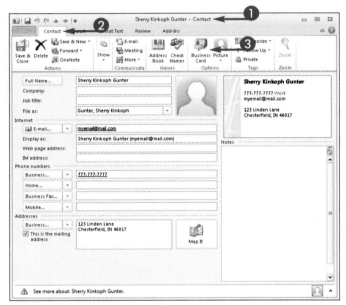

The Edit Business Card dialog box opens.

④ **To change the card layout, click here and specify where you want the image on the electronic business card to appear (here, Image Left).**

Note: *By default, the layout image appears on the far left side of the card.*

⑤ **To add a background color, click the Fill Color button to open the Color dialog box.**

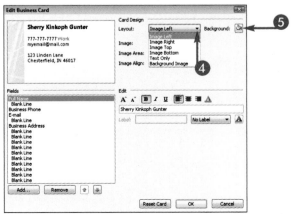

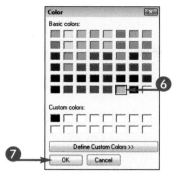

The Color dialog box opens.

6 Choose a background color for the electronic business card.

7 Click OK.

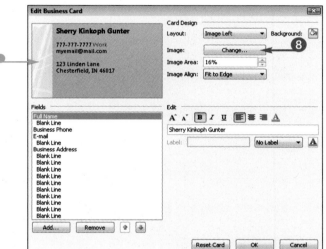

● Outlook applies the new color.

8 To change the image shown, click Change.

TIPS

Did You Know?

In addition to creating an electronic business card that contains your contact information to share with others, you can display all of your contacts in electronic business card form, much the way Rolodexes of old stored paper-based business cards did. To view your contact entries as electronic business cards, click the Home tab and click Business Cards in the Current View gallery. If the option does not appear, use the scroll arrows (⊟ and ⊡) to search for the Business Cards view option.

Customize It!

Rather than choose a background color from Outlook's Basic colors palette, display the custom color palette and choose a softer color shade from the various shades available for the selected color choice. Just click the Define Custom Colors button in the Color dialog box to expand the palette, and then choose another hue from the bar at the far right.

Outlook adds a default graphic design to your business card. You can certainly use the default graphic and choose how you want it positioned on the card, you can even control the size of the element. However, if you have another graphic in mind, you can replace the default graphic with something more appropriate, such as a company logo, a product picture, or even a photograph of yourself.

You can also assign a background color to the card. Keep in mind that solid colors and small business card text are not always a good match. Legibility is often an issue, so choose your

background color wisely. If you pick something too dark, you may not be able to see the business card text on the card. You may need to make some adjustments to the text color or background color to get just the right effect.

In addition to an image, consider adding an extra field to your card to type up, such as a slogan. For example, if your company's tagline is "over 50 years' experience" you can add this to your card as a blank line and type the tagline.

The Add Card Picture dialog box opens.

⑨ Locate the image you want to include on your electronic business card and click it to select it.

Note: *You need not use a photograph on the card; an image file containing, say, your company's logo would also work.*

⑩ Click OK.

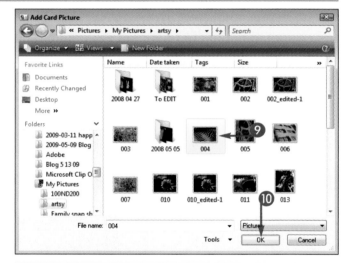

⑪ Click the Image Area spinner arrows to increase or decrease the image size.

⑫ To change the image alignment, click here and choose another alignment option.

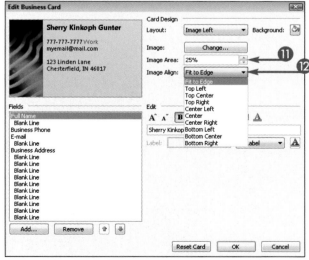

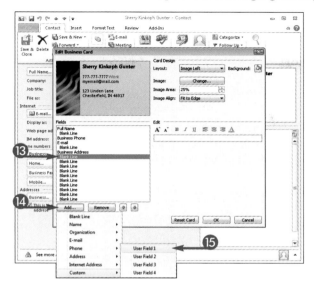

⓭ To add an additional field to the card, click a Blank Line where you want to place the line.

⓮ Click Add.

⓯ Click the type of field you want to insert.

⓰ Type the text you want to add.

● To change the order of the fields on your card, click the field you want to move, and then click one of these buttons.

● These buttons enable you to format the font and alignment of the selected field.

⓱ When you finish formatting your business card, click OK.

The business card is saved in your contact record.

⓲ Click Save & Close to exit the contact record window.

Note: *If you make too many changes to your card, or are unhappy with the way it turned out, you can click the Reset Card button to reset the card to the way it first appeared when you opened the Edit Business Card dialog box.*

More Options!

Instead of having a separate field for, say, your job title, you might add that information as a label to the Full Name field. Labels let you add another design element to the card that appears separately from the main information. To do so, specify in the Edit Business Card dialog box whether the label should appear to the left or the right of the existing text, type the label, and choose the desired font color.

Apply It!

To attach your business card to an e-mail message, open the message window and compose your message. Then click Attach Item on the window's Message tab, click Business Card, and choose the card you want to include with the message. Outlook adds it to the message window and as a file attachment.

If you plan to visit someone listed in Contacts, and if that person's contact record includes an address, you can use the Contacts map feature, called Map It, to pinpoint the person's location. With an online connection and a little help from the Bing Web site, you can quickly locate an address from any contact in your list.

By default, the Contacts map feature opens your browser window to the Bing Web site and displays the address in Road view, like a typical map. You can, however, switch to Aerial view, which is a satellite image of the location. The tools in the top left corner of the map let you change views, switching between Road

and Aerial. In addition, the Contacts map can be displayed in Bird's Eye view, which combines elements of the Road and Aerial views. To switch views, click Aerial and then click Bird's Eye. You can also choose to view the map in 2-D or 3-D modes.

In addition to enabling you to view a map pinpointing the contact's location, you can obtain driving directions from your location to your destination, as well as fine-tune those directions to show the shortest route or the quickest route. You can even forward the information to your mobile phone.

① **With the desired contact's window open in Outlook, click here and choose Home, Business, or Other to select the address you want to map.**

② **Click Map It.**

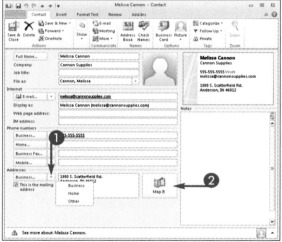

● **A Bing Web page opens, pinpointing the contact's location.**

● **For a better look at the map in any view, drag the Zoom slider to zoom in and out.**

③ **To obtain directions from your location to the contact's location, click the Directions link under the address.**

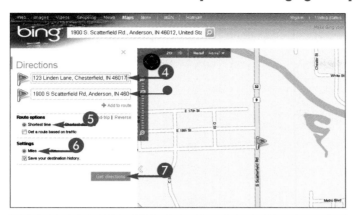

The Directions pane opens.

④ Type your starting address.

● The contact's address already appears as the destination.

⑤ Choose any route options you want to apply, such as shortest time or shortest distance (◎ changes to ◉).

⑥ Choose whether you want the direction in miles or kilometers (◎ changes to ◉).

⑦ Click Get Directions.

The map changes to show your route.

⑧ To print the directions, click here and select whether you want to print the map of the route, text directions, or both.

⑨ To send the directions to your mobile device or via e-mail, click here, choose the appropriate option, and follow the on-screen prompts.

More Options!

You can also find your way to the Outlook Map It feature through the Communicate group of tools on the contact window's Contact tab. Click the More button and click Map It.

More Options!

In order to use Outlook's mobile features, you must first configure a text messaging account. Outlook can help you with this by walking through the required steps to set things up. To start the process, click the File tab to open Backstage view, then click Options. From the Outlook Options dialog box, click the Mobile tab and click the Mobile Options button. Follow the on-screen prompts to set up your account.

Do you like to keep your Outlook items really organized? Then consider using categories. If several Outlook items pertain to a particular project, company, or what have you, you can create a category for those items. Outlook items in the same category are color-coded so you can easily tell what the item pertains to at a glance. The process for categorizing an Outlook item is essentially the same regardless of what type of item it is.

One of the best things about categorizing Outlook items is that you can then sort them by category. To sort tasks and contacts by category, display the Home tab and click a category in the Current View gallery. To sort e-mail messages, click the Arrange By heading at the top of the message list and choose Categories. (Note that Calendar entries cannot be sorted by category.)

To expedite the categorization process, Outlook provides a Quick Click function, which enables you to apply a category to an Outlook item with the click of a button.

Create a New Category

1. Click an Outlook item you want to place in a new category.

2. Click the Home tab.

3. Click Categorize.

4. Click All Categories.

   The Color Categories dialog box appears.

5. Click New.

   The Add New Category dialog box appears.

6. Type a name for the new category.

7. Click here and select the color you want to associate with the category.

● Optionally, click here and select a shortcut key to associate with the category.

Note: *If you associate a shortcut key with a category, then you can simply press that key combination to apply the category to a selected Outlook item.*

8. Click OK to close the Add New Category dialog box.

9. Click OK to close the Color Categories dialog box.

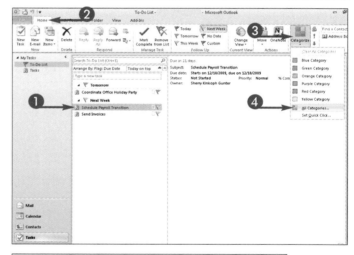

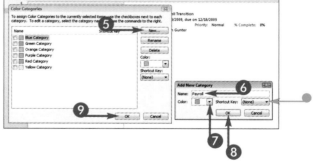

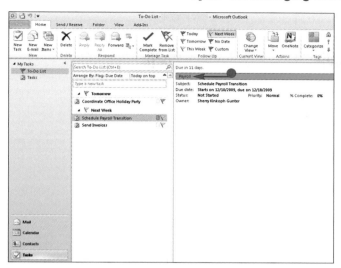

● Outlook creates the new category and applies it to the selected Outlook item.

Assign an Existing Category to an Outlook Item

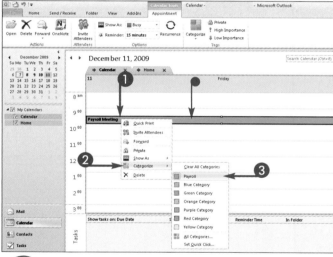

① Right-click the item you want to categorize.

② Click Categorize.

③ Click the desired category from the list that appears.

● Outlook categorizes and color-codes the selected item.

TIPS

Try This!

If you frequently use the same category, or need to add several items to a category in one sitting, you can use Outlook's Quick Click feature. To do so, choose Set Quick Click in the Categorize submenu and, in the Set Quick Click dialog box, click the down arrow and choose the desired category. Then simply click an Outlook item's Categories column to apply the selected category. To turn off Quick Click, choose No Category in the Set Quick Click dialog box.

Important!

The Categorize menu contains categories used most recently. If the category you want to apply does not appear in the list, choose All Categories and select the desired category in the Color Categories dialog box that opens.

Send a Calendar Snapshot

You can e-mail a calendar snapshot to others — that is, a static view of your calendar as it appears at the moment it is sent. When you create a calendar snapshot, you are creating a graphical representation of your calendar. If the recipient of your calendar snapshot also uses Outlook, he or she can drag items from your calendar snapshot into his or her own calendar. If the recipient does not use Outlook, he or she can still view your calendar.

In addition to sending calendar snapshots to others, you can view calendar snapshots sent to

you. To do so, click Open This Calendar in the e-mail message containing the snapshot. When prompted, click Yes to confirm that you want to add the snapshot to Outlook; Outlook displays it side by side with whatever calendar was already displayed. To copy an entry from one calendar to the other, click the entry and drag it.

Note that calendar snapshots are static. When the owner of the calendar makes a change to it, the change is not reflected in the calendar snapshot.

① With Calendar open, click E-mail Calendar.

The Send a Calendar via E-mail dialog box appears.

② Click the Calendar drop-down arrow and select the calendar you want to send.

③ Click the Date Range drop-down arrow and select the date range you want to include in the snapshot.

④ Click the Detail drop-down arrow and select the calendar snapshot's level of detail.

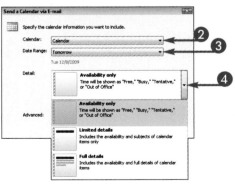

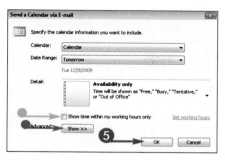

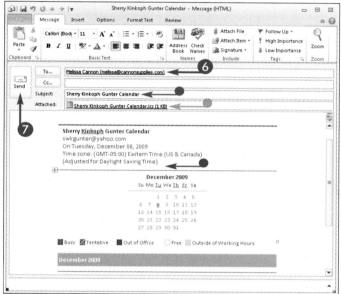

- Optionally, click Show Time Within My Working Hours Only to shorten the calendar to working hours (☐ changes to ☑).

- You can click the Show button to display additional settings for revealing private items or attachments.

⑤ Click OK.

  Outlook launches a new message window.

- The subject line is filled in automatically.

- The calendar snapshot is added as an attachment.

- Additionally, the calendar snapshot is embedded in the body of your message.

⑥ Enter the necessary recipient information and any additional text you want to include with the snapshot.

⑦ Click Send.

More Options!

You can also save your Outlook calendar in the iCalendar file format and share it with others. To do so, click the File tab to open Backstage view and click the Save As option. This opens the Save As dialog box you are used to seeing in all the other Office 2010 programs. Edit the calendar file name, if desired, and choose a destination folder for the saved file. Click the More Options button in the Save As dialog box to open the same dialog box described in steps 2 to 4 of this task. You can fine-tune the settings as needed. Click Save; the calendar is saved and you can share the file with others.

Caution!

When you create a snapshot of your calendar, Outlook assumes you are free during the before and after periods of your regular work hours. If you do not want the recipients to know you are available during the early morning or late evening hours, make sure you check the Show Time Within My Working Hours Only check box (☐ changes to ☑).

You can use multiple calendars in Outlook. For example, you might keep track of a calendar for work appointments and a completely separate calendar for home or personal appointments. You can then flip from one to the other to view calendar items. You can also view those multiple calendars either side by side or in overlay mode.

In overlay mode, the calendars appear transparent and stacked, enabling you to see the appointments, events, and meetings in both. The active calendar appears highlighted in brighter color than the calendar at the

bottom of the stack. To make the other calendar active, click an appointment or click the calendar name at the top of the viewing area.

If the calendars are displayed in overlay mode, you can revert to side-by-side mode by clicking the arrow button in the tab of either calendar. You can also close one of the calendars by clicking its Close button. At least one calendar must always be displayed on-screen. You can display up to 30 calendars in Outlook and view them all side by side or in overlay mode.

Add a New Calendar

① With the Calendar open, click the Home tab.

② Click Open Calendar.

③ Click Create New Blank Calendar.

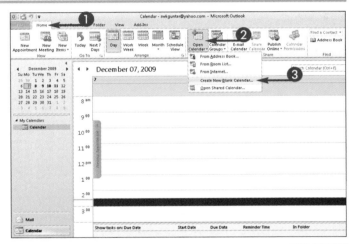

Outlook displays the Create New Folder dialog box.

④ Type a name for the new calendar folder.

● Calendar Items is selected by default.

⑤ Click OK.

● Outlook displays the new calendar name in the Navigation pane.

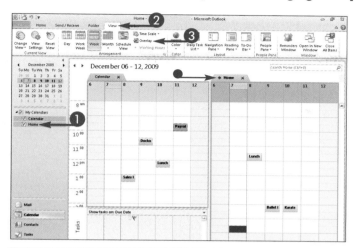

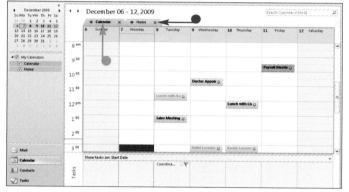

Overlay Two Calendars

1. In the Navigation pane, click the second calendar you want to view in addition to the one already open.

   A check mark indicates the calendar is shown.

2. Click the View tab.

3. Click Overlay.

● You can also click the left arrow in the tab at the top of the calendar on the right to switch to overlay view.

Outlook displays the calendars in overlay mode.

● In this example, the main calendar overlays the Home calendar.

● Click here to close the calendar.

TIPS

More Options!

When viewing multiple calendars, you can use Outlook's Arrange tools on the Home tab to change the way in which you view calendar dates, just as you do with the regular calendar view. For example, you can view the calendars by day, work week, or month.

More Options!

Just a reminder — if you need more viewing area on-screen for your Outlook calendars, you can always collapse the Navigation pane and free up some space. Simply click the Minimize the Navigation Pane arrow button ([◄]) located in the top right corner of the pane. When clicked, this minimizes the pane to a vertical bar on the left side of the screen. Click the Expand the Navigation Pane button ([►]) to bring back the full pane again.

To keep track of your interactions with contacts and other activities, such as the amount of time spent on a particular project, you can use Outlook's Journal feature. Perhaps the most efficient way to use this feature is to configure it to log certain activities automatically.

In addition to configuring Outlook to log journal entries automatically, you can enter them manually. These journal entries can pertain to Outlook items or activities relating to other files on your computer. To manually record an Outlook item, click the Home tab, click Journal Entry, and enter the desired information in the window that appears.

To ensure that your journal entries do not consume more than their fair share of space, Outlook archives them automatically using default archive settings. Clicking the AutoArchive Journal Entries button in the Journal Options dialog box opens the Journal Properties dialog box, where you can change these AutoArchive settings.

① **Click the File tab.**

② **Click Options.**

The Outlook Options dialog box opens.

③ **Click Notes and Journal.**

④ **Click Journal Options.**

The Journal Options dialog box appears.

⑤ **Click the items for which you want to generate automatic journal entries (☐ changes to ☑).**

⑥ **Click each contact for which items should be automatically recorded (☐ changes to ☑).**

● **Optionally, you can record activities related to other Office programs (☐ changes to ☑).**

⑦ **Specify whether double-clicking a journal entry opens the entry or opens the item to which the entry refers (◉ changes to ◉).**

⑧ **Click OK.**

⑨ **Click OK again to close the Options dialog box.**

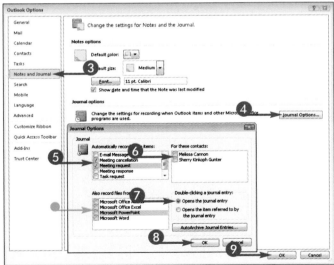

Delegate a Task

You can delegate a task to another person, who can accept or decline the assignment. When someone accepts a task, that person becomes the task's "owner"; only he or she can make changes to the task. If a task is declined, the person who created the task can revert ownership back to him- or herself.

When the person to whom you delegate a task updates the task, all copies of the task — including the version in your Outlook — are

also updated automatically (assuming you checked Keep an Updated Copy of This Task on My Task List). When the person marks the task complete, you are automatically sent a status report notifying you of the task's completion (assuming you checked Send Me a Status Report When This Task Is Complete).

To view tasks that you have delegated to other users, click the View tab while in Task mode, click Change View, and click Assigned.

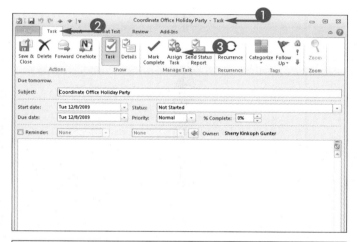

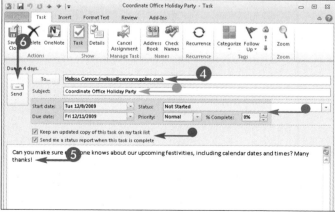

① Create or open the task you want to delegate.

② Click the Task tab.

③ In the tab's Manage Task group, click Assign Task.

The task window changes to a message window.

④ Type the name or e-mail address of the person to whom you want to delegate the task.

● The name of the task becomes the subject of the mail message.

● The Start Date, Due Date, Status, Priority, and % Complete fields reflect the settings you established when you created the task.

● The managerial actions are selected by default. Click an action to turn it off (☑ changes to ☐).

⑤ Type a message to the task recipient.

⑥ Click Send.

Adding Power to Publisher

Many Microsoft Office users go right for the big guns — Word, Excel, and PowerPoint — when using the applications, often overlooking the power and potential that lies within Publisher. Publisher is a desktop-publishing application geared to nondesigners. The program is easy to use and offers plenty of exciting tools and features for creating professional publications. You can use Publisher to whip up newsletters, brochures, flyers, stationary, calendars, catalogs, business cards, and just about any other printed media you can think of. The program includes dozens and dozens of templates you can use — just pop one open and fill in your own text or photos and you are ready to go.

Although it started out its history as a small-business and consumer-targeted program, each new version of Publisher has introduced more commercial features, making it a great alternative to pricier software that accomplishes the same thing.

New to Publisher 2010 is the Ribbon and other general enhancements to the user interface, along with the File tab, which offers you access to the Backstage view where all the file-related commands are grouped together. The Page Navigation pane lets you view page previews in the same way you view slide previews in PowerPoint. The Print and Print Preview features are joined in Publisher 2010, and you can view how your document is set up to print. You can also now save your publications as PDF and XPS files. Microsoft has also made improvements to the way in which users can work with pictures. With an online connection, you can immediately access loads of templates online at the Office.com Web site that you can download with a click. You can also find a greater number of building blocks to help you create professional-looking pages. In this chapter, you tap into a few techniques that can help you get more out of Publisher 2010.

Quick Tips

Find Templates Online

Microsoft Publisher comes with a seemingly endless supply of publications you can choose from, and you are bound to find one that meets your needs in some way. You can always edit any of the existing templates to create a custom template, deleting elements, adding new ones, and so on. With an online connection, you can access even more templates.

By default, Publisher displays both installed templates and online templates whenever you click the File tab and click New. Of course, the online templates appear only if you are connected to the Internet. As you begin to peruse the various categories, the Backstage view displays a navigation bar allowing you to move from one page to the next as you examine the templates and preview what they look like.

If you do not see a template you like, you can search for a particular kind of template using the Search tool. Whenever you encounter an online template you want, you must download it in order to use it. Depending on your connection speed, the process takes only a moment or two.

---

1. Click the File tab.

2. Click New.

   ● Backstage view displays Installed and Online Templates by default unless you specify otherwise here.

3. Scroll down the list to view the various template categories.

4. Click a category you want to view.

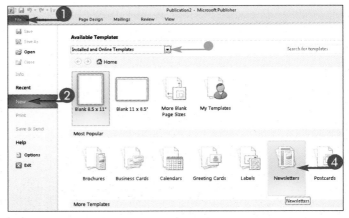

5. Click a template to preview it.

   ● You can click the navigation buttons to move back or forward a page.

   ● You can click the Home button to return to the first page of templates at any time.

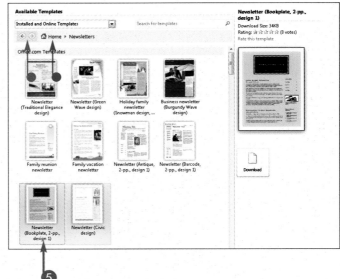

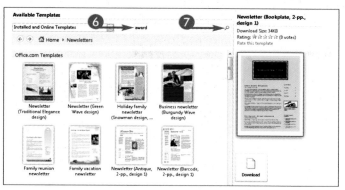

6. Click the Search for Templates field and type the keyword or words describing the type of template you want to find.

7. Click the Search button or press Enter.

● Publisher displays any matches.

8. To download a selected template, click Download.

   If the template is already installed on your computer, the Create button appears instead.

TIPS

Did You Know?

If you create a particularly useful template, you can share it with others on the Office.com site. Submitting a template for consideration requires uploading the template file and filling out a form. You need a Windows Live ID to do this. It takes a couple of days for review, and then, if it passes, the template is posted for others to download. Use this Web address in your browser window to open the Submit a Template page: https://services.office.microsoft.com/en-us/templates/start.aspx. Be sure to check out the Templates Home page to find more resources, blogs, and partner sites.

More Options!

If you create a publication you really like, you can save it as a template you can reuse or share with others. Click the File tab and click Save As to open the Save As dialog box. Click the Save as Type drop-down arrow and select Publisher Template. Give the file a unique name and click Save to create the template file.

Many of the documents you create in Publisher require gathering content from another source. For example, you might be working on a newsletter and your colleague has composed a story in another program. You can import text-based files into Publisher to use as newsletter articles or to use in as content in other types of publications.

So how do you bring in a text file and place it into a publication? Ordinarily, you might think copying and pasting does the trick. However, Publisher offers you another method to use. You can import a text story without having to open the originating program. This saves you some time and steps.

When you import a text file with the Insert File command, it flows into the text box where you want it to appear. Any extra text that does not fit into the text box flows into the next frame or into overflow.

① Select the text box in which you want to place a text file, or create a new text box to hold the story.

② Click the Insert tab.

③ Click Insert File.

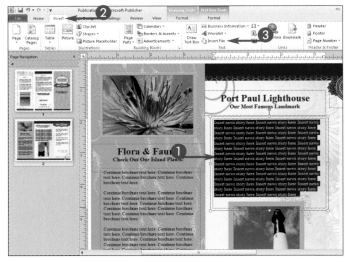

The Insert Text dialog box opens.

④ Navigate to and select the file you want to import.

⑤ Click OK.

● Publisher inserts the text.

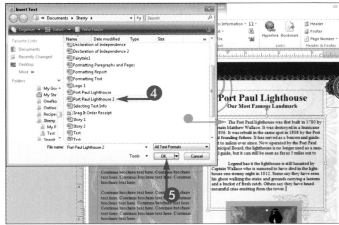

Nudge a Text Box

When you select a text box in Publisher, you can move it around the document wherever you want it. Sometimes, however, you need to move it only a small amount of space. With the box selected, you can press the keyboard arrow keys to nudge a text box ever so slightly up, down, to the left, or to the right, depending on which arrow key you press. This is a handy little trick for when you need to move a box, but dragging it moves it too much or not precisely enough.

The nudge feature is set up to move a selected box 0.13" every time you press the arrow key for the direction you want to move. You can change this setting to be more or less. Using the program's Options dialog box, you can specify a different amount to suit the way you work. You may want to nudge boxes more or less than the default setting. Just enter your own value into the field.

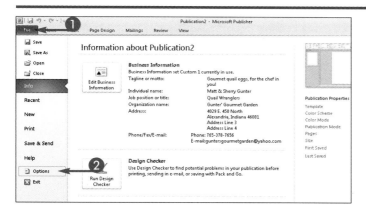

① Click the File tab.

② Click Options.

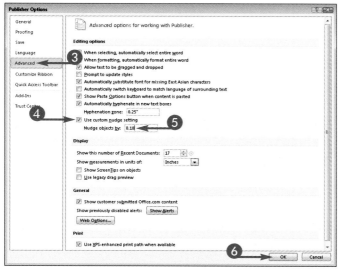

The Publisher Options dialog box opens.

③ Click the Advanced tab.

④ Click the Use Custom Nudge Setting check box (☐ changes to ☑).

⑤ Type a new value in the box.

⑥ Click OK.

You may find yourself working on a longer publication using lots of pages, such as a newsletter or brochure. What happens if you need to move a story, associated graphics, and all the other objects found on the page to another location in the document? For example, maybe the story you placed back on page four is now a front page story. You can certainly use the tried-and-true practice of copying and pasting each element to its new location on a new page, but you may prefer a more direct method. Thankfully, Publisher has just the tool for the job — the Move Page dialog box.

You can specify exactly where you want the page inserted, either below or above another page. If your document has a two-page spread, both of the pages move as a unit.

If you want to move a single story instead of a page, use the Cut and Paste commands instead.

① Display the page you want to move in the publication.

② Click the Page Design tab.

③ Click Move.

The Move Page dialog box opens.

④ Click whether you want to move the page, before or after (⊙ changes to ◉).

⑤ Click the page that you want to move the current page before or after.

⑥ Click OK.

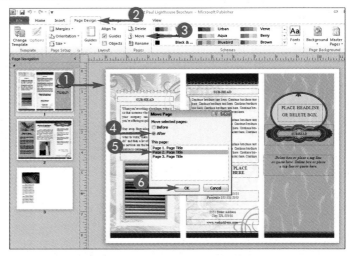

● Publisher moves the page; you can view the new location in the Page Navigation pane.

Note: If your publication has a few pages, you can just drag and drop the page into a new location on the Page Navigation pane.

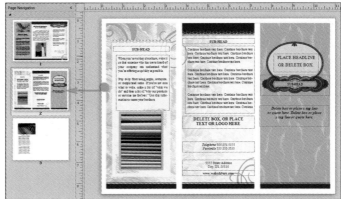

Text boxes are the receptacles for your publication stories and content, and depending on the template you use, how much text fits into a box is limited by the box size. If you try to place too much text into a box, it overflows to another. When this is not a solution, you can try Publisher's Text Fit commands to remedy the problem.

The Text Fit control gives you four distinct options to try for fitting text into a text box.

The Best Fit option automatically resizes the text to fit every time you resize the text box. The Shrink Text On Overflow option shrinks the text inside the text box if any overflow text exists. The Grow Text Box to Fit option does just what its name implies: It resizes the text box to fit the text. The Do Not Autofit option tells Publisher not to automatically adjust the text size to fit.

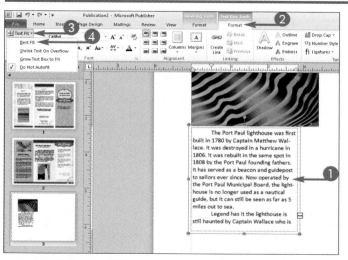

① Select the text box you want to edit.

② Click the Format tab for Text Box Tools.

③ Click Text Fit.

④ Click a text fit option.

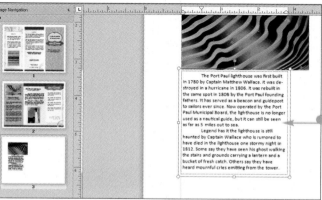

Publisher immediately applies the new setting.

● In this example, Best Fit was applied to fit all the text within the text box.

Publisher automatically hyphenates text to help display as much text as possible in a text box. Hyphens break up words that do not fit at the end of a line. As a space-saver idea, this is a good one. However, not every publication you create needs or warrants hyphenated text, and in some cases, the hyphenation ends up looking far worse than the space it saves. You can control whether hyphenation is applied or not, and even control it manually.

The Hyphenation dialog box offers controls for turning off automatic hyphenation or controlling it manually on a case-by-case basis. By default, hyphenation is set up to occur

when text breaches the 0.25" area at the right border of the text box. You can set a smaller hyphenation zone, such as 0.05" to achieve less hyphenation. If you enter a larger value, you can expect more hyphenated words.

When you turn off the feature, hyphenation is no longer applied to the selected text box at all. You can also activate the Manual feature and manually determine what hyphenated words you keep or dismiss in a text box.

If you insert your own hyphens, Publisher does not remove them if you turn off the automatic hyphenation feature. You must remove them yourself.

Turn Off Hyphenation

1 Select the text box containing the hyphenation you want to change.

2 Click the Format tab for Text Box Tools.

3 Click Hyphenation.

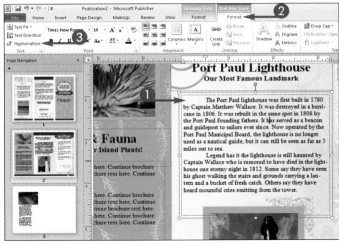

The Hyphenation dialog box opens.

4 To turn off hyphenation, click this check box (☑ changes to ☐).

● To adjust the hyphenation zone, click here and enter a new value.

5 Click OK.

Automatic hyphenation is turned off.

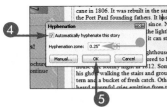

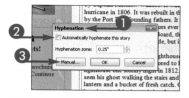

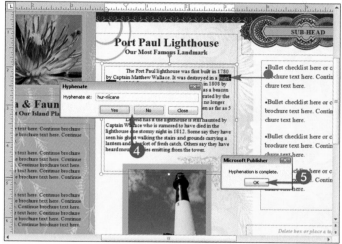

Turn On Manual Hyphenation

① Select the text box you want to edit and open the Hyphenation dialog box (see the previous steps).

② Click the Automatically Hyphenate This Story check box (✓ changes to ☐).

③ Click Manual.

● The Hyphenate dialog box opens and highlights the first occurrence in the text box.

④ Click Yes to approve the hyphenation, or No to remove hyphenation.

Repeat step 4 to continue editing each occurrence.

⑤ When all the hyphenation has been checked, click OK.

More Options!
You can turn off the hyphenation settings for new text boxes you add in Publisher. To do so, you must open the program's Options dialog box. Click the File tab and click Options to open the Publisher Options dialog box. Click the Advanced tab and uncheck the Automatically Hyphenate in New Text Boxes check box (✓ changes to ☐). You can also set a default value for the hyphenation zone by entering a new value in the Hyphenation Zone box. Click OK to exit the Options dialog box and apply your changes.

Did You Know?
If hyphenation is causing you problems, you can always try resolving the issue by resizing your text box or adjusting the Hyphenation Zone setting.

Send Your Publication as an E-mail

You can e-mail your publication to share it with a colleague or boss, or even a friend. Microsoft Publisher gives you a variety of options for e-mailing files. If you have a multipage publication, for example, you can choose to e-mail just the current page. This option inserts the page in the message body of your e-mail as an HTML element. You can also e-mail all the pages and insert them as a single page into the message body.

Another option is to simply e-mail the publication as a file attachment. When you select this option, the publication is attached to the message, and in order for recipients to

open the file, they, too, must have Publisher installed.

If the recipient does not have Publisher installed, you can try sending the publication as a PDF or XPS file. Both formats retain the formatting of the publication, but the contents cannot be easily edited. The recipient must open the file before viewing its contents.

This task demonstrates the Send Current Page option and the E-mail pane that opens for filling in a recipient. If you choose the Send All Pages option, Publisher prompts you to save your file in a separate dialog box first, and then opens the E-mail pane.

---

1. Click the File tab.
2. Click Save & Send.
3. Click Send Using E-mail.
4. Click a send option.

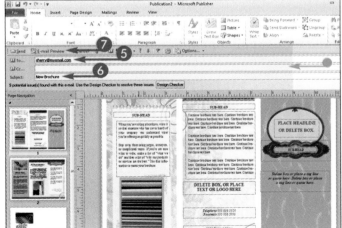

● Publisher opens an e-mail pane at the top of the publication.

5. Type the recipient's e-mail address.
6. Type a subject heading for the e-mail.
7. Click E-mail Preview.

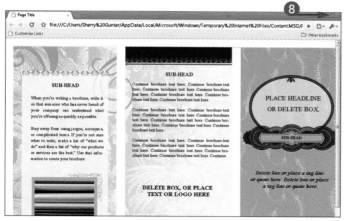

The default browser window opens and displays the publication page.

⑧ Click the window's Close button to return to Publisher.

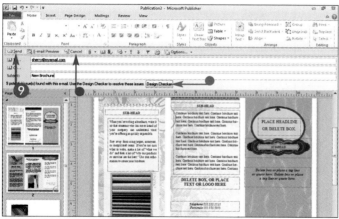

● To check the publication for any design issues, click the Design Checker button.

⑨ When you are ready to send the publication, click the Send button.

● To exit the E-mail pane without sending the publication, click the Cancel button. This turns the display off and returns you to publication view.

Note: *You must be logged onto your Internet account in order to send the e-mail.*

Try This!

You can also preview a publication for e-mailing before you open a particular e-mail option. Display the File tab, click Save & Send, and then click the E-mail Preview option. Click the E-mail Preview button that appears in order to view your publication as an HTML e-mail message using your default browser window.

More Options!

If you choose to send the publication as an attachment, regardless of whether it is a Publisher file, a PDF file, or an XPS file, a separate default Message window opens for including a personal message along with the file attachment. In the case of sending a PDF or XPS file, Publisher first converts the file to the designated format and then attaches the file to the message.

Save a Publication for a Commercial Printer

Some of your Publisher publications may require professional printing, especially if your desktop printer cannot handle all the binding, trimming, and finishing required, or if you need to print out large quantities of materials. Commercial printers can take over and help you reproduce your work on professional printing presses and various equipment. Thankfully, Publisher 2010 can assist you in starting the process with options to help you prepare the publication.

You can choose from several quality settings when preparing your file. The Commercial Press setting creates the largest file and saves the file to the highest quality settings for offset printing.

If you prefer to optimize the publication for desktop printing at a high-end copy shop, choose the High quality printing option. Use the Standard option to create a compressed file suitable for online viewing, or the Minimum size option for regular old computer display.

In addition to a quality settings, you can also specify whether you want to create a PDF or Publisher format file or both.

After deciding on your commercial printer options, you can then follow the Pack and Go Wizard prompts to copy your publication to a disk or other location. The wizard packs the publication and its linked files into a single file you can take or send to a commercial printer.

---

① Click the File tab.

② Click Save & Send.

③ Click Save for a Commercial Printer.

④ Click the quality setting drop-down arrow and select a file quality.

⑤ Click the file type drop-down arrow and select whether you want to create both a PDF and Publisher file, or just a PDF or Publisher file.

⑥ Click Pack and Go Wizard.

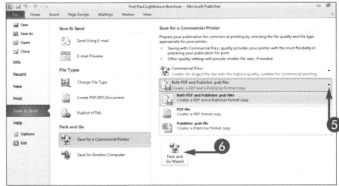

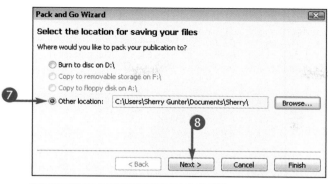

The Pack and Go Wizard opens.

⑦ Click a destination for the publication (◎ changes to ◉).

⑧ Click Next.

● Optionally, to print out a composite of the final product, leave this check box selected.

⑨ Click OK.

Did You Know?

When preparing a publication for commercial printing, first and foremost you need to find out if the commercial printer can handle your Publisher file. Most printers do. If not, you can save the file as a PDF or XPS file, other common formats for printing. Saving publications to Publisher 98 or Publisher 2000 is also a good idea to make sure everything is compatible. You should also be very clear about what you need regarding the printing project, such as paper size, quality, deadlines, file size limitations, and so on. Publisher's help files offer some great tips on readying your file for professional printing.

More Options!

You can utilize Publisher's Design Checker to check your publication for any potential printing issues. Design Checker looks over your document for problems like overflow text, or pictures scaled disproportionately. To activate the Design Checker, click the File tab, click Info, and then click the Run Design Checker button. Publisher opens the Design Checker pane and lists any issues it finds. You can address each one as needed.

Creating Pizzazz with Office Graphics

What exactly are "graphics?" Whether you call them pictures, photographs, images, or visual objects, graphic elements help you create a polished Office file and go the extra mile in conveying your message. This chapter uses the terms interchangeably. Graphics can include pictures you insert from a digital camera, clip art you insert from a clip art collection, shapes you draw using the Office Shapes feature, or even WordArt objects that turn text into artwork. For practical purposes, and unless stated otherwise, graphics are the elements you add to an Office file to create visual impact or further convey a message in some form or fashion.

In this chapter, you learn techniques to help you take your Office graphics to the next level. Included are tasks on how to use the new Screenshot tool to take a picture of your Office screen, and how to use the new Background Removal tool to apply a quick photo-editing technique to your digital images. You also learn how to take control of your clip art collections and keep things organized in the Clip Art Organizer, one of the extra applications installed in the Microsoft Office 2010 Tools folder, and how to assign new artistic effects to turn a regular graphic into something spectacular.

Ever wonder how to create a perfect watermark or wrap text around a problematic graphic element? This chapter shows you how. You also learn how to use the grouping and ordering commands to their best advantage, and apply the Ungroup command to customize clip art.

So if you are ready to get graphic, then dive in!

Quick Tips

Capture a Picture of Your Screen

An exciting new feature to Office 2010 is the screen clipping tool, called Screenshot. The screen clipping tool lets you take a picture of your screen, also called a *screen capture*. The screen clipping feature first appeared with OneNote, and is now available in Word, Excel, PowerPoint, and OneNote with the new and improved Office 2010 features.

You can find the Screenshot tool on the Insert tab in Word, Excel, PowerPoint, or OneNote. When you activate this command, and you have any other application windows open, the Screenshot tool assumes you want to take a

picture of one of the currently opened windows, so it displays the windows in a gallery of screenshots. To use one, just choose the one you want to insert into the current document.

The other option is to take a new screenshot by dragging over the area of the screen you want to capture. This technique lets you control exactly what to include in the screen clipping.

Once you grab a clipping, it is immediately inserted into the current document window wherever you have clicked in the file.

---

① In Word, Excel, PowerPoint, or OneNote, click where you want to insert a screen clipping.

② Click the Insert tab.

③ Click Screenshot.

④ Choose a screenshot from among the existing open applications.

● The screen clipping is added to your file.

⑤ To capture a new screenshot, click the Screenshot button.

⑥ Click Screen Clipping.

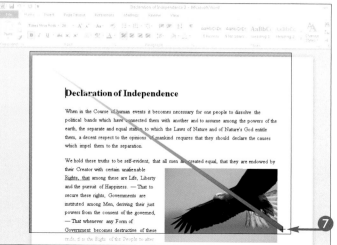

⑦ Click and drag across the area of the screen you want to capture and it is immediately added to your file.

TIPS

More Options!

Once you add a screen clipping to your file, you can treat it as any other image. You can resize it, move it, wrap text around it, add a caption, or save it as a graphic file to reuse again later. Resizing and moving are probably the first two tasks you will perform on the clipping. To move it, click the image and drag it to a new location in the file. To resize it, click and drag a corner icon of the selected image.

Try This!

A neat trick you can do with a captured image is turn it into a hyperlink that, when clicked, takes the user to the file from which the image was captured. To do so, right-click the image and choose Hyperlink. This opens the Insert Hyperlink dialog box. Navigate to the original file and click OK. The image now acts as a link to the original file.

Hidden among the Microsoft Office 2010 Tools folder is a little gem of an organizer tool called, appropriately, Microsoft Clip Organizer. This stand-alone mini-application helps organize drawings, photos, sounds, videos, and other media clips as well as access clips from the Microsoft Office Web site. In previous renditions of Office, you could access the Organizer through the Clip Art pane; now you must go through the Windows All Programs menu.

Microsoft Clip Organizer is its own separate window complete with a menu and toolbar, a Collection List pane listing all the folders and categories of clip art, and a viewing pane for displaying the clips. By its very nature, the Clip Organizer keeps track of your clip art collections, including photographs, sound clips, video clips, and of course, clip art graphics. You can also use the Organizer's feature to access more clips online, organize clips into unique categories by moving and copying them into different categories and collections, or the Organizer's Search tool to look for specific clips in your collections.

Like other files and folders stored on your computer, the Organizer lists clip art collections in hierarchical order, with folders and subfolders, and categories you can expand and collapse to change the view.

① Click Start.

② Click All Programs.

③ Click Microsoft Office.

④ Click Microsoft Office 2010 Tools.

⑤ Click Microsoft Clip Organizer.

The Microsoft Clip Organizer window opens.

⑥ Double-click a collection name to expand the collection and view its categories.

⑦ Click a category to view associated clips.

Some categories include subcategories; double-click the category name to display all the related subcategories.

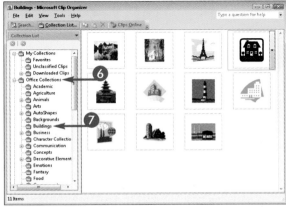

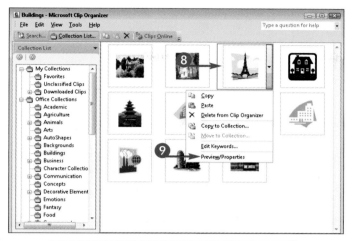

⑧ Click a clip to reveal a menu of commands you can apply.

⑨ To learn more about a clip's properties and preview the clip, click Preview/Properties.

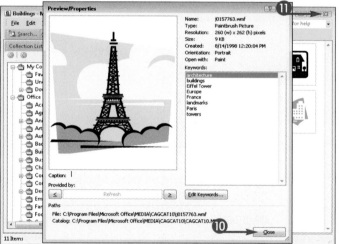

The Preview/Properties window opens.

⑩ Click Close to exit the preview.

⑪ Click the Organizer window's Close button to exit Microsoft Clip Organizer.

TIPS

Try This!

To search for a particular clip, click the Search button in the Microsoft Clip Organizer window to open the Search pane, type the keyword or words you want to search for, and then click the Go button. The window displays any matching results. Among the Search Options, you can search for all media file types, or just for certain types, such as clip art or photos. Click the Results Should Be drop-down arrow and click the media types you want to include in the search. If you want to include items from the Office.com Web site, leave the check box selected.

Apply It!

When you find a clip art or other media clip you want to use in an Office program, you can copy and paste it. Click the clip and choose Copy from the pop-up menu. Open the program where you want to insert the clip and click where you want it to appear. Right-click and choose Paste from the pop-up menu. The clip is pasted into place.

Find More Clip Art Online

One of the best parts of using Microsoft clip art is being able to look for more clip art online. As an Office 2010 user, you are entitled to use any of the clip art from Microsoft's huge online clip art collection. With a connection to the Internet, the clip art is always at your disposal.

The first time you use the Office.com site to download clips, you may be asked to accept a service agreement. Once you pass this hurdle, you can download as many clips as you want.

Clip art is added to the Microsoft Clip Organizer, one of the Office 2010 stand-alone programs that installs with the suite. To learn more about this, see the previous task. With the clip art safely added to your computer, you can use it with any of the applications that utilize clip art. You can use the Clip Art pane to search for your downloaded clips and add them directly to your documents.

---

① Click the Insert tab.

② Click Clip Art.

● The Clip Art pane opens.

③ Click the Find More at Office.com link at the bottom of the pane.

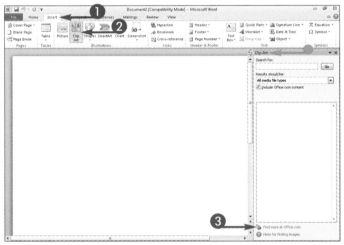

The default browser window opens to the Microsoft Office Clip Art site.

④ Click in the search field and type the keyword or words you want to look for in the online clip art collection.

⑤ Click the Search icon or press Enter.

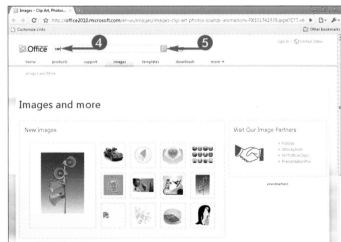

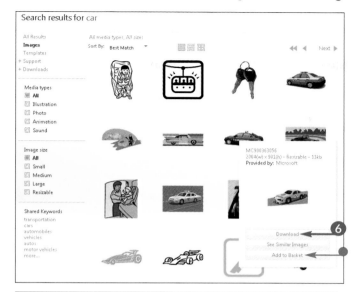

The browser window displays any matches.

⑥ When you find a clip you want to use, move the mouse pointer over the clip and click Download.

● If you want to download more than one clip during your session, click Add to Basket and download all the clips together when you are ready.

To view details about a clip, click it to view a larger version of the clip and view dimensions, file size, and so on.

Note: Depending on whether you have used the Web site before, the Microsoft Service Agreement window may open. Click Accept to continue with the download.

● The clip art is downloaded and added to the Microsoft Clip Organizer.

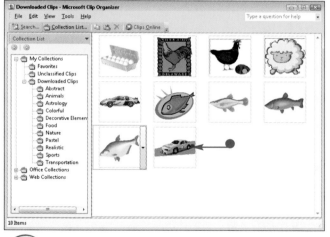

TIPS

Apply It!

Once you have downloaded a clip, you can use the Clip Art pane to look for the clip and insert it into your file. Type the clip's keyword into the Search field of the Clip Art pane and click Go or press Enter. The pane displays any matches. Click the one you want to insert into your document.

Try This!

You can search for a particular type of clip on the Office.com site. On the search results window, you can find a variety of options you can use to narrow down your search based on media type and image size as well as find links to other clips with shared keywords. Look on the left side of the page to find options you can turn on or off to narrow down your search results.

Remove an Image Background

New to Office 2010, you can edit an image, such as a photo, and remove the background. This technique basically cuts out the subject of the image and allows you to use a different background behind the image, which opens a variety of possibilities. You might use the image with closely wrapped text, or place the image over a solid color background that matches your document's color scheme.

Normally you have to use a program like Photoshop to remove a background. With the new Background Removal feature, you can designate areas of the background to remove or use the marquee to cover what areas you

want to keep. When you first open the feature, a magenta color overlays the image.

Background Removal tries very hard to figure out what part of the image you want to keep and what background to remove. The Background Removal tool includes a tab of tools you can use to fine-tune the procedure. You can then choose to keep your changes to the image, or discard them entirely. After editing an image, you can save it as a new picture file and reuse it again later.

The Background Removal feature is available in Word, Excel, PowerPoint, and Outlook.

---

① Insert and select the image you want to use.

The Picture Tools Format tab appears on the Ribbon.

② Click Remove Background.

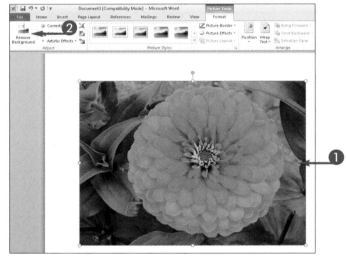

The Background Removal tools appear.

③ Reposition the marquee rectangle to cover the area you want to keep as the subject of the image.

● Click and drag a corner handle to resize the two sides of the marquee at once.

● Click and drag a side or top handle to resize a side of the marquee.

You can also move the marquee to a new location over the image.

- You can also click the Mark Areas to Keep button and click where you want the background to stay.

  You can connect the markers that each click creates to select an area to keep or single-click a spot in the area you want to keep.

- For more detailed removal, click the Mark Areas to Remove button and click where you want the background removed.

- To remove a mark, click the Delete Mark button.

- ④ Click anywhere outside the image to view the removal or click the Keep Changes button.

- The background removal is applied to the image.

TIPS

More Options!

If you want to remove a background from a piece of clip art, you can use another technique. First you must ungroup the clip art and then delete the background element. To learn more about this, see the task "Customize Clip Art with the Ungroup Command" later in this chapter.

Try This!

The tighter the marquee around the area you want to keep, the better job the Background Removal tool does to keep the part you want in the image. Be sure to move the marquee as close as possible to the subject you want to keep. You can also use the Mark Areas to Remove button to mark along areas that prove to be difficult to remove on the first try.

Assign Artistic Effects to a Picture

You can use the Office Artistic Effects to turn a regular picture into something eye-catching. For example, you can turn a photo into an instant chalk sketch or a negative glow with edges. If you are looking for ways to bring attention to pictures in your document, workbook, or presentation, artistic effects may be just the technique for you.

With Live Preview on, you can preview what each artistic effect looks like before you actually apply it. Live Preview is turned on by default, but if yours is not you can click the File tab, click Options, and then click the Enable Live

Preview check box in the General tab to turn it on again.

With over 20 different effects you can try, it is not likely that you will run out of ideas anytime soon. However, if you do, you can also fine-tune each effect to create a new look. The Format Picture dialog box offers a tab for Artistic Effects with several tools to change settings pertaining to a particular effect, such as transparency, smoothness, and so on. Try experimenting with the options to see what kind of new looks you can create.

Assign an Effect

① Insert a picture, such as a digital photo into your Word, Excel, or PowerPoint file and select it.

Note: *Artistic effects do not work on clip art pictures.*

② Click the Format tab under Picture Tools.

③ Click the Artistic Effects button in the Adjust group of commands.

④ Click an effect.

● The artistic effect is immediately applied to the image.

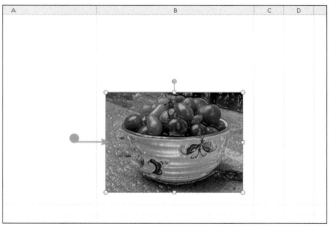

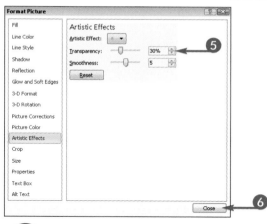

Customize an Effect

1. Select the picture containing the artistic effect you want to edit.

2. Click the Format tab under Picture Tools.

3. Click the Artistic Effects button.

4. Click Artistic Effects Options.

The Format Picture dialog box opens to the Artistic Effects tab.

5. Adjust the settings for the effect.

6. Click Close to apply the new settings to your picture.

TIPS

Did You Know?

It is easy to confuse artistic effects with picture styles, especially because they are both located on the Picture Tools Format tab. Artistic effects change the entire appearance of a picture, whereas picture styles are specialized formatting for a picture that merely changes how it is presented in a document. Picture styles revolve mainly around borders and shapes, such as turning a picture into an oval by lopping off the corners, or adding a thick frame to create a border around a picture.

More Options!

You can use the Color button, also found on the Picture Tools Format tab, to change the color saturation of a picture. This feature is helpful if you want to match the image to a color scheme or theme in your document. To use the tool, click it to display a gallery of color tone, saturation, and recolor options.

Control Graphic Placement with Ordering

Here is a technique often overlooked by Office users — the ability to change the order of elements in a document. You can create layers or *stacks* of graphic objects in your document, such as placing a shape on top of a photo, or moving a clip art object underneath a WordArt object. Using the ordering commands, you can control which object appears in which position in a stack. You can use this technique to create logos, letterhead, and other graphical elements.

You can apply ordering controls to text boxes, clip art, shapes, pictures, WordArt, charts, and just about any other graphic object you place in a document, workbook, presentation, or publication.

Ordering objects boils down to sending an object to the back of the stack, or to the front of the stack, or positioning it somewhere in between. To place an object at the very front, choose Bring to Front. To simply move it up in the stacking order, choose Bring Forward. To place an object at the very back, choose Send to Back. To move it backwards in the stacking order, choose Send Backward. The steps in this task show a shape object being moved through the stack of other objects.

① **Click the object you want to reorder.**

In this example, an object is being moved from the middle of the stack.

② **Click the Format tab in the Picture Tools or Drawing Tools on the Ribbon.**

③ **To move an object to the foreground, click the Bring Forward drop-down arrow.**

④ **Click either Bring Forward or Bring to Front.**

The object moves forward.

● In this example, the object is placed forward one spot in the stack.

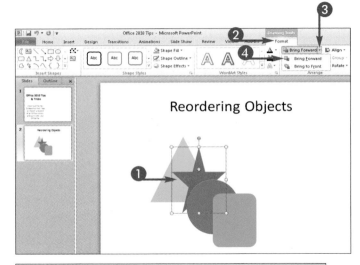

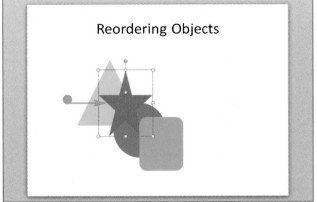

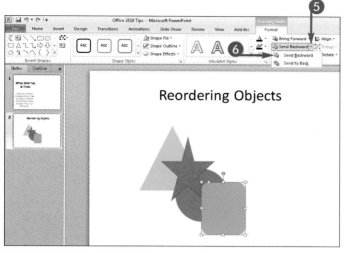

⑤ To move an object to the background, select the object and click the Send Backward drop-down arrow.

⑥ Click either Send Backward or Send to Back.

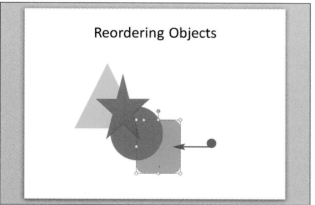

● The object moves backward.

Try This!

If you are having trouble selecting objects on-screen, open the Selection and Visibility pane. Click the Selection Pane button on the Format tab for the Drawing Tools or Picture Tools. This opens the pane on the right side of the window, and you can click which item you want to select and then apply an ordering command. You can also use the Bring Forward (▲) or Send Backward (▼) arrows at the bottom of the pane to reorder the selected item in the stack.

Did You Know?

You can use the alignment tools on the Drawing Tools or Picture Tools tab to align shapes and other graphic elements in a document. You can align selected objects to the left, right, or center, or you can align them vertically to the top, middle, or bottom of the page. You can also choose to distribute the objects evenly across the page or up and down the page. To find all these controls, simply click the Align button and choose an alignment.

You can group several objects together in a document and perform formatting tasks to every item in the group at the same time. For example, perhaps you have a shape, a WordArt object, and a text box in your document that you want to reposition. Rather than move each object individually, you can place them all in a group and move them at the same time.

You can also group items to apply formatting, such as align them all at once, or add the same border to each one. You can even group items simply to create one large object in a document. For example, you might group three or four shapes and turn them into a graphic object you can reuse again later.

The key to grouping is learning to select multiple objects at the same time. You can do this by pressing Shift or Ctrl while clicking all the items to include in a group.

You can find grouping commands on the Format tab for Drawing Tools or Picture Tools on the Ribbon. Once you group objects, you can easily ungroup them again later to return them to their individual states.

Group Objects

1 Select the objects you want to group.

To select multiple objects, press Ctrl or Shift while clicking objects.

2 Click the Format tab in the Picture Tools or Drawing Tools on the Ribbon.

3 Click the Group button.

4 Click Group.

● The objects are grouped in a single selection box. You can edit or move the objects as a group.

Ungroup Objects

1. Click the group.

2. Click the Format tab in the Picture Tools or Drawing Tools on the Ribbon.

3. Click the Group button.

4. Click Ungroup.

● The objects are ungrouped. You can now move or edit them individually.

Note: *If you use a lot of SmartArt graphics, you can apply the Ungroup command to ungroup the graphic into individual shapes. The only caveat to this, however, is once you ungroup SmartArt, you cannot turn the individual elements back into a SmartArt object again.*

Caution!
In previous versions of Office, you used to be able to group WordArt objects with shapes and pictures. You cannot easily do so in Office 2010. The workaround for this is to pursue the steps shown in the task "Turn a WordArt Object into a Picture File" and utilize the Windows Paint program to turn the WordArt into a graphic. Copy the file back over to your Office 2010 document and paste it in; then apply the group command to group it with something else.

Did You Know?
You can nudge a selected object on-screen to position it in small increments. Simply press the appropriate keyboard arrow key. For example, press the right arrow key to nudge the selection to the right.

Customize Clip Art with the Ungroup Command

Do you ever have trouble finding just the right piece of clip art to illustrate your work? Maybe you can find one that is close to meeting your requirements, but it needs to be another color or lose a portion of the background. Fret no more. You can use the Ungroup command to customize a piece of clip art to meet your needs.

You can convert a clip art object into a Microsoft Office drawing object and make changes to the image's individual elements. To do this, you must apply the Ungroup command.

Once you ungroup the various parts that comprise a clip art drawing, you can edit those parts to create a different piece of clip art. For example, you can change a shape's fill color, or remove an outline or delete an entire background behind the main subject.

After editing individual elements of the clip art, you can regroup the parts again to create a single object.

Note that this technique does not work for all clip art objects!

① Insert and select the clip art you want to edit.

② On the Picture Tools, click the Format tab.

③ Click the Group button.

④ Click Ungroup.

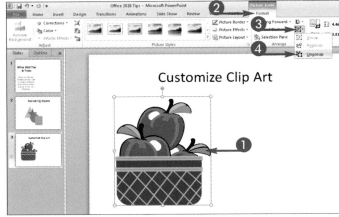

A prompt box appears asking if you want to convert the picture.

⑤ Click Yes.

Even after okaying the conversion, you may have to repeat steps 2 to 4 again to fully ungroup the elements.

Note: *Depending on the clip art's complexity, you may need to apply the ungroup command more than one time to break down individual components.*

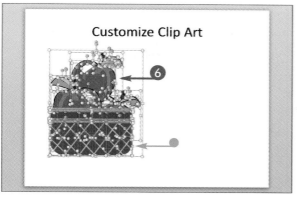

● Individual components of the clip art appear with their own separate selection boxes.

⑥ Click a component you want to change.

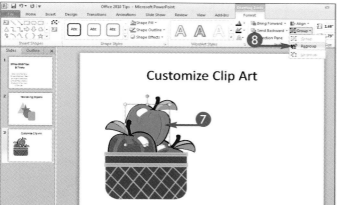

⑦ Edit the selected item, such as changing its color, size, or position in the picture.

⑧ When you finish editing the image, you can regroup the components; click the Group button again and click Group or Regroup.

Note: You can remove all the edits you perform on a clip art image. You can use the Undo button (⌔) to undo each change, or you can click the Reset Picture button (🖼) to return the entire clip art piece back to its original state.

More Options!

You can make adjustments to a clip art's brightness and softness settings through the Format Picture dialog box. Right-click the clip art you want to edit, and then click Format Picture. This opens the dialog box to the Picture Corrections tab. You can also find additional formatting options through all the other tabs in the dialog box, such as adding a glow or cropping the clip art.

Try This!

Looking to get rid of a background color in a clip art image? Use the Set Transparent Color tool. With the clip art selected and the Picture Tool's Format tab displayed, click the Color button and click the Set Transparent Color command. Next, click the background you want to make transparent. The background fill is immediately removed.

Add a Caption to a Graphic

You can add captions to any graphics you insert into your Word or Publisher documents. Captions can really help explain what you are illustrating, such as a photo, a chart, or a graph. For a particularly long file, like a Word document, captions can help you keep track of figures by numbering them, such as Figure 1, Figure 2, or Table 1, Table 2.

The captioning feature offers you several preset captions to use, such as Figure, Equation, or Table. You can also enter your own label. You

do not have to use a label. You can turn this feature off if you want.

Captions normally appear directly below the image. The captioning feature lets you control the location of your captions. For example, you might want to place a caption above a picture.

You can type your caption directly into the Caption dialog box and then apply it to the selected image.

① Right-click the graphic.

② Click Insert Caption.

In Publisher, click the Format tab and click the Caption button in the Picture Styles group.

The Caption dialog box opens.

③ Click the Label drop-down arrow.

④ Choose a caption label.

- To change the position of the caption, click here and choose another.

- To create a new label, click New Label and fill out label text.

- To change the numbering system applied, click Numbering and choose another.

- To leave off the label and keep the number only, click this check box (☐ changes to ☑).

⑤ Click OK.

- The caption is added.

⑥ Type any additional caption text you want to include.

When in the Course of human events it becomes necessary for one people to dissolve the political bands which have connected them with another and to assume among the powers of the earth, the separate and equal station to which the Laws of Nature and of Nature's God entitle them, a decent respect to the opinions of mankind requires that they should declare the causes which impel them to the separation.

We hold these truths to be self-evident, that all men are created equal, that they are endowed by their Creator with certain unalienable rights, among these are Life, Liberty and the pursuit of Happiness. — That to secure these rights, Governments are instituted among Men, deriving their just powers from the consent of the governed, — That whenever any Form of Government becomes destructive of these ends, it is the Right of the People to alter or to abolish it, and to institute new Government, laying its foundation on such principles and organizing its powers in such form, as to them shall seem most likely to effect their Safety and Happiness. Prudence, indeed, will dictate that Governments long established should not be changed for light and transient causes; and accordingly all experience hath shewn that mankind are more disposed to suffer, while evils are sufferable than to right themselves by abolishing the forms to which they are accustomed. But when a long train

Figure 1 American Eagle

TIPS

Did You Know?

You can use the AutoCaption button in the Caption dialog box to turn on the automated caption feature. This tool automatically inserts captions for you as you go. You can select from a list of items, such as Microsoft Excel Chart or Bitmap Image. Whenever you go to insert the designated object, AutoCaption adds the appropriate caption with the sequential number assigned.

Try This!

Another way to add a caption to an image is to insert a text box directly below the image. Use this method if you do not want to rely on a numbering system and prefer to just use text captions only. To add a text box, click the Insert tab on the Ribbon and look for the Text Box button. Once activated, you can click and drag where you want to insert a text box, and then fill it with the text you want to use.

Turn a WordArt Object into a Picture File

You can use the Office 2010 WordArt feature to create custom text designs, such as arched text for a logo or shaded text for a document title. For example, if you create a company logo in a Word document using a WordArt object, you can convert the logo into an image file that you can use with another program, such as a page-layout application, or with another Microsoft Office program.

Although you cannot save a WordArt object as its own file type in Word or Excel, you can use another easy avenue to convert the object into an image format that non-Office programs can use. By using the Windows Paint program, an application that installs with Windows, you can copy the WordArt object and paste it into the Paint window, and then save the object as a graphic file. Popular graphic file formats include bitmap, GIF, JPEG, and PNG.

The real trick to this technique is remembering to crop the graphic in the Paint window so you end up with a properly sized graphic object.

---

① Use the WordArt tool to create a text object.

② Press Ctrl+C to copy the WordArt object to the Clipboard.

③ Click Start.

④ Click All Programs.

⑤ Click Accessories.

⑥ Click Paint.

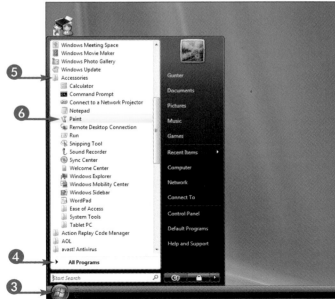

The Paint program opens.

⑦ Press Ctrl+V to paste the WordArt object into Paint.

⑧ Crop or resize the image to the dimensions you want to use.

● To resize the image, click and drag a selection handle.

● To crop the image, click Image and Crop and then drag around the area you want to keep.

Note: If you are using Windows 7, you can use the Crop command on the Ribbon's Home tab to crop an image.

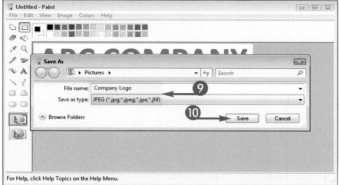

⑨ Press Ctrl+S to save the object as a new graphic file with a new file name and the preferred file type.

⑩ Click Save.

You can now insert it into other programs as a picture.

Note: When it comes to choosing a file format, you cannot go wrong with JPEG, GIF, TIFF, or PNG formats. Any of these four file types are commonly used among applications and the Web.

Try This!

PowerPoint and Publisher are the only Office 2010 programs that let you save a WordArt object as a picture file. Just right-click the object and choose Save As Picture. This opens the Save As Picture dialog box where you can name the file and save it as a specific file format.

More Options!

Windows Paint is not the only program you can use to turn a WordArt object into a graphic file. You may have other drawing programs installed on your computer you can use instead. Windows Paint, however, is already installed as part of the Windows applications that come with the operating system.

Add a Custom Watermark

A watermark is a recognizable background image or words that appear faded yet still discernable behind the document's content. Apart from the realm of computers, watermarks are typically security features found on paper money, passports, and postage stamps, usually as a way to verify authentication and prevent counterfeiting. Over in the world of business and computer-generated documents, watermarks are commonly used in official letters, a way to brand output, or as Web page backgrounds.

In this task, you learn how to insert a graphic as a watermark. In Word, the Watermark feature is set up to insert text watermarks. You can use a text watermark to mark a document as a copy, an original, confidential, or urgent. Going the extra step of using a graphic takes a little more planning. For example, you might want to use a company logo as a watermark, or a branding logo.

When using an image as a watermark, legibility is the key issue. You want to make sure the document's text is clearly readable over the image. As you create a custom watermark in Word, you can control the scale of the image. The Washout setting is selected by default, to create the faded appearance for the background.

---

① In Word, click the Page Layout tab on the Ribbon.

② Click Watermark.

③ Click Custom Watermark.

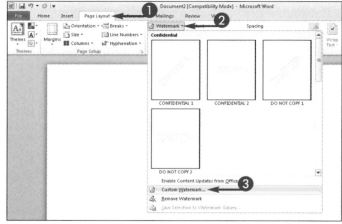

The Printed Watermark dialog box opens.

④ Click the Picture Watermark option (◯ changes to ◉).

⑤ Click Select Picture.

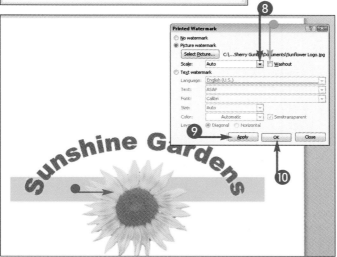

The Insert Picture dialog box opens.

6 Select the picture you want to use as a watermark.

7 Click Insert.

8 To scale the image, click the Scale drop-down arrow and choose a percentage.

● Click the Washout check box if you want the image to appear faded (☐ changes to ☑).

9 Click Apply.

● The watermark is applied to the document.

10 Click OK to close the dialog box.

TIPS

Try This!

You can also create your own text watermarks rather than choose from the preset list. To do so, open the Printed Watermark dialog box and click the Text Watermark option (⊙ changes to ⊙). Replace the default text listed in the Text field with your own.

Try This!

You can simulate a watermark in Excel by assigning a picture as a workbook background. To do this, you must first make sure the image you want to use is set to the degree of transparency needed so your data is clearly legible on top of the image. You can use a photo-editing application to adjust the image transparency before using it in Excel. Once you have an image ready, click the Page Layout tab on the Ribbon, and then click the Background button. The Sheet Background dialog box opens, where you can navigate to the file you want to use.

If you plan on inserting graphic elements into your file, it is a good idea to learn the various ways in which you can wrap text around the graphic. Text wrapping refers to the way in which text flows around a graphic object in the document. Whether you insert a photograph, clip art, or a basic shape, you can use the text wrapping tools to assure just the right fit. You can find text wrapping tools in Word and Publisher.

As far as wrapping options go, you can choose from a variety of settings. By default, text is set up to wrap an object inline, which simply means the object sits on the same horizontal line as the text. Alas, this setting is a bit limiting and the object sits there like a sore thumb without blending into the document. Instead, try choosing one of these text wrapping settings: Square, Tight, Through, Top and Bottom, Behind Text, or In Front of Text.

Thankfully, the names are pretty accurate as to how the text wrap is going to appear in the document. If you choose Tight wrapping, for example, the document text flows fairly closely to and around the object. Try them all to see what works best for your document.

Apply Text Wrapping

1. In Word or Publisher, click the graphic object to which you want to assign text wrapping.

2. Click the Format tab for Picture Tools (Word) or Drawing Tools (Word or Publisher).

3. Click Wrap Text.

4. Click a text wrapping command.

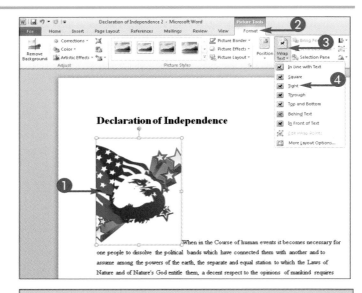

The text wrapping is assigned.

● In this example, Tight wrapping is applied.

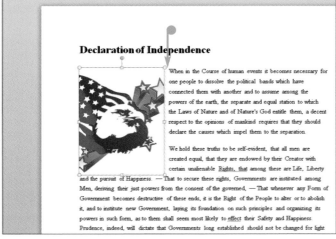

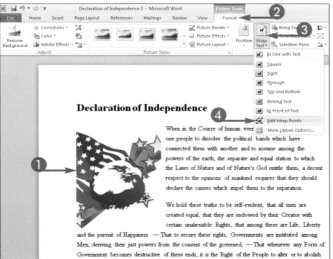

Apply Custom Wrapping

① In Word or Publisher, click the graphic object to which you want to assign text wrapping.

② Click the Format tab for Picture Tools (Word) or Drawing Tools (Word or Publisher).

③ Click Wrap Text.

④ Click Edit Wrap Points.

⑤ Click and drag a wrap point to change the wrapping for that particular area of the object.

● In this example, a corner is moved to allow text to wrap more closely to the clip art image.

⑥ Click outside the wrap points to turn them off.

Note: *To turn off text wrapping, click the Wrap Text button and choose In Line with Text.*

TIPS

Did You Know?

Excel also has a text wrapping option you can apply in cells, but it works a bit differently than wrapping around an object. If you type a line of text or numbers that exceeds the column width, you can tell Excel to wrap it to the next line rather than expand it across columns. Click the Wrap Text button located on the Home tab among the Alignment controls to turn the feature on.

More Options!

You can find a few more text wrapping controls in the Format dialog box for the object you are trying to wrap. To open the dialog box, select the object, click the Wrap Text button and click More Layout Options at the bottom of the menu. This command opens the Layout dialog box to the Text Wrapping tab, and you can find several additional controls for wrapping text on one side or the other, or specifying an exact distance (this option is available only when you choose Square text wrap).

Organize Pictures with Picture Manager

When you install Microsoft Office, it includes several extra applications stored in the Microsoft Office 2010 Tools folder. One of these extra apps is Microsoft Picture Manager, a simple image-editing program that allows you to manage, edit, and share your digital picture files. The program provides you with a centralized location for viewing all picture files stored on your computer.

You can easily find pictures located in other folders on your computer and view them in the Picture Manager window. The program includes several useful tools for editing your pictures, such as cropping, reducing red eye,

adjusting brightness and contrast, and resizing. After you edit your pictures, you can share them with others. Picture Manager includes tools for e-mailing pictures or placing them in a SharePoint Picture Library to share with a workgroup.

You can also send pictures directly to an Office program. You can insert a selected image directly into an open file, or add the image to a new file.

If you make changes to a picture, such as resizing or cropping, Picture Manager keeps track of your unsaved edits and keeps them in the Unsaved Edits folder.

---

1. **Click Start.**

2. **Click All Programs.**

3. **Click Microsoft Office.**

4. **Click Microsoft Office 2010 Tools.**

5. **Click Microsoft Office Picture Manager.**

6. **You can expand or collapse various picture folders in the Picture Shortcuts pane; double-click a folder to expand or collapse.**

7. **Click a view button to change how you view the pictures.**

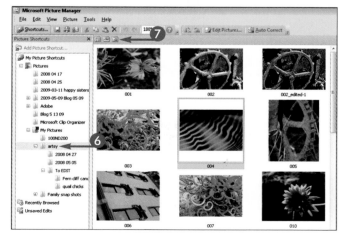

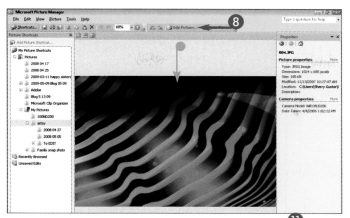

- Single Picture view is applied to this image.

⑧ To edit your pictures, click the Edit Pictures button on the toolbar.

- Microsoft Picture Manager opens the Edit Pictures pane.

⑨ Click an editing tool to apply edits to the image.

⑩ Click the Save button to save any of your changes to a picture.

⑪ When you finish viewing and editing pictures, click the Close button to close the program window.

More Options!
You can find a bevy of editing tools in the Edit Pictures pane. You can edit the brightness and contrast of an image, adjust the color, crop a picture, rotate and flip a picture, remove red eye, resize a picture, and compress the picture file size. Do not forget to save the changes before closing Microsoft Picture Manager. You can also save a copy of the picture and keep the original intact. Just click the File menu and click Save As.

Try This!
To remove a picture you no longer want, select it and click the Delete button (☒). A Delete File dialog box appears asking if you really want to remove the file to the Recycle Bin. Click Yes. The image is not permanently removed until you empty the Recycle Bin.

Index

A

Access (Microsoft)
    adding background reports, 256–257
    applying input masks, 230–231
    assigning themes to forms, 252
    attaching files to records, 234–235
    automating tasks with macros, 248–249
    changing form tab order, 253
    collecting data from Outlook, 222–225
    conditional formatting, 258–259
    copying previous records, 229
    creating mailing labels, 246–247
    default values, 226
    displaying summary statistics, 240
    documenting databases, 242–243
    exporting reports to Word, 244–245
    importing data from Excel, 218–221
    inserting OLE objects, 236–237
    overview, 214, 250
    pictures in forms, 254–255
    PivotCharts, 262–263
    PivotTables, 260–261
    primary key fields, 227
    saving filters as queries, 238–239
    setting data validation rules, 232–233
    setting field captions, 228
    templates, 216–217
    viewing object dependencies, 241
action buttons, 170–171
archiving (e-mails), 290–293
author permissions, 36–37
AutoArchive feature (Outlook), 290–291
AutoCorrect (Word), 62–63
AutoFill feature (Excel), 102–103
AutoFilter feature (Excel), 131
AutoText (Word), 60–61

B

backgrounds, 256–257, 334–335
bibliographies, 82–83
blog posts, 50–51
bookmarks, 56–57
borders, 70–71, 140–141
building blocks, 14–15, 46–47

C

Calculator tool, 114–115
calendars, 306–309
captions, 213, 228, 344–345
CDs, copying presentations to, 184–185
cells
    borders, 140–141
    changing text orientation, 153
    data-validation rules, 132–133
    generating random numbers in, 110
    joining text from separate, 113

    protecting, 108–109
    setting constraints, 125
    Watch window, 106–107
certificates, 274
chart objects, 146–147
charts (Word), 78–79. *See also* PivotCharts
citations, 83
clip art, 202–203, 330–333, 342–343
color
    background, 142–143
    gridline, 138
color-coding, 104, 144–145
comments, inserting in formulas, 112
compressing media files, 180–181
conditional formatting, 144–145, 258–259
conversations (e-mail), 286–287
cover pages, 88–89
cross-references, 94–95

D

data. *See also* text
    automating, 102–103
    collecting from Outlook, 222–225
    color-coding, 144–145, 258–259
    importing/exporting, 218–221
    printed, 154
    setting validation rules, 232–233
data forms, 128–129
data-validation rules, 132–133, 232–233
Database Documenter feature (Access), 242–243
database tables, 126–127
datasheets, 260–263
definitions/synonyms, looking up, 54–55
Design Checker (Publisher), 325
digital signature, 34–35
distribution lists, 270–271
documents. *See also* files
    adding line numbers, 96–97
    assigning properties, 28–29
    bookmarks, 56–57
    checking compatibility, 24–25
    comparing, 74–75
    converting to presentations, 158–159
    encrypting, 32–33, 274–275
    marking as final, 38–39
    PDF, 26–27
    recovering unsaved, 40–41
    removing sensitive information, 30–31
    searching through, 52–53
drafts, 40–41
Drop Caps feature (Word), 64–65

E

electronic business card, 273, 298–301
e-mails. *See also* Outlook (Microsoft)
    archiving, 290–293
    electronic business cards to, 273, 298–301

Index

N

O

P

Index